B

the

The Campaigns of Montrose

The Campaigns of Montrose

A Military History of the Civil War in Scotland
1639 to 1646

STUART REID

THE MERCAT PRESS
EDINBURGH
1990

First published in 1990 by Mercat Press
James Thin, 53 South Bridge, Edinburgh EH1 1YS

© Stuart Reid 1990

ISBN 0 90 182492 5

Printed by Butler & Tanner Ltd, Frome and London

Dedication

This book is dedicated to my grandfather,
Jack Milton, a regular soldier 'Out Since Mons'
with the 2nd Battalion Highland Light Infantry,
1914–1918.

Contents

Maps

Acknowledgements

This book would never have been written without the active encouragement of David Ryan, editor of *English Civil War Notes and Queries* and the publisher of an invaluable series of monographs on the Civil War period. In 1987 he invited me to contribute a short piece on the battle of Kilsyth, to which I readily consented. Having access to all the important Royalist sources and being well read in modern accounts of the battle I assumed that a short monograph could be written without any real difficulty. All that I lacked, I somewhat rashly thought, was the defeated General Baillie's account of the affair, which I anticipated would provide some useful quotations. No sooner had I obtained what turned out to be a set of papers laid before a commission of inquiry into the defeat, than I realised that there were serious discrepancies between Baillie's very clear evidence and all the modern accounts of the battle. Some further investigation and a visit to the site convinced me that, although quite incompatible with the modern reconstructions, Baillie's narrative was entirely compatible (making allowances for their differing viewpoints) with other contemporary accounts. Thus intrigued, I launched into a detailed re-assessment of the other battles in this period, the results of which form this present book.

It would also be fair to acknowledge the part played by the members of the English Civil War Society, an organisation devoted to re-enacting battles and some less martial episodes of the Civil War, in helping me to appreciate some of the practical aspects of seventeenth-century military science. In particular, I should like to mention the members of the recreated Sir John Tyldesley's Regiment and the thirty or so individuals drawn from both armies who followed me in 1980 retracing the march of Montrose's army over the mountains from Kilchumin to Inverlochy.

Introduction

Montrose, the Covenant and the Art of War in the Seventeenth Century

The proliferation of books and articles about Mary, Queen of Scots, and her great, great grandson, Charles Edward Stewart, has long been held to be cause for crying 'Hold, enough!' and the same might in justice be uttered upon the appearance of yet another book on James Graham, 1st Marquis of Montrose. The advent of this particular volume therefore begs some explanation.

Montrose, arguably, was one of the greatest soldiers Scotland has produced. Since he was also dashingly handsome, has left some scraps of poetry to posterity and was executed by his enemies after leading a doomed uprising on behalf of a Stuart king, his status as a warrior hero has long been assured. George Wishart, his chaplain, was only the first in a long line of adulatory biographers. Of late, it is fair to say, biographers have grown somewhat more critical of Montrose's character and his motives, but on the other hand it would be equally fair to say that such revelations of his shortcomings serve only to enhance rather than diminish his status as one of Caledonia's favourite sons. By so being humanised he becomes a real person rather than a mythical hero, and his achievements may be accounted all the greater for his having so spectacularly surmounted his shortcomings.

Yet herein lies the paradox. Montrose was neither a statesman nor a warrior king. Unlike Robert de Bruce his fame rests not upon what he accomplished for his country, but upon his impressive military victories, most of them won within a single year. The evidence indeed suggests that he was an indifferent administrator and a tactless diplomat, all too frequently alienating those with whom he ought to have made common cause. Without his skill as a soldier, his ability to win battles, he would long since have vanished into obscurity like many another servant of King Charles, yet it is precisely this quality which has been least considered by his biographers. There has never been, strangely enough, a serious study made of the civil war period in

1

Scotland from a military point of view, and the quite remarkable victories won by Montrose have been for the most part treated of in a most unsatisfactory manner, chiefly anecdotal. Not since Samuel Rawston Gardiner's classic but flawed reconstructions in the 1880s has a serious attempt been made to establish properly what happened where and why. Far from such an enquiry taking place, the fighting has all too frequently been dismissed in the most perfunctory manner in a couple of paragraphs—usually thinly disguised reworkings of Gardiner—and rather more attention then devoted to the brave words said to have been uttered by individuals, and exaggerated accounts of the personal prowess of others. This less than happy approach was pioneered by the earliest of the biographers, George Wishart, for example; who devotes more space to relating a merry tale of an Irish soldier cheerfully amputating his own shattered leg than he does to describing the Justice Mills fight at Aberdeen in which the Irishman was wounded. This emphasis on brave deeds has been followed only too well by the subsequent biographers, and there has above all been little evident appreciation of time and distance, of seventeenth century weapon characteristics and tactics. Colonel Fitzwilliam Elliot's reconstruction of Philiphaugh and Dr. David Steven's recent reconstruction of Auldearn are notable exceptions, although neither is entirely satisfactory.

In short it would probably be hard to find a similar instance of a soldier whose life and career have been so frequently recounted, without any serious attempt to address the matter of his generalship.

This present study is not intended to be merely another biography of Montrose, and indeed he may at times be conspicuously absent from the narrative as related operations are discussed. It is indeed a quite straightforward attempt to describe the conduct of military operations in Scotland from the Trot of Turriff on 14 May 1639, to the storming of Aberdeen seven years to the day later on 14 May 1646, two engagements which effectively began and ended the civil war in Scotland. Inevitably this exercise involves a very considerable re-assessment of the several actions and of Montrose's part in them. It is not however by any means a debunking exercise of the type all too frequently encountered of late. The purpose of this study is not to try to prove that Montrose was not responsible for the victories attributed to him, but rather to examine the battles anew, and demonstrate how it was that an ill-trained and poorly equipped rabble, stiffened by a surprising number of regulars, was able time and time again to defeat the best that the government could send against them.

James Graham, 5th Earl and later 1st Marquis of Montrose, was born in 1612 and succeeded to the earldom in 1626 at the age of fourteen. In January of the following year he was admitted to St. Andrews University, where he appears to have been chiefly distinguished in such manly sports as hunting, hawking, archery and golf. This was by no means unusual at the time, since the education imparted was supposed to be a 'universal' one in contrast to the rather narrower disciplines of modern institutions, and his studies, we are assured, did not suffer thereby: but even if this was indeed the case, it betrays a certain want of application and attention to detail—an unfortunate trait which was to be all too apparent in his generalship. Arguably the Marquis of Montrose was the very image of a cavalier—a *beau sabreur* certainly—but hardly a professional. His want of attention to detail, or to put it less charitably, his carelessness, was to cost him dear upon a number of occasions, and was ultimately to undo all that his brilliant dash had gained and lead him to the gallows.

Married at seventeen to Magdalen Carnegie, daughter of David, Lord Carnegie of Kinnaird, and Margaret Lindsay of Edzell, he moved in with his in-laws for the next three years, and the unsatisfactory nature of this arrangement may be readily gauged by the alacrity with which he fled the country upon his coming of age in 1633, embarking upon a three year long Grand Tour of the continent—without Magdalen Carnegie. Here a belated attempt at intellectual improvement was made, and during the winter of 1633–4 he studied at Angers before moving on to Rome the following year. It is worth speculating whether this period spent in two of the foremost Catholic states of Europe may have been responsible for his later toleration of Catholicism, despite a firm adherence to the tenets of Calvinism. Military matters are also said to have interested him, and although there is no record of his having done so, it is possible that he may have looked in upon a siege or even a general engagement, since such an excursion was commonly regarded as an essential feature of the Grand Tour. There was certainly ample scope for it. Although Montrose does not appear to have visited Germany, the Imperial armies were on the march in northern Italy, and in May 1635, shortly after his arrival in Rome, France and the Empire went to war. Nevertheless there is no evidence that he emulated Richard Fielding, a son of the Earl of Denbigh whom he met in Rome, by taking service with one of the armies. (Fielding, later a Colonel in the Royalist army, curiously enough appears as the companion of Daniel Defoe's 'Cavalier' in the interesting if semi-fictional account of a Grand Tour in France and Italy in the early 1630s, which forms the early part of the apocryphal *Memoirs of a Cavalier.*)

In 1636 domestic affairs recalled Montrose to Scotland. He stopped en route in London where he was for some reason coldly received by the King. In 1633, shortly after Montrose's departure for sunnier climes, Charles I had belatedly condescended to visit his northern kingdom for his coronation—eight years after his accession to the throne on the death of James VI. Outwardly, all might have been thought to have gone well, and the Edinburgh Militia even tricked themselves out in feathered hats, white satin doublets and black velvet breeches, but a train of events was set in motion which within five years led to war. The Scotland to which Montrose returned in 1636 was a rather less than contented realm.

Unlike the English Parliament, the Scots legislature was divided not into two semi-independent houses, Lords and Commons, but into three Estates sitting together in one hall. In place of the Lords Temporal and Spiritual were the two Estates of the Nobility and the Kirk, and in place of the Commons the Burgesses, representatives of Scotland's Royal Burghs. The latter were elected at conventions, and there was in places a hard struggle to maintain a degree of independence from the neighbouring feudal landowner. The real problem, however, lay with the Kirk. Before the Reformation this Estate was comprised of the Bishops, but abolition of them and diocesan government of the Kirk in favour of presbyteries, gave this third estate very largely into the hands of the lesser lairds serving as elders of the Kirk. In 1610, however, James VI reversed this to some extent by re-introducing the Bishops as presidents of their presbyteries, thus restoring the status quo in political if not religious matters. This was far from popular, but it was at least an effective compromise, which served well enough until Charles I rode north. On his accession to the throne in 1625, an Act of Revocation was rushed through, and thereafter both the nobility and a great many of the lairds lived in terror of the King's repeated threats to resume possession of all the lands possessed by the Kirk before 1540, gathered in by the Crown and then re-distributed to deserving members of the nobility.

In 1633 the Parliament assembled for his coronation was directed to ratify the Act, and the blow at last fell. This had two important results. In the first place the tiends or tithes which had fallen into secular hands were claimed by the Crown. Secondly, former Kirk lands were similarly reclaimed, or more accurately the feudal superiorities were reclaimed. Although the analogy is not quite accurate, this in effect altered the tenure from freehold to leasehold; and as much of the land possessed by the Lords of Erection, as they were known, had been in turn feued out, these feus became payable directly to the Crown. In both instances compensation at ten years purchase was to be made for the loss of revenue, but none was made, or could be made, for the concomitant loss of influence. For its part, the Kirk was dismayed at this settlement, since none of the lands were returned to it (albeit provision was made for payment of ministers' stipends out of the revenue now accruing to the Crown); and the Act, while arguably just, managed to alienate influential elements of society just at the moment when radical changes were about to be imposed in religious practice.

4

These changes were to appear to many to fly in the face of all that the Reformation had achieved and to herald a return to Rome. In short, it was the imposition of Laud's Anglican forms of worship: the prayer book, bishops and episcopal government of the Kirk. Of themselves it is questionable whether either of these measures would have resulted in rebellion, but now a sizeable section of the nobility, disgruntled by the Act of Revocation, made common cause with the lairds and ministers dismayed by the apparent imminent destruction of presbyterian worship.

Montrose's active involvement with the opposition seems to have begun in November 1637, when he was elected as one of the four representatives of the nobility to the 'Tables', opposition committees, which also included representatives from the lairds, burgesses and ministers—in effect an unofficial forerunner of the Committee of Estates which exercised executive power in Scotland during the civil war. More dramatically, on 28 February 1638, Montrose was one of the first to sign the National Covenant binding the country to the defence of the Protestant religion.

Throughout that year negotiations were conducted between the Tables and James, Marquis of Hamilton, the King's commissioner. The role played by Hamilton at this critical juncture in his master's fortunes was an equivocal one, and perhaps the most charitable explanation of his actions is that he did not know what he was doing. On the one hand he acted for the King both in the council chamber and in assembling allies, chiefly in the highlands and in Ireland, both ominously Catholic or at least reputedly so, for a military solution; yet at the same time secretly encouraged the Covenanters, as they were now known, to stick by their demands.

By the beginning of 1639 war was very nearly inevitable. Montrose was appointed a colonel both for levies raised in Perthshire and in Forfarshire; and on 1 February he arrived at Forfar to oversee the mustering of the shire's fencibles, and promptly fell out with his father-in-law, now Earl of Southesk. A week later he was on the march for Aberdeenshire at the head of 200 men.

His military career thus embarked upon will be followed in the first chapter, but before describing the early skirmishes it is necessary to pause and look at the art of war as it was practised in Western Europe in the second quarter of the seventeenth century.

Most infantry, who made up the bulk of the fencibles being mustered in February 1639, were armed with matchlock muskets—relatively unsophisticated firearms, effective enough when used en masse—although between thirty and forty per cent of infantry still carried the traditional pike, varying in length from twelve to sixteen feet. In order to be able to handle either weapon effectively a soldier needed some

1·5 metres of front: there was no question of standing shoulder to shoulder. In theory an infantry regiment would be drawn up six men deep, though five was probably commoner, and on occasion it might, as will be seen, be only drawn up three deep. This generally came about because under-strength units—as most were—tended to sacrifice depth in order to maintain a broad frontage. An infantry regiment some 500 strong, drawn up in five ranks, would therefore occupy a total frontage of some 150 metres. Furthermore, in order to be able to carry out the rather limited repertoire of manoeuvres of which it was capable, the regiment would also require to maintain a distance of around 50 metres between it and any neighbouring units. Cavalry for their part required more space still, needing a minimum of two metres for each horse and rider in the front line.

Appreciation of this simple factor alone is sufficient to warrant a re-examination of a number of Montrose's victories, since the armies concerned clearly occupied rather more ground than has been appreciated in the past, and the battlefields in consequence must have been somewhat larger than is generally realised.

It is probably fair to say that even regular infantry units, although certainly capable of jockeying for position in the early stages of a battle, found it rather difficult to actually manoeuvre in the face of the enemy, and once committed to combat they could really only go forward, stand fast or retire—and even these could be difficult enough in some circumstances. It is little realised, for example, that musketeers can march appreciably faster than pikemen, and co-ordinating the movements of a regiment comprising both pikemen and musketeers is not therefore quite as simple as may at first appear.

Lacking a sophisticated communications system, a general's skill was chiefly displayed in getting his men to the battlefield and then drawing up the various units comprising the army to the best advantage on the most suitable site, deciding where the weight of his attack should fall or the bulwark of his defence should lie, making a suitably inspiring oration if time and circumstances permitted it, and then very largely leaving his regimental officers to get on with it—unless of course the need arose to lead a particular attack in person.

As to getting on with it, it may be said of the minor tactics employed in the mid-seventeenth century that even at this early date they centred round the firefight, despite the relatively high proportion of men in each regiment unprovided with firearms. In 1746 General Henry Hawley was to remark in his fighting instructions issued shortly before the battle of Falkirk that a 'large musket shot' was three score yards, or not much more than fifty metres, and fire was not infrequently reserved until the opposing bodies of troops were well within this range. The old saying about waiting until you could see the whites of the enemy's eyes has a firm base in actual practice. Such at any rate was the ideal. Nervous and ill-trained troops might on the other hand rather more frequently blaze away at greater distances, and indeed in theory could subject formed bodies of soldiers to harassing fire for up to about 200 metres, although this was rare. Accurate casualty figures for firefights in this period are impossible to come by—although a hundred years later the French general Maurice de Saxe was acidly to comment that he had seen volleys fired by whole battalions killing no more than four men—but it is unlikely that they were particularly high. A firefight, then as now, was more a matter of nerve than attrition, and once a unit's nerve was lost and it began to give way, the fight moved into a very different phase.

Loading a matchlock musket, or for that matter the firelock muskets which many of the Royalists were equipped with, is by no means the marathon session sometimes suggested by writers who have done no more than idly leaf through the elegantly illustrated drill manuals of the day. A reasonably well trained musketeer can in fact be expected to have reloaded well within sixty seconds, and a veteran can do it in half that time. Moreover, in order to avoid a tense pause after a volley had been delivered while the musketeers hurriedly reloaded, firefights were generally conducted by a process known as *extraduction*. That is, a unit drawn up in four, five or six ranks, would discharge its muskets not all at once but rank by rank, the front rank firing first then falling away to the rear of the formation in order to reload. By this means the commander of a regular unit could be reasonably certain of maintaining a steady rolling fire, since he could expect that by the time the last rank had discharged their muskets in the general direction of the enemy the original front rank, who had been the first to fire, would have completed the process of reloading and would be standing ready to begin the whole cycle anew. Were highlanders, as popular legend has it, really to throw themselves flat just before their opponents fired, with the object of jumping up immediately afterward and rushing upon them as they struggled to reload once more, they would receive a very rude shock in the form of successive volleys from the other four or five ranks. Under certain conditions a unit might indeed fire off all its muskets at once—firing by *salvee*—but this was only used to preface either a violent assault with swords and the butt-ends of their muskets, or else to receive an attack at point-blank range. This was something which the Irish mercenaries working for Montrose, and later Huntly, were to make something of a trade-mark.

The pikemen, who might compromise up to forty per cent of infantry regiments in both the government and the rebel forces (units armed only with muskets were not very common), were in fact for the most part fairly ineffective except under certain conditions. Their main job was to protect musketeers from cavalry, although as this narrative will reveal they seldom had an opportunity to exercise this role in Scotland. As far as infantry fighting was concerned, in order to engage the enemy they had to advance into actual physical contact—or something very close to it—yet already the firepower of the flanking musketeers was more than adequate to ensure that such an advance, against a unit not already dominated by the attacking regiment's own musketeers, would result in unacceptably high casualties and not improbably the effective neutralisation of the attackers. The battle of Auldearn, on the other hand, provides a good example of how a successful attack might be managed. The musketeers of Sir Mungo Campbell of Lawers' Regiment won the firefight with a scratch battalion led by Montrose's Major General, Alasdair MacColla, and then provided covering fire as the pikemen literally pushed the rebels back into the village. Combat between two opposing bodies of pikemen was quite literally a matter of pushing and shoving, since the pikeheads tended merely to lodge in thick clothing and protective jerkins rather than impale people. This was indeed a fairly harmless proceeding unless one of the contending bodies physically collapsed or was overthrown by main force, whereupon the victorious party would commonly set about them with swords as they struggled to extricate themselves from the crush and make their escape.

It is all in all fair to say that in this era there were comparatively few men slain in hand to hand combat (and most of them shot rather than hacked or stabbed or bludgeoned to death), and that most battle casualties actually occurred after a firefight as the defeated party tried to run away. In Kipling's words two and a half centuries later, it was 'ruin to run from a fight'.

Perhaps because there were so few of them, the cavalry element in the Scots armies of both persuasions has generally been overshadowed by the infantry in general, and by the highlanders in particular, yet especially in Montrose's later battles they were to have an effect on the outcome out of all proportion to their meagre numbers.

Cavalry tactics of the time were generally speaking sedentary, in that rather than getting in and mixing it, 'banging it out braifly' as the saying was, they preferred to hang back and bang away with pistols and carbines instead; although should one side give way, then, as with their pedestrian comrades, the eagerness of the victorious party to set about the runaways knew no bounds. There were exceptions to this general rule, of course: some Scots cavalry lacking the requisite complement of firearms were equipped instead with lances, and at Auldearn Lord Gordon's Regiment executed a series of cavalry charges which were pressed home with unusual vigour.

8

Artillery played little part in the campaigns about to be described, largely because of the difficulty of transporting it about the Scottish landscape. Montrose, for example, had problems in shifting his guns in the two day battle for the Bridge of Dee in 1639, while at Kilsyth, six years later, the government's artillery train was captured after the battle without having been brought into action. The only real use made of artillery was, not surprisingly, in the siege or defence of fortified positions.

These, briefly, were the tactics which Montrose would have learned either from his studies or from Alexander Leslie and the other professional soldiers working with him in the early months of 1639. They were, of course, the conventional ones of the day, and their relevance to some of the forces raised by the rebels and to the highland contingents in particular may justifiably be questioned. This study is in part devoted to examining this question, and the role played by highlanders in some of Montrose's battles is vigorously re-assessed. For the moment however it is sufficient to say that the evidence suggests that conventional tactics predominated. It is certainly true to say that after he had changed sides and was fighting for rather than against the King, Montrose appears to have been much exercised by his shortage of sufficient regular troops, and as will become apparent, the strategy which he adopted was designed to use those few regulars, both cavalry and infantry, at his disposal, to their best advantage; and not to commit the less reliable elements of his forces, in particular the peasant levies from the western highlands, until a favourable opportunity had been created by the regulars. Highlanders were, in short, used not as shock troops, but to finish off an enemy already shaken by the onset of Montrose's regular troops.

This however lay in the future, and Montrose's first campaigns were to be fought by and against soldiers who, save for their blue bonnets, could have belonged to any Western European battlefield in the middle of the seventeenth century.

9

1

All the King's Castles and All the King's Men

Although concerned that the Marquis of Huntly in the north was resisting both their blandishments and threats, the provisional government in Edinburgh saw the most pressing threat as coming from the south: from an English army led by the King himself, from an Irish army led by Lord Wentworth, and from another English army led by the maladroit Marquis of Hamilton which was supposed to sail north to join Huntly. In addition the Covenanters also had to face the task of reducing a number of castles in southern Scotland still held by the King's soldiers or adherents: most notably, of course, Edinburgh Castle.

Sitting as it did quite literally overlooking the Parliament House, the Covenanters simply could not afford to ignore this stronghold, and it was the first of the castles to be taken by them. Guides at the castle will today proudly relate that the castle has never been taken by storm, yet on the morning of 21 March 1639 that was precisely what did happen.

Early that morning the Covenanters' military commander, General Alexander Leslie, a greatly respected veteran of the Swedish service, ordered his muster-master to select some companies of foot and draw them up in the 'outward courtyard' of Holyrood House. Doubtless after an inspection and a few brave words such as are appropriate to such desperate occasions, Leslie then led them up the High Street and concealed them behind those houses nearest to the castle. The castle approaches in 1639 were of course rather different from their present appearance, and in place of the magnificent Esplanade there was a long narrow outwork with a gate on the south side, called the 'Spur'. This imposing ashlar edifice was, however, something of a white elephant, as Leslie's assault was to demonstrate, and it was subsequently demolished between 1649 and 1650. The problem, as Leslie seems to have realised, was quite simply that the Spur masked any attackers from the castle guns. The actual storming of the castle was extremely

10

sudden and apparently quite bloodless. Two companies of foot—probably slightly less than 200 men—abruptly left the cover of the houses and rushed the gate. A petard—a cast iron bucket filled with gunpowder—attached to it by the artillery expert Sandy Hamilton, promptly blew it in; and the Covenanters, led on by Leslie, burst in sword in hand, and breaking down two inner doors made their way to the Half Moon Battery where, according to James Gordon of Rothiemay, the governor, Captain Archibald Haldane (brother to the Laird of Gleneagles) and his soldiers simply stood looking on helplessly amongst their useless cannon.[1]

Two days later the King's house at Dalkeith was seized after, if it were possible, even less resistance, entrance being effected on this occasion through a window.[2] Dumbarton Castle fell on 26 March, and it seems obvious that in this instance at least there was some collusion between the garrison and the Covenanters, for the entire garrison save a few sentries was captured, together with the governor, when he marched them out to attend divine service at a nearby church. Although the Tables may have slept more securely in their beds with Edinburgh Castle taken, the capture of Dumbarton was probably in the long term of greater significance, since it deprived Wentworth of a bridgehead for his Irish army. Since he was pretty unenthusiastic about the project in the first place, this was sufficient excuse to call off the expedition and thus one of the three armies was neutralised.

The Marquis of Hamilton for his part had been intended to land at Aberdeen with something in the region of 5,000 men, and to join with Huntly and the Gordons. In consequence Huntly received some rather odd orders from Hamilton not to engage in hostilities until he arrived, but by the time he was in a position to do so, Huntly had been arrested. In view of this development Hamilton instead sailed no further than the Firth of Forth, arriving off Leith on 1 May. The Covenanters, naturally enough, declined to let him land, and so he spent the rest of the brief war riding at anchor having achieved nothing. He has been much criticised for this inactivity; but quite apart from an understandable desire not to be seen to be leading an English invasion of his native country, or to face his pistol wielding mother, herself a stout supporter of the Covenant, or for that matter his ordinary inability to make up his mind, he had an utter lack of faith in the quality of the troops aboard his ships. His army comprised three regiments of militia from Kent and East Anglia, and by the testimony of the professional soldiers appointed to lead them they were indeed a sorry lot. Sir Nicholas Byron had few complaints about his men, but Sir Simon Harcourt, embarking men from Suffolk and Cambridge at Great Yarmouth on 18 April, reported that his regiment's arms were defective and old-fashioned: the muskets were too heavy and the pikes rotten.

Sir Thomas Morton's regiment, raised in Kent, was however the worst of the three, as a melancholy letter from Edward Rossingham to Viscount Conway reveals:

> The officers of those trainbands which were to go out of Kent, when they came to Gravesend last week, examined their arms, which they find very unserviceable, many of their muskets having no touch holes, and some others having them so large as one might turn ones thumb in them, and the pikes were so rotten as they were shaken many of them all in pieces; some few of the muskets were reasonably good; the captain commending one of those muskets wished they had all been so good. Nay saith the musketeer, my master sought to have found a worse musket, but he could find none in all the town, if he could I should have had it. These ill arms and the poor undisciplined [untrained] men being hired for £8, £10 and £12 by the trained men to go in their stead, being taken into consideration, they sent to the Council to complain of the county for providing no better for the Kings service ...[3]

Hamilton may therefore have felt that he had good reason not to force a landing, and, perhaps with little to do other than reflect upon his unenviable situation, he may also have recalled previous English military operations which had ended in disaster, such as the Isle of Rhé expedition of 1627, and his own mishandled participation in the German wars. Nevertheless he ought to have realised that the Covenanters were in no better state, and had his original instructions been adhered to, a landing at Aberdeen in mid-May might have made a considerable difference to the King's affairs.

Preoccupied as they were with the threat of an invasion from England, it is clear that the Covenanters still saw the Gordons as a considerable threat, and accordingly took steps to deal with them; though at first it may have seemed that in fact they presented very little threat at all. The key to this seeming paradox was George Gordon, 2nd Marquis of Huntly. Broadly speaking, this nobleman was master of all Scotland from Aberdeen to Inverness and perhaps beyond, or at least should have been, were it not for his weak and irresolute character. Sympathetic contemporaries such as Gordon of Rothiemay and Gordon of Ruthven are quick to stress that Huntly was under orders from Hamilton not to engage in hostilities without his express command, while at the same time being required to muster men for the King's service, and so create a threat which the government would find it impossible to ignore. A more resolute personality might have acted and let the results justify the deed—as indeed his vassals were shortly to do—but Huntly, not for the last time, was torn by a fatal indecision and was unwilling to act thus, so providing the government with the excuse and opportunity to arrest him and disarm his followers, without his having achieved anything.

12

A not inconsiderable part of Huntly's problem was that a sizeable number of families in the North-East of Scotland, partly from stout Protestant conviction, and partly from a just as potent and unashamed rivalry with the House of Gordon, adhered to the government; and this led to the first, bloodless, clash at Turriff on 14 February 1639.

Although a market town of no great size, Turriff was centrally situated in the lowlands of Aberdeenshire, and consequently ideally placed as a rendezvous point. The Covenanters therefore convened a meeting there attended initially only by the local Covenanting lairds; but it was suspected that Huntly would attempt something, and they were quickly joined by the Earls of Montrose and Kinghorn with their followers, and thus, protected by no fewer than 800 heavily armed men, they squeezed into the tiny church and began their deliberations. Having taken these steps, they were by no means surprised when Huntly duly turned up with a large following. The circumstances and outcome of the events which followed are by no means as simple and straightforward as is sometimes represented. According to John Spalding, Huntly had been attending a funeral in Aberdeen the previous day with his two eldest sons, the Lord Gordon and the Lord Aboyne, and other Gordon lairds, and since Turriff lay on his road home to Strathbogie he took the opportunity to lay on a show of strength.[4]

Accordingly he summoned all his dependents to escort him past the village with a view to suitably impressing if not actually intimidating the Covenanters gathered within. Although the fact that he had ordered his men to muster armed only with muskets and swords might support the impression that his intentions were for the most part peaceful, the Gordons themselves stated that Huntly in fact intended to go further and occupy Turriff if he could, and so intimidate the Covenanters from meeting. Sir George Gordon of Gight indeed had arrived there ahead of the main body of the Royalists, and casually entered only to find the streets thronged with the heavily armed Covenanters; he had therefore withdrawn in some embarrassment. Huntly on his arrival was offered the use of the young Earl of Erroll's house to refresh himself by some no doubt straight-faced Covenanters, but conscious of his dignity he declined. While this brief exchange took place, the Covenanters crammed themselves into the churchyard and prepared to defend the (still extant) walls against Huntly's host; but that tragic figure had no intention of initiating hostilities at this stage, and instead he rode past, 'hard under the dyckes of the churchyarde, westward within two picke lenth to Montrose company without salutatione or worde speaking on either side.'

This incident was clearly felt by some of the Gordons to have been rather humiliating, and the Covenanters naturally made the most of it, though Spalding in Aberdeen, being able to view it with a degree of

13

detachment, seems to have believed that Huntly had achieved his objective in 'showing the flag' without engaging in as yet unwarranted hostilities. Nevertheless, although he may on this occasion have been constrained by his instructions from Hamilton, the lack of more positive action was a portent of things to come. Another factor in Huntly's unwillingness to act, however, which has been little considered, is that at this stage in the proceedings he had neither experienced officers nor adequate supplies of arms for his men; and while at Aberdeen he had dispatched Sir Alexander Gordon of Cluny to the King with a request for an adequate supply of arms and a contingent of regular soldiers. Cluny returned to Aberdeen on 9 March aboard one of the King's yachts, escorting a collier laden with 1,000 pikes and 2,000 muskets, with armour and other warlike supplies, but no soldiers. Huntly took delivery of these arms on the 17th and at once began raising his men in earnest; but as Gordon of Ruthven observed, the arrival of these arms was in some ways a mixed blessing:

> The comeing of the armes without the aid both discovered Huntlyes res-
> olution and incouraged the Covenanters suddenly to raise and bestir there
> forces, whereby he was constrained to make the best of ane evill day; raising
> such forces as he could upon the sudden, and many of them but coldlie
> affected and all of them, through a long continued pace, ignorant of all
> militarye discipline. When he had brought them to the randewowes, and a
> counsell of warre held tuo severall dayes most wotes carried it that they
> sould dissolue for that tyme and not to wrong the Kinges cause vpon vnequall
> termes to hazard a battle, being all vntrained men without commanders
> (save only Leautennent colonell Johnstoune) with divers other reasons but
> chiefly the want of the promised aid.[5]

Not all of the Royalists were quite so unenthusiastic. Some of the equipment was leased by Huntly to the Aberdeen Militia, as well as to his dependants, as far afield as Strathavan and Glenlivet. The Aberdonians indeed seem to have thrown themselves into warlike preparations with some enthusiasm, and under the direction of Lieutenant Colonel Johnston, a professional soldier who was also the son of a former Provost of the city, wooden bulwarks were raised, cannon mounted and the citizen soldiers drilled daily on the Links. According to Spalding the wearing of swords was socially essential.

But then, abruptly, Huntly disbanded his forces as related above; and needless to say this caused consternation amongst the Aberdonians, who suddenly felt very vulnerable indeed. The swords disappeared and many fled in panic, though sixty of them stoutly took ship to join the King at Berwick: 'weill armed with suord, musket and bandilier as excellent cavillieres. They took one of the toune's cullouris and John Park their drummer with thame.'[6] A number of Royalist gentlemen similarly took ship for the south, including the Lairds of Drum, Pitfodels,

Foveran and Balgownie, but all of them were to find themselves back in Aberdeen rather sooner than they might have expected.[7]

Meanwhile the Covenanters were not slow to take advantage of this sudden collapse of the 'anti-covenanter' or Royalist party, and on 30 March they entered Aberdeen in some strength led by the Earls of Montrose and Kinghorn and the Earl Marischal, sporting for the first time the blue ribbons which were to be the emblem of their party, and marching behind banners which declared them to be 'FOR RELIGION, THE COVENANT, AND THE CUNTRIE'.

Pausing only long enough to install the Earl of Kinghorn as Governor of the city, (which must have upset the Earl Marischal, who undoubtedly regarded Aberdeen as belonging to his own sphere of influence), and to give orders for the slighting of Johnston's defences, Montrose marched out to Inverurie where he met Huntly on 4 April.

What happened next was to have far-reaching consequences, yet it is unlikely that we will ever know what was said and what was not said. The upshot was that Huntly came to Aberdeen under a safe-conduct, but was arrested and subsequently incarcerated none too uncomfortably in Edinburgh Castle. It has been surmised that he deliberately chose to be arrested in order to escape from the impossible position in which he found himself, and this idea may have some merit; though it is also true that having been arrested while under safe-conduct, Huntly later refused to trust or co-operate with Montrose after the latter's defection to the Royalist party. Whether his arrest was engineered by Montrose, by Alexander Leslie who was at this time serving as a military adviser to Montrose, by the Covenanting ministers, or even by Huntly himself, the result was the same: Huntly departed from the scene, the Gordons were left leaderless, and the Covenanters battened on them, disarming them and plundering them, cheerfully oblivious of what was to happen next.[8]

Montrose departed southwards with Huntly, doubtless congratulating himself on having neutralised the Gordon threat without a fight: but in fact he had achieved the opposite result. Led by the irresolute Huntly, the Gordons posed little real threat, but now that he was out of the way the smaller lairds, or the 'Barons' as they became known, took matters into their own hands. Despite their dramatic success, the Covenanters' control of the north-east was far from effective as yet; and Sir George Ogilvy of Banff, concerned as much as anything by the imminent possibility of his lands being plundered, persuaded Sir George Gordon of Gight and some others, including Lieutenant Colonel Johnston, whom Huntly had left at Strathbogie in command of an infantry regiment, to join with him in an attack on Towie Barclay Castle near Turriff.

The attack on Towie Barclay Castle was, except in one important respect, an inconsequential affair, and Spalding's account of it is sufficient:

> There wes together the Laird of Banff, the Laird of Geight, the young Laird of Cromartie, with sum vtheris, who with Lieutenant crouner Johnstoun, vpone the 10th of May intendit to cum to the place of Tollie Barclay, and thair to take out sic armes, muscatis, gunis and carabinis as the Lairds of Delgatie and Tollie-Barclay had plunderit from the said young Laird of Cromartie, out of the place of Baquholly, bot it hapnit the Lord Fraser and maister of Forbes to sie thair cumming. Thay manit the house of Towy, cloissit the yettis, and schott diverse schottis fra the house heid, whair ane servand of the Laird of Geight's wes schot, callit David Prat. The baronis, seeing they culd not mend thame salffis, left the houss, thinking it no vassalage to stay whill thay war slayne; syne, but more ado rode their way.[9]

The death of David Prat, the first man to be slain in the Civil Wars, seems to have given both parties something to think about, and they were not slow in realising that the dispute was now to be considered in earnest. For their part the Covenanters assembled again at Turriff, raising, according to Spalding, 1,200 horse and foot led by Lord Fraser, the Master of Forbes, Hay of Delgaty, the Laird of Towie Barclay, Keith of Ludquharn, Forbes of Craigievar, Forbes of Tolquhon and the Lairds of Skene, Echt and Waterton. The Royalists similarly banded together at Strathbogie included Ogilvy of Banff, Gordon of Abergeldie, Gordon of Haddo, the Lairds of Cromartie, Grag Auchindoir, Foveran and Crombie, Gordon of Gight, Gordon of Newton, Leith of Harthill, Forbes of Blacktoun and Lieutenant Colonel William Johnston. They only appear to have mustered 800 horse and foot, but although out-numbered, they possessed two considerable advantages over the Covenanters: one was Lieutenant Colonel Johnston, the only professional soldier in sight, and the other was the Strathbogie Regiment, six companies of regular infantry raised by Huntly, equipped with the King's muskets and pikes and trained by Lieutenant Colonel Johnston. The Covenanters could match neither of them.[10]

The 'Trot of Turriff', 14 May 1639

Once again the prime mover amongst the Royalists was Sir George Ogilvy of Banff, who according to Rothiemay:

> loved not to see the Covenanters so near himself in arms, there being but six short myles betuixt Turreffe and Banfe's house. Besyde, if the businesse carryd, he would be sure to ascribe the praise to himselfe; if otherwayes the losse that should be sustained should alight amongst the Gordons and not on him, who had but few ther to lose; or, if he wer called to ane accoumpt for it afterwardes, he could easily lurke amongst the multitude, and pass with the rest, as having but one vote and not command ther, so that goe the world as it pleased, he did not think himself a gainer or no loser. Ther

16

were many handes but few heades; and Banfe had a number of gentlemen of his acqwayntance ther whom he used as adjutators, to sett on the multitude to call for that which he projected.[11]

Turriff is only about 15 miles from Strathbogie (Rothiemay's estimate of 11 miles is a little optimistic), and it was soon agreed that the Royalists should sally forth and beat up the Covenanters' quarters in the night; but as they were on the point of setting off, it occurred to them that someone ought to be in command, and on this question they could not agree. One of the first to be proposed was Huntly's brother, Lord Adam Gordon, but apparently his brains were 'craicted', and attention then focused on the third of Huntly's sons, Lord Lewis Gordon; but as he was a 12 year old schoolboy, he was similarly rejected, and doubtless because he had been so keen on the enterprise, Ogilvy of Banff was proposed after all for the command. This was quickly assented to, but because he was not a Gordon, Sir John Gordon of Haddo was also appointed to command with him jointly. Both, in Rothiemay's acerbic view, were brave men, 'but Banfe the wittier of the two, and Hadda supposed to be plyable to Banfe's councells and advyce'.[12]

Having thus settled the command, the Royalists then turned to the equally weighty matter of 'What commissione they had for to fight': but here they were on surer ground, and Alexander Gordon of Carnborrow proposed that a Band of Association be drawn up, declaring that they were taking up arms for the maintenance of the King's prerogative, for the service of Huntly and his family, and for their own mutual 'preservatione'. This was enthusiastically agreed, and thus prepared, the first of the Royalist armies took the field.[13]

No sooner did the cavaliers set off but the wrangle over the command was seemingly forgotten, and the actual management of the army passed almost by default to Lieutenant Colonel Johnston. In view of his being the only professional soldier present, he was given command of the van, but no-one seems to have objected or indeed even raised any eyebrows when he liberally interpreted this to mean the whole army, and no one was in any doubt that he was in command by the next morning. Banff and Haddo cheerfully acquiesced in this takeover, probably because the former wanted to stay in the background and the latter was all too conscious of his inexperience. In any case, since the Royalist army at this point comprised only two weak troops of horse and the Strathbogie Regiment which Johnston had himself been training, they were already in some measure superfluous.

By this time it was ten o'clock at night, and it would seem likely that the Royalists marched by what is now the A97 from Strathbogie (or Huntly as it is now called) as far as Haddo, and then either turned east along the path of the B9024 or perhaps simply followed the river Deveron to Turriff. Spalding declares that they came by an unexpected way, which would suggest the river rather than the road—this would have prevented them from getting lost in the dark, and may also account for a reference to a 'troublesome' march.[14] At any rate, by the 'peip of day' they arrived before Turriff, at which point the carriage of one of their four brass field pieces broke, and there was an anxious pause whilst it was repaired as 'weall as the time wold permitte'.[15]

The Covenanters were taken completely by surprise: as is often the case, they themselves were planning to attack the Royalists, and it never occurred to them that they might be set upon first. Most, obviously, were asleep; though others, evidently not of a puritanical disposition, were drinking and smoking, or even walking up and down, and the sudden peal of trumpets and the loud rattle of the Strathbogie Regiment's drums which greeted the dawn inspired a fearful consternation. This confusion was made worse by the fact that unlike the Royalists, they had not yet appointed a leader, so that 'as it befalls in such cases, all commanded, and no bodye obeyed'. Johnston, perceiving this confusion, took advantage of it to march along the deep valley of Idoch Water which lies below the south side of the town. Gordon of Rothiemay's account of the opening moves of the fight is perhaps the best, although he differs from Gordon of Ruthven in the matter of where the Covenanters were drawn up:

> ther marche was along a valley which lyes east and west under the village of Turreff; which stands upon highe and steepe grounde upon the north syde of the valleye. They could not enter it in aeqwalle termes upon any syde but either on the north or upon the easte, but best upon the east syde, though it wer the ende of the village farrest removed from them, who wer come from the west that night. Ther marche about the village, as it gave leisour to ther enemyes to draw upp within the large street of the village, which runnes from the east to the west, so it gave the Gordons a great advauntage for to macke ane infall; the east ende of the street being opne, without any gate or porte, and it capable to receave a number of horse or foote a breaste; besyde, the feeld hard by the streete levell and usefull for drawing upp a greate number of men for reserve, to second the persewers. The Covenanters made a fashione for to baricade that ende of the street, as the short tyme and few materialls, which wer ill to be founde, but most of all ther confusione and trepidatione, would permitte; for within the village all was in a confusione.[16]

Ruthven on the other hand declares that the Covenanters brought all their men out of the town and drew them up in order of battle to face the Royalists, but otherwise is in agreement with Rothiemay. Perhaps they did so initially but then fell back. At least, despite the confusion, the Covenanters were hastily able to agree that they should be commanded by a local Laird, William Hay of Delgaty, who seems to have been a soldier; but otherwise the choice was not a happy one, for he was a secret Royalist, and indeed during the Civil War proper in the 1640s he fought under Montrose.

The battle was opened by two musket shots fired out of the Earl of Erroll's house and promptly answered by two cannon shots from the Royalists. These may have done no harm save to the Covenanters' nerves, but greatly encouraged the Royalists, and the Strathbogie Regiment 'could not by their commanders be restrained from a present charge upon there enemies, notwithstanding of there long and trouble-som march all the night before'.[17]

The Covenanters' foot battalion refused to face them, and either, depending on whether you follow Rothiemay's or Ruthven's version, fell back into the town or back down the street from their barricades. Since the defences were incomplete, Ruthven's version seems likelier, but the two are not incompatible. The Strathbogie men immediately set to tearing down the barricades before sending a volley crashing down the street accompanied by a third cannon shot. Both Delgaty and Sir William Keith of Ludquharn did their best to keep their men in order 'first by there faire persuasione, and then by threttings, but all in vaine'. A fourth cannon shot and the appearance of the two small Royalist cavalry troops (both, as the chroniclers emphasise, markedly outnumbered by their Covenanting counterparts) proved too much for them, and all incontinently fled in all directions, including the Lord Fraser, who according to Spalding filled his breeches. So sudden indeed was their flight that Johnston, fearing a trap, restrained his own men from pursuing. The Covenanters were so scattered and frightened that pursuit was in any case unnecessary, and in consequence casualties were very light. Indeed only three are known to have been killed outright, two of them Covenanters, and the third an unfortunate common soldier of the Strathbogie Regiment killed 'by the unskill-fullnesse of his owne comerades fyring ther musketts, as was thought'.[18]

Two prisoners were also taken, James Skene, the Laird of Skene, and Arthur Forbes of Echt, though both were extremely unfortunate in that they were taken not by Johnston's men but by 'ane old cavallier Sir George Gordon of Gight who coming that morning with his servants towards Turriff mett them in the way unexpectedly and made them prisoners'.[19]

Gight had clearly been making his own way to the battlefield, and the gallant old gentleman probably regarded his prisoners as ample compensation for his earlier humiliation at Turriff when Montrose had been there. Both men were released later that day, but probably not before witnessing yet another farcical incident. Doubtless because they were feeling at something of a loose end after quite literally beating the

King's enemies before breakfast, the Royalists decided to accord the now unknown Royalist soldier who had been shot in the back a full military funeral. He was laid to rest in the burial place of Walter Barclay of Towie (died 1636) within the church of Turriff. Having lowered him into his grave a party of musketeers proceeded to fire a volley or two over him within the tiny building! For some reason they had loaded with ball and the bullets ripped through the ceiling to the terror of the minister, Mr. Thomas Michell, 'who all the whyle with his sonne, disgwsed in a womans habite had gott upp and was lurkinge above the syling of the churche'.[20]

The Royalists had brought no provisions with them, and with the proprieties observed, they broke into houses in search of oatmeal; though inevitably perhaps the plundering quickly got out of hand. Next they convened all the inhabitants who had not already fled and administered the King's Covenant before marching on Aberdeen. There was no resistance to their occupation, but although they were soon joined by several hundred highlanders led by Huntly's delinquent schoolboy son, Lord Lewis Gordon, and by Huntly's Baillie, Donald Farquharson of Monaltrie, they abruptly lost their nerve and retreated northwards again; so that when Montrose arrived at Aberdeen on 25 May with 4,000 men, he found that it had already been re-occupied by the Earl Marischal. The first occupation of the city by the Covenanters had been quite peaceful and their soldiers well behaved, but this time it was a different story, and Aberdeen had been fined and thoroughly plundered by the time Montrose moved north in search of the Royalists. No sooner had he done so, however, than a report was received that another of Huntly's sons, Lord Aboyne, had appeared off the coast in one of the King's ships. It seems to have been assumed that he had brought thousands of soldiers with him, and Montrose obviously decided that he needed to recruit more men from the friendly Mearns and his native Forfarshire.

In actual fact Aboyne had brought only the fifty musketeers who had fled from Aberdeen earlier, and what might be termed a military mission—several English captains to train the Gordon levies, and Colonel William Gunn, a Scots professional soldier, who was to serve as Aboyne's military adviser.[21] Few though they were, the presence of the Lord Aboyne was enough to put fresh heart into the Royalists, and by mid June Aberdeen was occupied by no fewer than 5,000 Royalist soldiers. Meanwhile Montrose was by this time in Forfarshire still raising men, and now beset by orders to march south to join the main Scots army at Duns on the border; but on receiving frantic messages from the Earl Marischal, who was still trying to muster his own men at Dunottar Castle, he marched north and precipitated the dramatic climax to the war in the north.

20

MEGRAY HILL, 15 JUNE 1639

The English captains were a useful addition to the Royalist forces, but Colonel Gunn proved to be a rather controversial figure. Until now William Johnston had enjoyed an unrivalled ascendancy, and if Ogilvy of Banff and Gordon of Haddo were the political leaders of the insurrection, he was its military commander. Now Aboyne had supplanted Banff and Haddo, doubtless to the relief of both (Banff had already withdrawn pleading ill-health), and he had brought his own military adviser with him. It is hardly surprising that there was friction between the two professional soldiers, and this may account for much of what followed. Johnston was clearly popular with the Gordons, he was an Aberdeen man and so not an outsider, his ability was recognised and respected and they were used to working with him. Had he not been so respected he could hardly have assumed command as he did at Turriff. William Gunn, on the other hand, was a Sutherland man, a stranger, and overbearing in his manner. The Gordon chroniclers unequivocally accused him of treachery in the fighting which followed, but it is hard to see what his motives might have been; and rather than treachery it is just as likely that jealousy and distrust on the part of Johnston's partisans, and arrogance and a certain incompetence on Gunn's part, were all that was involved. Afterwards he returned to the Imperial service, and one might have expected that if he had indeed been playing the Royalists false, that he would instead have taken service under the Covenant.

At any rate, probably rather late on Friday 14 June 1639, Aboyne marched out of Aberdeen across Bishop Elphinstone's seven-arched brown sandstone bridge and south towards Stonehaven in an attempt to bring the Earl Marischal to battle. The army only got as far as Muchalls, about halfway to Stonehaven, that night, and encamped at the castle. This slow progress therefore gave the Earl Marischal a chance to send to Montrose for help, and thus reinforced the Covenanters barricaded themselves into the small fishing port of Stonehaven. Nevertheless they had only some 1,200 men and 14 guns,[22] all but two of them light ones, and when the Royalists arrived next morning a vigorous assault should have cleared them out of the village in short order. Indeed, anticipating this, the Earl Marischal sent word to the small garrison left in Dunottar Castle to have the gates open ready to receive such of the Covenanters as could make their escape.

The Royalists marched from Muchalls at dawn 15 June with 2,500 horse and foot, including 500 highlanders; and finding the Covenanters waiting for them, drew up on Megray Hill a little to the north of Stonehaven. Then, incredibly, Gunn went off for breakfast, taking Aboyne with him. Led by Johnston, who was commanding the cavalry, some of the more active of the Gordons recovered from their surprise, and interrupting the breakfast party they won from the reluctant Gunn permission to skirmish with the enemy. Accordingly 24 'cavaleers' rode down towards the village and encountered an equal number of Covenanters, though neither party evidenced much desire to come to hand-strokes.

> This was the first tyme that ever the Covenanters stoode ther ground at the distaunce of shott. Many pistoll shott wer exchanged, but at too great distaunce on both sydes most shottes; otherwayes the continuall motione of ther horses preveened all hurt. Some, by the restivnesse of ther owne horses wnused to service, wer throwne to the grounde. All the losse that was sustained at ther first rencounter was the killing of William Seaton of Shethinn his horse, not by the Covenanters horse, but by ane hardye fellow, ane Aberdeens traidsmane, who had fledd to the Covenanters as fancying them most; who, tacking the advauntage of a plott of high grounde that overlooked the place wher both partyes piched, did lett flee about a dosen of muskett shott amongst Abynes cavaliers and then gott of: any hurt that was done was by him.[23]

After a time the Covenanters fell back, perhaps because they had run out of ammunition; but they were reinforced by a second party of volunteers, and the Royalists had in turn to give way before being reinforced in their turn: 'the rest of that troop to which they belonged, impatient to see ther freends reteer, fell in to ther rescwe, without order; such as pleased falling in, and such as wanted courage keeping off.'

These were presumably the troop of 'volunteer gentleman cuirassiers' who had taken the van with a handkerchief tied to a lance by way of a standard; and the Covenanters fled from them, drawing them within musket range of their infantry in Stonehaven. Johnston realised the danger at once, but his calls to retire were ignored, and they rode into what amounted to an ambush:

> But no sooner did the Covenanter horsemen fynde a mor considerable number of horse drawing neer, but instantly they tacke them to ther heels and runne towards Stonehyve; not for want of courage but for to draw the Anti-Covenanter horsemen fully under ther shott, as it fell out. For most pairt of them, upon a mistacke did persew them so eagerly that, ere they wer aware they wer under the muskett shott of Stonehyve; Johnston only being sensible of ther error, and calling to them to reteere; but that was in vaine, till Montrosse pairty beganne to lett flee at them both with his two half canon and with severall feeld peeces tackne off of Dunotyre for that purpose, as also with muskett shott after that he had seen his owne horsemen safely under cover; so that now they who but immediatly befor wer so eager in ther pursuite wer glade to runne of in disorder, not having any enemy to cope withall but canon and muskett shot.[24]

All the while, the Royalist foot brigades, commanded by Colonel Gunn, had stood motionless on Megray Hill watching the skirmishing. It had been Johnston's proposal that while he engaged the Covenanters' attention by skirmishing, Gunn should march the foot around the high ground to the west and so outflank the Stonehaven position. To his dismay he now realised that Gunn had not stirred an inch, and now the Covenanters' artillery turned its attention to the Royalist infantry. Unfortunately no Royalist order of battle exists, but we do know that the 220 men of the Aberdeen Militia stood on the right of the front line and that the rest of the front line was comprised of the Strathbogie Regiment and other Lowland levies.[25] Curiously, in view of the prowess with which (largely Victorian) mythology has invested them, the 500 or so highlanders were relegated to the rear. All seem to have agreed that while they had their uses they were not fit to stand in the front line, and this low opinion was dramatically vindicated when after a few cannon balls had landed, either amongst them or the front line (accounts are not clear but the latter seems likeliest), they took to their heels and precipitately fled, not stopping until they had found refuge in a bog fully half a mile to the rear. Aboyne and other officers rode after them, but all their entreaties and threats proved unavailing and the rabble refused to budge. According to Rothiemay 'two or three wer either maimed or killed', none of them seemingly highlanders; but the panic flight of the tartan-clad rabble 'made the rest of the foote for to reele, for the most pairt; who beganne now to mutinee against Gunne, so that in the ende he gave order to draw them in covert backwarde from the sight of Montrose his two so formidable carthawes' (20lb cannon).

Had he not done so, Rothiemay claims they would have retired of their own accord, but in actual fact it made little difference. By early afternoon the highlanders, still lurking in the bog, decided that there was no profit in remaining and 'beganne to dropp awaye and marche off in whole companyes'; and once again infected by their pusillanimous example, the lowland foot, gathered about the farm of Logie, did likewise in twenties and thirties.[26] Only the horse could be persuaded to stand facing the enemy to cover what quickly became a general and disorderly retreat, and sensibly Aboyne dispatched two officers to Aberdeen to round up the stragglers as they arrived there. This they proceeded to do with the aid of a couple of the town's drummers, but hardly had they begun when Aboyne himself rode in. So many of his soldiers had run away that he had no army left to command, and he tactfully put it about that he thought it unwise to remain so close to the Covenanters overnight. In fact the Covenanters were at first quite unaware that they had won a famous victory. They had seen Aboyne's foot retire over the crest of Megray Hill about halfway through the

23

morning, and since then had sat tight behind their barricades, apprehensively awaiting an attack from some other direction. Indeed so sure were they that the Royalists were secretly marching around their flank that they forbore to fire upon the Royalist cavalry, taking the rearguard for a decoy. Consequently the Royalists, vulnerable as they were to the feeblest pursuit, got clean away, and Aboyne was given the chance to pull his shaken forces back together.

So unprepared for this surprise victory was Montrose that the Covenanters did not move forward until Monday 17 June, by which time the Royalists had recovered somewhat. Perhaps as many as 4,000 lowland foot were assembled at Leggatsden, a traditional rendezvous to the north-west of Aberdeen, and Aboyne was concluding arrangements for billeting and paying his troops in Aberdeen, but the highlanders were gone beyond recall. Plundering the Earl Marischal's estates as they went, they marched off back up Deeside, and in Aberdeen itself Aboyne could muster only his cavalry and what remained of the Strathbogie Regiment, now commanded by Captain Nathaniel Gordon[27]—a professional soldier later to win some renown. It must have been small consolation to retrieve the four brass cannon used at Turriff from the hold of the ship in which they had lain during the skirmish at Megray Hill.

Lieutenant Colonel Johnston meanwhile took out a party of horse, with Gunn's somewhat reluctant approval, to harass the Covenanters, which they did well enough but then clattered into Aberdeen at nightfall with the news that Montrose's men were on their heels.

THE BRIDGE OF DEE, 18 AND 19 JUNE 1639

A little before dawn on the morning of 18 June the drums beat through the streets calling the Aberdeen Militia to arms, and while they crept reluctantly from their beds Captain Nathaniel Gordon marched the survivors of the Strathbogie Regiment out to the Bridge of Dee, two miles above the town. There he set them to work strengthening the gate at the south end by piling up earth and turves behind it. Although the seven-arched brown sandstone bridge stood outside Aberdeen it was the only practical crossing point for some distance. In good weather and at low tide there was a useful ford a few hundred yards downstream and another a short distance upstream at Banchory Devenick, but the river on the morning of the 18th was in spate, and both were quite impassable. Consequently, outnumbered as they were with most of their men still at Leggatsden, the Royalists seized upon the bridge as being the only position from which they could defend Aberdeen, since the Covenanters had no other means of attacking the town, save across it.

24

It seems to be generally agreed that Montrose had something in the region of 2,000 men with him, though details appear to be lacking. It is nevertheless possible to speculate with a fair degree of certainty as to their composition. The Earl Marischal's Regiment of foot would have been present, though probably somewhat under strength, since in later years it included an Aberdeen contingent which was certainly lacking on this occasion; and perhaps also a troop or two of horse. Montrose was to raise two regiments of foot in Forfarshire (Angus) in 1640, and there is no reason to suppose that he did not do so in 1639. At any rate a strong contingent is known to have been present from Dundee, and a company from Arbroath, which would suggest a regiment raised on Tayside as well as one from the Montrose area. Given the haste with which these troops had been levied, it is likely that both were under strength. Again also some troops of horse formed part of the Forfarshire contingent. As at Megray Hill, Montrose could call upon the services of two 20lb cannon, together with a number of lighter pieces, though their performance was at first to be rather disappointing.

Captain Gordon's Strathbogie men were soon followed to the bridge by Aboyne and the Royalist cavalry, but their arrival coincided with that of the Covenanters who greeted them with a salvo from their big guns. The cannon-balls fell short, however, and the Royalists prudently stayed well clear of the bridge: though oddly enough they had gained a considerable advantage, for the artillery so hastily emplaced to fire upon them could not easily be re-deployed to fire effectively on the bridge. As a result the Covenanters' artillery fire was to be totally ineffective throughout the day—as, it has to be admitted, was the fire of the Royalists' four brass cannon. Finally Lieutenant Colonel Johnston arrived at the head of the Aberdeen Militia and assumed command of all forces on the bridge, posting his men for the most part in the 'ravelins' or passing bays. Just how many men he brought is a matter of some dispute. The unknown author of *True Rehearsall* states that 500 men manned the bridge, and although they must have been very tightly packed this is not inconsistent with Rothiemay's account, which speaks of the 'Aberdeens companyes, about four colours'. On the other hand, the normally reliable John Spalding, who was probably himself present in the ranks of the Militia, categorically states that only 100 men were present. The discrepancy is at first sight a considerable one, but it is likely that Spalding was correct, and that the remaining 400 men—of the Strathbogie Regiment and Captain Grant's Company—provided covering fire and moral support from the north bank of the river.[28]

On the first day the Covenanters got nowhere. Their cannon on the hill-top could only fire obliquely on the bridge, and although they doubtless gave some encouragement to the various parties of commanded musketeers who were pushed forward from time to time, their fire was quite inaccurate and caused no casualties. Indeed this artillery-fire was so ineffectual that after two or three hours the wives and servants of the Aberdeen men joined them on the bridge, bringing welcome supplies of food and drink.[29]

Thus fortified 'the Aberdeens men stoode to it gallantlye, and all that day continowed giving fire'. A brisk rivalry has always existed between Aberdeen and Dundee, and the success of Johnston's men in holding the bridge roused the jealousy of some of Montrose's men, who begged him to give them the chance to show their mettle:

> After noone the companyes of Dundee, aemulouse of the Aberdeen citizens, desyred to be lettne storme the bridge, which Montrose readily yeelded too. Two companyes fell on, under the commande of one captain Bonner* but they founde so hotte a welcome from the Aberdeens men that they made a quick retreat; which was seconded with the whooping and hallowing of such as wer looking on who mocked ther poor bravado.[30]

Although fighting between the two factions had unquestionably been in earnest, it is evident that the majority of the combatants were still civilians at heart. Shortly after the repulse of the Dundee men one of the Aberdeen Militia, a burgess named John Forbes, was shot through the head by the Covenanting Laird of Dunsmill; and incensed by the fact that Dunsmill had clearly been seen to have taken deliberate aim at Forbes, one of the Strathbogie Regiment, John Gordon of Instomack, retaliated by shooting dead in turn one Captain James Ramsay on the Covenanters' side.[32] Only one other Royalist casualty is recorded on the 18th, William Gordon of Gordons Mills—one of the Old Aberdeen men—'rakleslie schot in the foot',[33] presumably by his own or his comrades' carelessness; but the death of Forbes was to have quite disastrous consequences for the Royalists.

Although it never properly gets dark in those latitudes at that time of year, both sides gave over firing early in the evening, though there was certainly no lack of activity as the night wore on. On the south side of the river Montrose had his two big guns dragged further to the east, and as the light improved sufficiently had them levelled directly against the bridge gate. The Royalists meanwhile committed a serious error. Early in the morning of Wednesday 19 June, fifty, that is half of the Aberdeen Militia, marched off back to the town, taking the corpse of John Forbes for burial.[34] Johnston was thus left only with fifty militiamen on the bridge and the Strathbogie men lining the north bank of the river.

On the previous day the Covenanters' cannon had done little more than shatter one of the two stone watch-towers flanking the bridge gate,

* A Lieutenant Colonel Boner fought at Marston Moor in Viscount Dudhope's Regiment which had been raised in Forfarshire.[31]

but now when the cannonade was resumed their fire was at first much more effective. Notwithstanding the earth and turves piled up behind it by Captain Gordon's men, the gate was soon blown in, and thereafter the cannonballs 'scoured the way of the bridge all alonge'. Unnerving though it may have been to see the heavy shot crashing along the roadway, the defenders were to begin with quite unscathed, since the 'ravelins' although low-walled afforded a considerable degree of protection, and perhaps a little paradoxically the cannon actually kept the militia at their posts. After all, in order to run away they would need to brave the shot-torn roadway. Aboyne, nevertheless, having sat inactively throughout the previous day's proceedings, now felt that the bridge ought to be reinforced and ordered his cavalry forward.

Seeing this movement, Montrose, who may have had rather less cavalry, ordered some of his own troopers to ride upstream as though making for the ford at Banchory Devenick. In turn Colonel Gunn, who, it seems, had already opposed the forward movement of the Royalist cavalry, ordered them now to follow the Covenanters upstream and prevent them from crossing. The Gordon lairds vehemently protested to him that the ford was impassable and the errand fruitless, but he insisted and led them on. Hardly had he done so however but they came within range of Montrose's artillery, and John Seton of Pitmeddan was instantly cut in two by a cannonball! This was all the excuse needed for the already unhappy Royalist cavalry to retreat once more, crying out that Gunn was betraying them.[35] Suitably encouraged by these highly visible (and perhaps audible) signs of distress, the commander of one of Montrose's foot regiments, Lieutenant Colonel John Middleton, cried out 'that ther cannon would mack them all arrant poultrons', and speedily assembled a storming party. In order to cover his assault the Covenanters' artillery was again switched to the bridge, and this time brought down one of the towers, burying the gallant Johnston in the rubble. He was quickly dug out by his men, but finding his leg broken they flung him over a horse and he was led away, crying out: 'Gallantis do for your selffis, and haist yow to the toune'.[36] This, according to Spalding, they were not slow to do. Captain Nathaniel Gordon then endeavoured to keep his Strathbogie men to their posts, but seeing Middleton's attack coming in they too lost their nerve and fled. Consequently the Covenanters took the bridge without further resistance, joyfully displaying their colours above it.

As soon as the news of Johnston's being injured reached Colonel Gunn, he announced to the cavalry that he was dead and the bridge lost, and ordered them to make swiftly for the town. The first was certainly untrue, and it is unlikely that the second had yet come to pass, so Gunn got 'slender obedience'; and indeed one of the Royalist officers, William Gordon of Arradoul, suggested forcefully that they

27

should instead counter-attack. Gunn refused to consider this, however, and instead fell to what Rothiemay called his old trick of threatening to complain to the King if his orders were not obeyed. All that this whining outburst produced were renewed cries that Gunn was a traitor, and Arradoul, in some heat, told him to his face that he was a villain and an arrant traitor; but nothing more was done, and the cavalry dispersed northwards allowing the Covenanters to make an unopposed entry into Aberdeen.[37]

Spalding records that three more of the Aberdeen Militia were killed that day, Patrick Grey, David Johnston and Thomas Davidson, with some others wounded; and that on entering the town the Covenanters took 48 of them prisoners—presumably the survivors of those who had stood with Johnston on the second day's fighting.[38] Rothiemay also mentions a Captain James Gordon—presumably another of the Strathbogie men—shot in the leg,[39] while Gordon of Sallagh in his history of the Earldom of Sutherland gives 14 of the Strathbogie men and the militia slain over the two days, and 'as many wer killed on the other side'.[40] Covenanting sources are generally in agreement with these last. Spang admits to only two Covenanters killed,[41] but Baillie speaks of 'some slaughter on both sides',[42] and the author of *True Rehearsall* mentions 'divers killed whom they buried in the mosses beyond the bridge',[43] and implies that Royalist losses were lighter. Certainly, given that the Royalists were for the most part ensconced behind stone walls and firing on the Covenanters in the open, it is highly likely that the latter would have suffered heavier losses.

Aberdeen being taken Montrose was pressed to allow its plundering, to which he acquiesced, but ordered a delay until the next day in order that it might fully be carried out in daylight, and a measure of control retained over the proceedings. Accordingly the army marched straight through the town and encamped upon the sea links; but to the intense disappointment of all concerned save the apprehensive citizens, at two o'clock in the morning a ship arrived with news of a cease-fire, and the Covenanters had to be content instead with levying a swingeing fine upon the town.

The King himself meanwhile had experienced some difficulty in assembling his army at Newcastle. Only about half the 30,000 men called for turned up (no Civil War army ever attained such a strength, so the King ought not perhaps to be judged too harshly on this score), and so on 14 May he issued a proclamation to the Scots stating that he was willing to discuss their grievances, but that in the meantime they should not approach within ten miles of the border. Far from invading Scotland and bringing the Covenanters to heel, the King was in effect now reduced to begging them not to invade England. Had he but known, the Scots had little intention at this stage of doing so, and in fact they too considered themselves to be quite incapable of mounting an invasion.

The basic problem was that although they had managed, albeit with some difficulty, to assemble an army, the forty days provisions which each man was supposed to bring with him were running short. Money was in short supply for the payment of the troops and the purchase of food, and though the Reverend Robert Baillie was to claim when the army was encamped at Duns Law that the men were well paid and well fed, this seems a little optimistic. In any case, the real problem seems to have been a lack of pack animals to carry food and other supplies, in the event of the army being called upon to move across the border. Indeed Baillie is quite categorical in stating that if the necessity had arisen, the army would have been quite unable to invade England, since Leslie had neither 'carried [pack] horses nor strong enough convoyes for it'.[44] Notwithstanding these difficulties, when the King joined his army at Berwick and sent a small detachment across the border, Leslie pushed southwards from his assembly area to Duns, and sent a detachment of his own to occupy Kelso. The King in turn countered by sending the Earl of Holland there on 3 June with about 3,000 men (most or all of them cavalry) to drive them out. Holland's expedition however came to grief when he encountered Colonel Robert Monro, a veteran of the Swedish service and the author of a tedious book on the famous MacKay's Regiment, with 1,200 foot, esconced behind a dyke. Monro knew what he was about and saluted Holland's men with a single thundering volley while they were still some distance off—more probably in warning than in deadly earnest—and was doubtless suitably gratified to see the English flee in disorder.[45]

The effect of this incident upon the morale of the King and his army was out of all proportion to its military significance, and both were greatly discouraged. Consequently when the Scots, two days later, offered to negotiate, the King agreed. The subsequent talks lasted nearly a fortnight, but neither side was in any doubt that the 'Pacification of Berwick', signed on 18 June 1639, was anything more than a cease-fire, notwithstanding stipulations that the armies should be disbanded.[46]

The Second Scots War was therefore but a continuation of the First, and although inevitable it was in some measure sparked off by the unexpected arrival of 100 English soldiers at Leith in early February 1640, as a reinforcement for the newly restored Royalist garrison, armed with a letter from the King instructing the Burgh to given them safe conduct into the castle. The Covenanters were taken completely by surprise; and the new governor, the King's Muster Master General of Scotland, Patrick Ruthven, Lord Ettrick, cheerfully reported that he was now capable of withstanding a siege of six to nine months—

notwithstanding a rather embarrassing partial collapse of a part of the curtain wall—and on 10 March 1640 the Covenanters responded by setting guards on the castle approaches, preventing tradesmen from making deliveries. Curiously, perhaps because Ruthven was rightly considered to be a somewhat more formidable proposition than the ineffectual Captain Haldane, a repeat of the previous year's *coup de main* does not appear to have been considered. That Ruthven was indeed determined to defend the castle vigorously was immediately made apparent by his threat to bombard the city, unless the shelters erected for the Covenanters' guards were at once demolished. The threat was received with defiance by the government and panic by the citizens, but was soon withdrawn when Ruthven received suitable assurances that the shelters were not intended to screen a battery raised against the castle. Despite daily desertions from his Scottish soldiers (sometimes three and four in a night) and an increasing toll from scurvy, Ruthven did indeed hold out for six months, not surrendering until 15 September 1640 with no hope of relief, having in the meantime slain 200 soldiers and civilians, caused great damage to the city and lost all his teeth to the scurvy.

In the meantime levies were ordered to be raised in March for another army. Leslie was re-appointed General on 17 April, and preparations made once more for a concentration on the border. Argyle, on the other hand, much to the disgust of Montrose who considered Perthshire and Forfarshire to be his own responsibility, received a commission on 12 June to proceed against 'the Earle of Atholl, the Lord Ogilvie and thair complices and assistantis as weill in Atholl as in the braes of Angus, the Farquhersones in the Braes of Mar, and thair complices and vtheris, our enemies and opposites in Badzenoch, Lochaber and Renoch.'[47]

No resistance was encountered by him in this, and indeed the episode is chiefly known for the burning of the 'Bonnie House of Airlie', and the exuberance of some of his men, whose enthusiastic references to 'King Campbell' caused Argyle some embarrassment shortly afterwards. Rather more positively, a blockade of Dumbarton Castle by some of his men produced its surrender on 27 August. With much the same view in mind, Monro, newly promoted to Major General, had been despatched northwards with a regiment to keep the Gordons and their friends in order. They comprised what sounds remarkably like a penal battalion, and the author of the *True Rehearsall* affords them scant respect: 'ane regiment of men to witt, sex or eight out of every parish and thes wes adulterers, furnicators, theives, murderers, drunkards, sabbath-breakers, who were given up be the minister of every parish and these were to plant the Covenant through Scotland'.[48]

Monro's men were assembled at Glasgow, Edinburgh and Haddington, which would suggest that most were in fact pressed in southern

Scotland before being brought to a general rendezvous at Musselburgh and marched north to Aberdeen. They arrived in the burgh at the end of May, and after a pause of about a month waiting for crops to ripen, Monro embarked upon a punitive sweep through Aberdeenshire and then beyond. Drum, Strathbogie and Auchindoun castles were all seized, and on 16 July the Bishop of Moray's palace at Spynie was also taken. In none of these cases was there much resistance, although Monro found himself in an odd three cornered fight at Auchindoun involving his own men, some cattle thieves and a party of Royalists led by the Laird of Auchindoun. A rather more congenial visit to his native Ross-shire netted him 200 highland recruits for his regiment, and returning to Aberdeen he went by way of Banff in order to plunder and demolish Sir George Ogilvy's 'palace'. This at least may have afforded the Gordons some consolation. Indeed the only black moment in this glorious *chevauchée* was a mutiny by some of his men at Strathbogie, dissatisfied with the share-out of the plunder—or more specifically the absence of a share-out. Characteristically Monro at once quelled the revolt by running through with a long sword the first mutineer he found. Not surprisingly the rabble 'wer quickly settled and by terror reduced to obedience again'.[49]

Not long afterwards Monro marched his regiment south to winter in the Merse, but Aberdeen had no respite, for Monro's regiment was succeeded by an equally rapacious unit raised in Aberdeenshire by the Master of Forbes—indeed for a few uneasy days both regiments had to be accommodated while the changeover took place. No sooner was Forbes' regiment in turn disbanded but a third regiment, yet worse than its predecessors, was quartered on the burgh. Lord Sinclair's regiment, like Monro's a penal battalion, remained in Aberdeen until ordered to Ireland in the spring of 1642, and by then they had long since overstayed their welcome.[50]

Also besieged in 1640 were the Earl of Nithsdale's castles, Caerlaverock and Threave. The capture of these fortresses lying near Dumfries had seemed unimportant in 1639, but now, with the arrival of one of Wentworth's Irish regiments in Carlisle, it was thought prudent to neutralise them lest a greater threat from Ireland should materialise. Colonel Robert Home was despatched to that purpose and despite a gallant resistance both castles fell. The main efforts were once again directed however towards the eastern end of the border. Leslie once again assembled the main Scots army at Duns in Berwickshire, while the King hoped to raise his own army at York. Once at Duns, though, Leslie realised that supplying his army was going to be as great a problem as it had been the previous year, and so on 20 August he invaded England with little better object in mind than eating off the English countryside rather than his own.

This year Montrose was with Leslie's army and only a Colonel. Already he was having his doubts as to whether he was on the right side. Whether these doubts arose from the conflict between conscience and loyalty to the crown, or perhaps more likely a growing rivalry with Argyle, exacerbated by that commission granted to the latter in June, is open to question. In early August he had gone so far as to draw up a band at Cumbernauld House, aimed at drawing together moderates and even some Royalists. Nevertheless, having put their names to this band, Montrose and his colleagues rejoined the army at Choicely Wood, some four miles south of Duns, in time for the invasion.

The army crossed the Tweed at three points: Montrose himself, having diced for the honour, was the first to cross at the head of his regiment at Cornhill, and units also crossed at Carham and Wark. Once on the other side they moved swiftly. According to intelligence reports Newcastle Upon Tyne was virtually undefended, and Leslie realised he might be in a position to capture it before the King's army came north. By the 27th the Scots had reached the Tyne. Some English forces were in the area under Viscount Conway, but were known to be heavily outnumbered; so Leslie felt secure enough to detach part of his army, including Montrose and his regiment, to march directly for Newcastle, while he faced Conway across the Tyne at Newburn a few miles upstream. The river is still tidal at this point, and although Leslie was ready to cross on the morning of 28 August he had to wait until mid afternoon before the ford was usable. As soon as the tide fell sufficiently Leslie made up for lost time. Covered by his guns, including two fframes (see page 38) mounted in the tower of the church of St. Michael and All Angels in Newburn, Leslie threw his army across, preceded by his cavalry. The English incontinently fled.

Two days later Newcastle itself surrendered on 30 August. For the first time in many hundred years of cross-border conflict, the city was in the hands of the Scots, and their first act was to demand the supplies which they so desperately needed.

The defeat of Conway and the capture of Newcastle was followed by the King's capitulation in the 'Treaty of Ripon' signed on 26 October 1640.[51] The Scots however remained in occupation of Newcastle for nearly a year—such a triumph was one to be savoured—only leaving it on 21 August 1641. There is no denying that the Scots came out well from both the Bishops' Wars as they became known: they had achieved all that they set out to do in the matters of religion and politics; their leaders too had benefited—Alexander Leslie, for example, was created Earl of Leven—but most of all it was the Scots' prestige and military reputation which was enhanced as never before at home and abroad.

Montrose on the other hand was in trouble. Immediately after the signing of the Treaty of Ripon he wrote to the King seemingly offering his support, and then had some explaining to do when his colleagues found out. Worse was to follow. On 19 October the Estates learned of the Cumbernauld Band, and although Montrose once again managed to talk himself out of the furore which followed, any hopes which he may have entertained of forming a party to oppose Argyle and the other grandees were wrecked. Further supposedly secret correspondence with the King got him incarcerated in Edinburgh Castle, where he remained throughout the King's visit to Edinburgh from August to November. This imprisonment did not at first stop him intriguing, though, and he managed to become involved in the abortive Royalist coup known as 'The Incident'. Nevertheless on 16 November Montrose was released and allowed to return home, without seeing the King who left two days later. Having burnt his boats with his erstwhile colleagues, Montrose could only turn ever more firmly towards the King. Reconciliations were attempted, and in the summer of 1643 he was even offered a command in the army being raised for another invasion of England in accordance with the terms of the Solemn League and Covenant, but turning this down he rode south to join his King at Oxford. Unfortunately it seemed that the King had little use for him.

2

Invasion and Counter-Invasion

Although ten regiments of foot, including three which had been retained in service after the Treaty of Ripon, had been sent to Ulster in 1642[1] to fight the Catholic rebels, Scotland was not at first involved in the English Civil War, or more properly, perhaps, the Great Civil War. On the other hand, a considerable number of Scots, both professional soldiers and volunteers, served with some distinction on both sides. Not surprisingly many of them, perhaps most, opted to fight for the cause of Parliament and the English presbyterians, although it is hard to believe that Nathaniel Gordon, whom we last met helping to defend the Bridge of Dee, chose to serve as Major to Sir John Browne's Parliamentarian dragoons at Edgehill from any feelings of religious zeal.[2] Some Scots occupied prominent positions in the Parliamentarian forces; Sir William Balfour, for example, served as Lieutenant General of the Horse under the Earl of Essex (although he had by 1642 become a naturalised Englishman). Others included Sir James Ramsay, who commanded the left wing of horse at Edgehill, and Laurence Crawford, who commanded a regiment of foot in the Dublin garrison before becoming Major General under the Earl of Manchester; and Colonel John Hurry, who was to achieve the dubious distinction of serving in each of the belligerent forces involved in the civil war, both north and south of the border.

Not all the Scots chose this course: the King's Lord General was Patrick Ruthven, Lord Ettrick, and now for his gallant defence of Edinburgh Castle created Earl of Forth (and shortly afterwards Earl of Brentford in the English peerage). Moreover, at least thirty of his regiments could boast at least one Scots officer, generally of field rank.[3]

Besides these there were also, it appears, a number of common soldiers enlisted for the most part into the Royalist forces. That they were to be found in the service of the King rather than Parliament can

34

most probably be attributed to the simple fact that until the Scots invasion in January 1644, the English side of the border was entirely under the control of the Royalists, and no Parliamentarian troops, far less recruiting parties, were able to penetrate north of Yorkshire and Lancashire. Although one of the charges levelled against the Marquis of Newcastle in 1642 was that he was recruiting Scots—foreigners—it is hard to assess just how widespread this recruiting was. The infantry regiment led by his military adviser, James King, Lord Eythin, had Scots officers, and their men may well have been Scots as well; while at least one troop in his cavalry regiment was also Scots—and commanded by a woman to boot! Examination of the 1663 *List* of indigent officers suggests that at least one other regiment in Newcastle's army, a small cavalry unit led by Colonel Francis Stuart (slain at Marston Moor), was Scots. Moving further south, Sir John Henderson, Newcastle's governor of Newark and himself a Scot, offered in early 1643 to raise a regiment of 300 Scots lancers to augment the garrison,[4] although there is no evidence of his having succeeded in doing so. There was even a regiment in the Oxford Army, a cavalry unit led by the Earl of Crawford, which certainly had Scots officers. Some of them were to march north with Crawford and Montrose in early 1644, but the regiment remained with the army under a new colonel, James Hamilton. There is little comparable evidence of Scots soldiers in Parliamentarian service, although there was a regiment, probably originally recruited by Lord Forbes for service in Ireland, in the garrison of Plymouth in 1642; and at Leicester in 1645 some of the defenders were Scots dragoons belonging to Sir Samuel Luke's Regiment, normally based in Newport Pagnell.

Although such recruitment of both officers and men clearly took place on a rather larger scale than may have been hitherto recognised, it was still limited, and as a stalemate in the war became ever more apparent in 1643, strenuous efforts were made by both sides to secure the aid of a Scots army. Notwithstanding the great concessions and personal rewards granted to the Covenanters in 1641, the King cannot realistically have entertained much hopes of persuading the Scots to assist him, and Royalist efforts were soon devoted to postponing the inevitable arrival of a hostile Scots army in what had until now been a secure rear area. All of Newcastle's field army was in Yorkshire, and it appears that only a single regiment was watching the border. The Marquis of Hamilton and his brother the Earl of Lanark were deeply involved in these efforts, but their behaviour was again eventually regarded, in part at Montrose's urging, as being at best equivocal, and the first ended up incarcerated in Pendennis Castle while Lanark only barely escaped.

The 'contract' for this army, the Solemn League and Covenant, was signed on 25 September 1643, though the actual preparations for the raising of the army had begun two months earlier. Originally it had been hoped to redeploy the Scots army in Ulster: this indeed had been the initial approach of the Parliamentarians, but for a variety of reasons it proved impractical. The army had been badly neglected for some time, and was unlikely to co-operate in such a move unless its substantial arrears were paid. There also seems to have been some doubts as to its political reliability, and at the end of the day it was still regarded as a necessary part of the Protestant forces in Ulster.[5] All in all it was easier to raise a new army from scratch, and this process began on 28 July 1643 when the Scottish Estates ordered the raising of five companies of foot and three troops of horse, to be mustered at Leith by 13 September. On 18 August a loan of £40,000 Scots was authorised for their equipment, and in order to distinguish them from the proposed regiments of shire conscripts they became known as 'The Levied Regiment'. Raised largely from amongst Edinburgh's law students and apprentices, the unit was at first commanded by Sir Alexander Gibson of Durie, a Senator of the College of Justice; but on 25 August, Lord Sinclair, who had left his regiment in Ireland pleading ill-health, took over. It was probably intended to serve as an internal security force during the raising of the army proper, but in the event was used to occupy Berwick on Tweed at the end of September, to the annoyance of the local Royalist commander, Colonel Edward Grey.

Meanwhile on 18 August the Estates issued a proclamation ordering a general muster within 48 hours of publication. In Scotland in the seventeenth century, military service was demanded of barons, freeholders and the inhabitants of Royal Burghs as a condition of tenure, and upon receipt of such a proclamation they were bound to present themselves in arms with their retainers. Enrolment of recruits did not actually take place at this preliminary stage. On 28 August the shire committees were formally appointed, all business up to that time having been conducted by an ad hoc grouping of the 'chiefest men' of the shire; and these committees were directed to meet at least once a week at the principal town in their locality and draw up, on the basis of the initial series of musters, a list of those men adjudged fit for service. The numbers thus being established, the Estates then set down the number of troops to be raised in each shire, and at a second series of musters held between 4 and 20 October the various colonels appointed by the Estates and the committees enlisted their men. Whilst they were obviously able to pick and choose to a certain extent, and the normal recruiting abuses were no doubt perpetrated, the numbers taken were limited to every fourth and every eight man ordered to present himself—and in later, supplementary musters, it was normal for only the eight man to be taken.[6]

In his study of the Army of the Covenant which prefaced his collection of the Ordnance Papers compiled for the Scottish History Society in 1917–18, Professor Terry assumed that these regiments bore 'county' titles corresponding to their recruiting areas, but in fact this was not the case.[7] Not only is there little contemporary evidence for such usage—regiments were in fact referred to by the name of their current colonel—but it is clear that a number of units were raised across shire borders. The Aberdeen area is a good example of this, with part of the shire allotted to the Earl Marischal, who also had troops raised in the Mearns, and the rest to Lord Gordon. This was also the position with the cavalry regiments. Conversely, bigger shires might raise more than one regiment. A few units did, it is true, bear titles: one such was the 'Levied Regiment', while another, raised by the exertions of the clergy—in actual fact the sweepings of each parish—was known as the 'Ministers' Regiment'. Only in two instances, Home of Wedderburn's 'Merse Regiment' and Colonel Rae's 'Edinburgh Regiment' were territorial titles used.

Recruitment by conscription, and certain peculiarities of dress, may outwardly have distinguished this army from its contemporaries south of the border, but in fact its most distinctive feature was its officer corps. There was a massive pool of professional soldiers, most though not all returned from the Swedish service, who had learned their trade in the German wars and were now, understandably, attracted by the prospect of war closer to home. The potential value of this large body of skilled professional officers was recognised from the first, and a simple system was devised which made the best possible use of their talents, whilst at the same time allowing the lairds and nobility the participation which they considered to be their due. The Colonel of each regiment was in the main a nobleman resident in the recruiting area, and consequently possessed of some local influence. The other field officers, upon whom the real work fell, especially if like the Earl Marischal the nominal Colonel declined to march off to the wars, were as far as possible professional soldiers, and this sensible arrangement was carried on down to company level.[8] Captains and Ensigns were local lairds or the nominees of Royal Burghs, and the Lieutenants and Sergeants were supposed to be professional soldiers. This intermingling of professionals and zealous amateurs also in theory counteracted any lack of militancy amongst the professionals, a point of some importance, since Patrick Adair, a presbyterian minister, had deplored the fact that the professional soldiers sent to fight in Ireland in 1642 '... had no inclination to religion except in so far as the times and State who employed them seemed to favour it'.[9]

The ever observant John Spalding provides an excellent description of the troops thus raised, in chronicling the departure of a company of Aberdeen men raised for the Earl Marischal's Regiment in February 1644:

> Upon Friday the 16th of February, Captain [*John*] Strachan marched out of Aberdeen with 130 soldiers, Captains and commanders furnished out by the said burgh upon their own charges and expenses. Ilk soldier was furnished with twa sarks, coat, breeks and hose, and bonnet, bands and shoon, a sword and musket, powder and ball for so many, and other some a sword and pike according to order: and ilk twelve of them had a baggage horse worth 50 pound, a stoup, a pan, a pot for their meat and drink and together also with their hire or levy money, ilk soldier estimate to 10 dollars: in furnishing and all to 100 merks.[10]

The Scots armies tended to be short of cavalry, and when it was agreed to send an army to Ulster in 1642, the cavalry, with the exception of the Lifeguard, were raised locally. A number of regiments were raised for the army of the Covenant, however, together with a single regiment of dragoons or mounted infantry, and further levies of both followed. Both the regular cavalry and subsequently the rebels evinced a distinct preference for using firearms, being armed with at least a brace of pistols and if possible a carbine as well. In the five months preceding the battle of Marston Moor the Earl of Eglinton's Regiment was to shoot away no fewer than 688 lb of powder, a third of that in June alone![11] Not all Scots cavalry relied on firearms though, and lances were also used. Regiments were normally divided in battle into two squadrons, and it seems to have been a fairly common practice to arm one of these squadrons with lances and the other with firearms. (The rebels too had their lancers and in 1644 Spalding noted that Gight's Horse had 'new whyte launces'.)[12]

Although well equipped with conventional artillery the Scots relied very largely for their close fire support upon 'fframes', a species of light cannon devised by Sir Alexander Hamilton, firing 3 lb shot and probably grapeshot as well. Made of cast bronze, they were about three feet long and carried on pack-horses. The famous leather guns were not introduced until after 1648, when Colonel James Wemyss succeeded Hamilton as General of the Artillery.[13]

The levies thus raised and equipped should have mustered 26,000 infantry and cavalry when they crossed the border on 20 January 1644, but many units were actually badly under strength. Three companies of the Earl Marischal's Regiment did not leave Aberdeen until 16 February, whilst levies for Lord Gordon's Regiment were equally delayed.[14] Whatever the true extent of these deficiencies the Scots army was still far stronger than the English forces immediately opposed to it, and Newcastle was invested by 3 February. Here Leven was halted for a time, but shortly after an inconclusive skirmish with some English cavalry at Corbridge on 19 February the Scots crossed the Tyne on the

22nd near Ovingham and seized Sunderland. A minor rearguard action took place at the foot of Penshaw Hill on 7 March, and a major battle at Boldon on the night of the 24th/25th: but the English, defeated by the inclement weather as much as by the Scots, were then forced to retire towards the Tees, although their retreat became precipitate with the news that Fairfax was threatening York.

Meanwhile, in a desperate attempt to divert the attention of the Scots, the Royalists attempted a counter-invasion of Scotland in conjunction with a rising. This plan was largely the work of the Earl of Antrim, who, with excellent logic but a total disregard for its impracticality, had proposed a grand combination of Irish, Scots and English Royalists in the summer of 1643. Nothing had come of it at that time, save for Antrim getting himself captured by the Scots army in Ulster, but after his escape a small force was despatched to Colonsay while he himself made his way to Oxford and entered into negotiations with the Earl of Montrose. Having changed sides in 1641, Montrose was finding it hard to gain the trust of those whom he now professed to support, and lent a ready ear to Antrim's hare-brained schemes. On 20 January 1644 Antrim was instructed by the King to persuade the Irish rebels (between whom and the King's forces a cease-fire or 'Cessation' had been signed on 15 September) to provide 10,000 men for service in England, and to despatch 2,000 men to Scotland. Armed with this authority, Antrim then concluded an agreement with Montrose on 28 January for a rising in Scotland by 1 April. The timescale was absurdly over-optimistic: Montrose was appointed Lieutenant General under Prince Maurice on 1 February, but presumably because the Prince proved to be unavailable, the commission was altered to exclude mention of him a fortnight later; and on or about 1 March Montrose finally left Oxford and headed north.[15] Time had obviously been required to prepare for the expedition, and the 200 cavalry who accompanied him were probably very largely drawn from the Earl of Crawford's horse. In addition to Crawford himself they included the Earl of Nithsdale, Lords Aboyne, Ogilvy and Reay, Colonel John Innes and Colonel John Cochrane.[16] Now, the assembling of this force may not have been straightforward. What remained of Lord Crawford's Regiment seems to have been taken over by Colonel James Hamilton, and some of the other officers, such as Innes, will have had to be replaced, but with time at a premium it should not have taken so long.[17]

Whatever the reason for the delay, by 15 March, with little more than a fortnight to go until the agreed date, they reached Durham and met the Marquis of Newcastle, who was of course in some difficulties and hardly well-placed to give Montrose the additional forces which he demanded. Leven's army was a far too immediate problem, and it was not until after the fight at Boldon Hill and the decision to retreat to the Tees that he at last gave Montrose some men. Wishart, speaking for Montrose, sourly commented:

> In the meantime all the aid he [Newcastle] could afford him in his present straits was about a hundred troopers but mounted on lean, ill-appointed horses (through no fault of his but owing to the envy of some men) with two small brass field pieces. He also sent orders to the King's officers and commanders of the militia in Cumberland and Westmorland to attend Montrose in his journey into Scotland with all the force they could muster, and give him every assistance.[18]

Given the appalling wintry conditions under which the Royalist cavalry had been marching and fighting for the past three months, it is hardly surprising that the horses were in poor condition. Furthermore it is evident from later events that rather more than 100 cavalry were involved, but here as in other cases it is apparent that Wishart is solely concerned with blaming Montrose's failures upon the malice and envy of others. The truth, self evident, is that the expedition was badly planned, and rushed through with inadequate preparation, and Montrose as its commander must shoulder the blame rather than those shadowy 'some men'.

On the road to Carlisle Montrose was joined by 800 foot and three troops of horse raised in Cumberland—assembling so many in such appalling weather at a few days notice deserves rather more credit than partisans of Montrose are usually willing to concede the militia officers—and thus augmented, his army crossed the border on 13 April 'in haste', according to Wishart, 'not to fail the Earl of Antrim at the time appointed'. A remarkable statement, in view of the fact that he was already two weeks too late. Hardly had he crossed the border but a mutiny broke out amongst the English soldiers, and according again to Wishart, most of them deserted rather than cross Annan Water. This he ascribes to the machinations of the servants of Sir Richard Graham, an English Parliamentarian; but some of their unease must have stemmed from the rapidly worsening situation in England. If Graham's men were indeed involved, they probably spread lurid tales of Belasyse' defeat at Selby and the imminent siege of York. At any rate Montrose pressed on and occupied Dumfries.[19]

At this point a totally unexpected factor emerged. Three of the Scots regiments serving in Ulster, disgusted at their long neglect by the government, had, contrary to orders, returned to Scotland; and now two of them, Lothian's and Sinclair's, offered to change sides, to join the rebels, and hand over Stirling Castle.[20] Montrose however was himself menaced by government forces led by the Earl of Callendar, and warned by Lord Johnston he evacuated Dumfries and fled back across the border. In all fairness to Montrose there was probably little else he could have done in the circumstances, but the futility of it emphasises how ill-conceived the expedition was in the first place. Antrim meanwhile had had no prospect whatever of meeting the 1 April deadline. In February the Irish agreed to let him recruit his men, and to provide them with 2,000 muskets and other supplies, but these were not to be handed over until 1 May at the earliest; and in fact Antrim's men did not arrive in Scotland until 8 July, over three months late!

HUNTLY'S RISING

Only in the north-east did the rising take place in time, and Montrose's utter failure to support Huntly cannot, perhaps, be overemphasised, as a factor in the antipathy which the two men afterwards displayed towards each other. Huntly was already much disposed towards a rising, since he was in trouble with the government for refusing to aid the raising of the army or provide cash for its support. So bad indeed were relations that the Sheriff of Banff, Abercrombie of Birkenbog, had attempted to arrest him on 6 February.[21] Nevertheless his position was far from desperate, since his eldest son, Lord Gordon, was actively supporting the government and raising regiments of horse and foot. Detachments of foot were despatched south throughout the early months of the year and fought at Marston Moor under Sir James Lumsden. Spalding's *Memorials* contain numerous details of incidents throughout the area connected with the raising of the army, some of them violent, but although there was obviously some unrest it was not significant enough to delay or disrupt the despatch of levies for the army. Whatever Huntly's own views upon the matter, the House of Gordon was not noticeably dragging its feet, and the rising was hardly born out of desperation. Huntly rose in response to Antrim and Montrose's plans, not because he had no choice.

The rising effectively began early on the morning of 19 March 1644, although it appeared at first to have its roots in some earlier bickering between Sir John Gordon of Haddo and local officials engaged in taxation and recruiting. Haddo, accompanied by Alexander Irvine of Drum, and the Lairds of Gight, Scethin and Tibertie, with about 60 horse, rode into Aberdeen, kidnapped the Provost in broad daylight, and then got clean away to Strathbogie. Even the Royalist John Spalding was appalled at this affront to civic dignity, not least because no resistance was made to the rebels or any attempt made to rescue the unfortunate Provost. The surviving members of the town council at once called out the militia and nominated officers to command it, but their resolution failed to match their indignation and when the rebels again descended on Aberdeen a week later they met with no resistance.[22]

Having taken the field and occupied Aberdeen, Huntly was seized by a fatal lethargy. He recruited men and they in turn plundered everyone in sight, but otherwise he made no real attempt to spread the rebellion beyond the borders of Aberdeenshire and Banffshire. In part, as he himself later pointed out, this was due to a fear of the northern Covenanters gathering at Elgin, including his own son and his regular regiment of horse, and partly no doubt a desire to wait and see how Montrose and the Irish got on. Nevertheless, a little more resolution might have alleviated his troubles. Montrose, one feels sure, would have dealt with the threat from Elgin by attacking the Covenanters there without more ado; and if later experiences may be drawn on, such a course of action would most likely have resulted in the utter dispersal of the government forces. Instead, Huntly's soldiers merely frittered their time away in pointless raids in search of arms, ammunition and plunder, of which this raid on Banff, described by Spalding, may be taken as a typical example: 'They took the town without contradiction, meddled with the keys of the tolbooth, took free quarters, and plundered all the arms they could get, buff coats, pikes, swords, carabines, pistols, yea and money also'.[23]

The government not unnaturally took rather a dim view of such proceedings, and as early as 20 March Argyle was given a commission to take charge of the suppression of the revolt. For this task he was given two regular regiments which had returned from Ulster, the Earl of Lothian's and Sir Mungo Campbell of Lawers'. Lothian's was, as it happens, far from reliable, although this was not to become apparent until later. In addition to these regulars and 1,000 of his own highlanders, Argyle was promised 800 from Perthshire led by the Earl of Tullibardine; the same from Fife led by Lord Elcho; and, as he advanced northwards, more from Forfarshire and the Mearns. In addition, of course, he also expected to be assisted by the northern Covenanters.[24]

Huntly's recruiting by contrast was not so successful. At first it had gone well enough, and although the Aberdeen Militia refused to muster for his service as they had done in 1639, a number of volunteers were enlisted from the city;[25] but as April wore on the situation worsened dramatically. In the first place the inactivity of itself sapped morale, and as the days went by his soldiers became discouraged, first by the news of Montrose's defeat, and then by the news of the army which Argyle was gathering. After calling a muster at Inverurie, ten miles to the north west of Aberdeen, on Saturday 13 April, when only 2,100 foot and 400 horse turned up, he took up residence in Aberdeen at Alexander Reid's house and had some colours made: 'whare upon ilk side was drawn a red rampand Lion, having a crown of gold, above his head C.R. for Carolus Rex, having the motto '*For God the King and*

Against all Traittoris' and beneath *'God save the King'*. There were divers other pincells made for the Barons'.[26]

Leaving a professional soldier, Major Hay, with some horse and foot as a garrison for Aberdeen, Huntly returned to Inverurie on the 17th escorted by 40 horse under Irvine of Drum; and next day ordered Donald Farquharson of Monaltrie to draw out 240 foot—most, although not all of them, highlanders—and march them south into the Braes of Angus. Having done that he returned again to Aberdeen, and had what remained of his army in the town drilled on the Links on Saturday the 20th. Their numbers must have been something of a disappointment, for there were only about 160 horse and no more than 800 foot.[27]

MONTROSE, 24 APRIL 1644

Notwithstanding this low turnout, Huntly permitted Drum to continue with the raid which he had authorised him to carry out on the town of Montrose, and at four in the afternoon, immediately after the muster on the Links was ended, nearly half his cavalry set off. Spalding's figure of 72 men, officers and all, equates pretty well with Ruthven's three or four score. They included what might be termed 'the usual suspects': Alexander Irvine of Drum, his brother Robert, George Gordon of Gight and John Gordon his uncle, John Gordon of Ardlogie, Urquhart of Craghouse, Innes of Tibbertie, Irvine of Kincousie and sundry others. Although Drum was in charge of the raid, Major Nathaniel Gordon commanded the horse.[28] He had lately returned from service with the English parliamentarians under the Earl of Essex, and had taken part in Haddo's raid on Aberdeen. A professional soldier, he was at this time under something of a cloud, having grievously upset Huntly in a ridiculous affair involving a Danish fishing boat and an English pirate ship. Ruthven states that the object of this present raid was simply to gain intelligence of Argyle's forces, and suggests that the assault on Montrose was all a dreadful mistake, but Spalding's version is much more convincing and attended as usual by a wealth of circumstantial detail.

Drum rendezvoused with Monaltrie and his foot somewhere on the river North Esk on 23 April, and moved that night on Montrose with the object of securing two brass 'cartows' or 24lb cannon which he knew to be there. Montrose was at that time, and very largely still is, built on a remarkably strong position. To the east was the North Sea, to the south the River South Esk, and on the west a huge tidal basin. Consequently the town could only be approached, let alone attacked, from the north; and at two o'clock on the morning of 24 April the rebels found the citizens armed and waiting for them, the common bell ringing, and a beacon fire blazing in the church steeple to summon aid from Forfar where some of Argyle's men were quartered. Nothing daunted, Drum ordered an immediate assault. While some men, probably highlanders, ran around the east side of the town and scrambled over the back dykes, he himself led a frontal assault on the North Port. With highlanders pouring through the alleyways into the market place, the militia abandoned the North Port almost at once, and a desperate milling fight took place inside the town. The Royalists first chased the militia off the streets, but they returned fire 'desperatlie' from the forestairs, which the rebels returned in equal measure, most notably the Tutor of Struan with some highlanders armed with carbines. Nathaniel Gordon, however, shot dead one of the town's baillies, Alexander Pearson, and thereupon resistance collapsed. Notwithstanding the violence, few or none of the rebels had been killed at this point, and only two or three of the militia including Pearson.[29]

Drum celebrated his victory by giving his men an hour's licence to plunder the town, and then set to dragging the two cannon down to the quay. As part of his preparations for the raid, he had arranged for a ship commanded by one Alexander Burnett to wait in the harbour of Montrose to collect the guns once captured, and transport them back to Aberdeen. Unfortunately, in his enthusiasm, Drum had overlooked the fact that Burnett's father was a loyal supporter of the government, and indeed a Captain in the Aberdeen Militia. The son duly stuck by his father's principles and warned the Provost of Montrose of Drum's approach. The Provost, James Scott, who was clearly a man of some prudence, left the defence of the town in the hands of Alexander Pearson, and himself boarded the ship with his movable possessions and 40 musketeers. It may be that he intended to assist in the defence of the town with the ship, but as it happened the tide was out in the basin when Drum attacked, and the ship was stuck fast in the mud. Unaware that Burnett had betrayed him and that the ship was stuffed full of musketeers, Drum waited patiently on the quayside for it to 'fleit'; but when it at last drew near the shore he was disagreeably surprised to receive a broadside and the fire of the musketeers. Perhaps because the light was bad, only two or three of the rebels were slain and some others wounded, but it sufficed to clear the quay of them. Drum, not surprisingly perhaps, lost his head at this point, and after breaking the wheels of the cannon and tipping them into the water, he returned to the town and set to plundering it with renewed energy. Spalding waxed quite lyrical in describing the rich merchandise stolen: clothes, silks, velvets 'and vther costlie wair', silver, gold and silver work, as well as arms and a pipe of Spanish wine, which the highlanders got in amongst with predictable results. Drum, furious at having been double-crossed, went around trying to set fire to the town, while the

44

rather more rational Nathaniel Gordon scurried around behind him quenching the flames. At length, about two in the afternoon, laden down with plunder and reeling drunk, the rebels staggered out of the town and made their way inland to the Earl of Airlie's house at Cortachie. Huntly had enjoined Drum to call upon the Earl and invite him to join with them; but already mindful of the fact that Argyle was virtually on his doorstep, Airlie took one look at the drunken rabble and declined. Next day they staggered northwards with Argyle by this time only hours behind them, picking up those stragglers too inebriated to march. Most of the highlanders in fact thereupon disbanded, and made for home with their spoils. Drum himself made straight for his castle a little to the west of Aberdeen, and it was left to Nathaniel Gordon to lead the undisciplined handful who remained back into the burgh. He brought with him also the unwelcome news that Argyle had reached Dunottar Castle, just outside Stonehaven.[30]

As it happened, Argyle had only an escort of 30 horse with him, but he was soon joined by the rest of his army which now included 800 men from Forfarshire under the Earl of Kinghorn, and 500 which the Earl Marischal and Viscount Arbuthnott had raised in the Mearns. The latter pair had presumably sat quietly in Dunottar Castle as the rebels passed by. The failure of the Montrose expedition and the approach of Argyle now began to result in the steady break-up of the rebel army. Gordon of Brasmoir deserted Huntly and took service with Lord Gordon, and thus encouraged the latter attempted to capture his father's castle at Auchindoun where the Provost of Aberdeen was imprisoned; but Gordon of Brinkinburn, the governor, refused to surrender and forced him to withdraw. Meanwhile on 29 April Huntly convened a council of war at Aberdeen[31] and defended his conduct to date, though this seems to have been little more than a formal prelude to the main business, which was a decision to evacuate the town since it was untenable, and withdraw northwards. Taking the field against Argyle was out of the question, given the disparity in numbers and the increasing boldness of Lord Gordon in the north.

According to Gordon of Ruthven Huntly had now decided to retire into the hills and hold out there in the hope of an eventual Irish landing. First, though, he marched for Banff in hope of surprising his son Lord Gordon there, but missed him. At Banff however, the lairds of Gight and Haddo, viewing the prospect of a campaign in the mountains with a distinct lack of enthusiasm, decided to retire to their castles and hold out there, cheerfully ignoring the fact that no relief could be hoped for if they were besieged. Huntly naturally was against this course of action, but was unable to prevent them; and their desertion so discouraged Huntly's remaining soldiers that they too deserted. Huntly thereupon retired to Auchindoun Castle.[32] Argyle meanwhile occupied Aberdeen without resistance. Indeed the citizens were probably at first rather glad to see him, since Huntly's stay had been expensive and far from happy, although their enthusiasm soon waned.

Argyle's own regiment marched up Deeside and harried the lands of Aboyne, Birse, Abergeldie, Cromar, Glenmuick and Glentanar, whilst Campbell of Lawers' Regiment was congenially quartered at Drum Castle, plundering both it and the surrounding countryside. Argyle himself continued northwards, and first laid siege to Kellie Castle, manned by Sir John Gordon of Haddo and his men. Ruthven merely states that Haddo's soldiers threatened to seize him and sur-render the house if he did not do so of his own accord; but Spalding adds the detail that they in fact asked him to assure them that he had taken appropriate measures both to stand a siege and to ensure their relief, and finding no satisfactory answer then mutinied.[33] Taking the gentlemen prisoner and releasing the common soldiers, Argyle then moved on Gight Castle which was likewise surrendered. Both Haddo and Gight were sent south to Edinburgh where Haddo was executed with indecent haste, but Gight managed to escape by bribing his jailers. Finally Argyle sent to Huntly inviting him to surrender, but the latter responded by fleeing north in an open fishing boat to hide in Strathnaver. Drum and his brother fled northwards too, but were betrayed by one Francis Sinclair, and only Major Nathaniel Gordon remained at large. He had at first offered his services to Lord Gordon, but on being rebuffed took to the hills and turned moss-trooper.

3

The Battle of Tippermuir,
1 September 1644

Following their abortive invasion of Scotland in mid April, Montrose
and Sir Robert Clavering returned to Tyneside and commenced a
vigorous little campaign against those Scots troops left behind by
Leven. Morpeth Castle was stormed on May 29 after nearly three weeks
under siege,[1] and in the meantime Captain Thomas Rutherford of
Ranfertlie, the governor of a fort captured earlier by the Scots at
South Shields, was persuaded to surrender (not surprisingly he was
condemned to death for it, but seemingly saved by the intercession of
the Earl of Lothian).[2] Sunderland was also attacked on 22 May,
although without success, and on the 26th the siege had to be raised;
partly because of the imminent arrival of Colonel Charles Fairfax with
a relief force, but primarily because Montrose and Clavering had been
ordered south by Prince Rupert.[3]

Clavering and Montrose met Rupert at Richmond on July 6,
shortly after his crushing defeat at Marston Moor. He had with him
no more than 4,000 men, and must therefore have greeted Montrose's
request for 1,000 horse with some incredulity. The accepted version of
events is that far from providing the men for which Montrose asked,
the Prince actually took Montrose's own forces to add to his own; but
on the contrary these soldiers actually belonged to Clavering, not
Montrose. It is extremely important in considering the refusal of this
request for troops to eschew the benefits of hindsight. In July 1644
Montrose was not only a turncoat but an unsuccessful one. At this time
most Royalists knew him as a rather unreliable individual. Arrogant
and given to extravagant promises and gestures, he and Antrim were
probably regarded as very much alike. Subsequent events have, of
course, shown Montrose in a different light; but before Tippermuir it
would have taken unusual prescience to detect his better qualities. The
fact of the matter is that on the basis of his previous track record no
general in his right mind would have given him the troops he demanded.

Nevertheless, the romantic vision of the lone hero, mocked and denied the assistance he needed through the jealousy or misjudgement of lesser men, riding forth to do battle against tremendous odds, has passed from the realms of legend (or indeed fairy-tale) where it properly belongs, into history. The problem basically is that Wishart, who more than anyone else created this image, wrote his famous biography of Montrose not as a chronicle of his campaigns for the information of later generations, or even as a posthumous eulogy, but as contemporary propaganda: and seventeenth century propaganda was far from subtle.

Montrose accompanied Clavering and other elements of Rupert's forces to Carlisle, and there his luck changed. Antrim's men had at last landed on the west coast of Scotland and were marching inland. Realising that his own regiment was at once too large to escape detection and too small to fight its way through to the Irish, he sent them south with what remained of Clavering's army (he had recently died of dysentery), and accompanied by only two companions made his way northwards in disguise. After hiding for a time in Methven Wood near Perth he received word that the Irish were in Atholl, and eventually met them at Blair Atholl on 29 August 1644. This Irish Brigade comprised some 1,600 men organised in three regiments, raised for the most part in Ulster, though some Connaught men and even an Anglo-Irish contingent appears on its rolls. Gardiner and many of his successors took the rather extraordinary line that most of the soldiers were not Irish at all but Scots exiles, perhaps because the notion of their hero leading a bloodthirsty band of proto-Fenians was rather uncomfortable; but while there were undoubtedly a number of Hebrideans amongst them, probably no more than a couple of companies, the overwhelming majority of the soldiers were native Irish officered in the main by O'Cahans, O'Neills, O'Haras, McQuillans, McHenrys and the like, with a few English such as Major Ledwich and Captain Dickson, and a lowland Scot, Captain Mortimer. The commander of the brigade was himself however a Scot, Alasdair MacColla, better if erroneously known as Colkitto.[4]

MacColla had sailed from Passage near Waterford on 27 June, having previously been driven back there by stormy weather after attempting to set out on the 24th. One of his regiments under Colonel Manus O'Cahan was landed in Morven to attack Kinlochaline Castle on 7 July, and the main body disembarked in Ardnamurchan the next day and applied itself to the capture of Mingary Castle. Kinlochaline surrendered to O'Cahan on the same day, but Mingary, held by a force of Campbells, did not surrender until 14 July, after which MacColla sent various emissaries to seek reinforcements, primarily from Sir James MacDonald of Sleat and the Earl of Seaforth. Both however refused— hardly surprisingly in the circumstances—and on 29 July the Irish marched into Lochaber and then to Kintail, where once again Seaforth refused to rise for the King, but under duress provided them with food and gave them free passage eastwards towards Badenoch. By 22 August they were at Ballachroan near Kingussie, where in some desperation MacColla took drastic steps to obtain reinforcements:

> he sendes a pairtie to euerie toune where the chiefe men and heades of the countray dwelt, and the nixt morning they ar all brought to him prisoners. Hee shows them his commission from his maiestie, and how he was come to aid the marquiesse of Huntly, and although it seemed he had come to late, yet he hopt to mende what was amisse before it ware long; and therefore he required there aid, which it was not tyme to capitulate vpon, naether for them to refuse for he was resolued to haue it.[5]

The result was a highly gratifying 500 recruits, most of them MacPhersons; but while these recruits were being gathered in, the shire committee of Moray had assembled forces of its own under the Laird of Grant on Speyside. Most of them were highlanders, including 1,000 (or so it is said) of Seaforth's men, but Lord Gordon's horse must also have been present and this army effectively prevented MacColla from pressing on across the Spey and into Strathavan and Strathbogie. Instead he turned south into Atholl. There too forces were being raised against him, but upon the unexpected arrival of Montrose, now a Marquis, they declared for the King and joined the rebels. One is tempted to wonder why they should suddenly have done so as the Irish were hardly welcome; Montrose may have been using his local contacts to the full. That the Tutor of Struan should join the rebels comes as no surprise, since he had recently been in arms under Huntly and had taken part in Drum's raid on the town of Montrose; but the Stewarts were not the only ones to change sides. Ruthven it is who best tells the tale which, he assured his readers, came from the mouths of both Montrose and MacColla, that the Athollmen and the Irish were on the point of battle when Montrose arrived to unite them so providentially; but since a further 500 men under Lord Kilpont and Sir John Drummond 'meate him by accident' the next day at Buchanty, and joined the rebels just as readily, it is hard to dismiss the suspicion that these defections were anything other than pre-arranged. The notion of so many men rushing so eagerly and spontaneously to his side out of love for him and loyalty to the King made rather better propaganda than the more prosaic truth. That the meeting took place at Buchanty is in itself further evidence of the defection being premeditated. Stevenson has already argued as much by way of an explanation for Montrose marching that way, rather than straight down Strathtay towards Perth; although having moved westwards to Aberfeldy in a vain attempt to enlist the support of Menzies of Weem, the logical route then to be followed would indeed have been down Glen Cochell and the Sma' Glen before turning westwards at Buchanty. What is significant however is that Kilpont, Drummond and the Master of Madderty were all lowlanders, not highlanders, and their estates lay to the south of Buchanty. Consequently in marching there they were actually marching *away* from Perth and the government forces. Madderty, moreover, was not only Montrose's brother-in-law, but his home was only a few miles from Methven Wood where Montrose hid before the Blair Atholl rendezvous.

TIPPERMUIR, 1 SEPTEMBER 1644

Early on the morning of Sunday 1 September the rebels found the government forces waiting for them on Tippermuir, a broad expanse of moorland a few miles to the west of Perth. (The village of Tibbermore now stands in the middle of it.) Royalist sources agree that they numbered about 6,000 foot and 700–800 horse, though it seems a rather generous accounting.[6] Orders for their assembly had been given on 28 August, that is four days earlier, so that although all fencible men in Perthshire were called out it was clearly impossible for them to have reached Perth by the 1st. Tullibardine had raised 800 men in April to fight Huntly, and these were presumably now on Tippermuir. A further 800 had been raised in Fife, but half of them were still in Aberdeenshire, and only Lord Burleigh's Regiment was present. Even if the 800 men raised in Forfarshire were available—and it is by no means certain that they were— this amounts to only 2,000 foot.[7] The Perth Militia may have added a further couple of hundred, and there may well have been fresh levies which did not follow Kilpont's example by defecting, but there is still a tremendous discrepancy between the numbers which can reliably be verified and the 6,000 claimed by rebel chroniclers. 3,000 foot is probably a much more realistic estimate (and even it may be on the high side), and one which is moreover consistent with reliable estimates of the numbers fielded by the government upon other occasions. It had been intended that these levies should be stiffened and led by the Earl of Lothian and his 'Irish' regiment, but both were still in Edinburgh on 1 September, and command was instead thrust upon Lord Elcho, who in Wishart's words 'had no great character as a soldier'. Perhaps conscious of his inexperience, he contented himself with taking personal command of the right wing—and probably only a single regiment of horse at that—while the foot in the centre were entrusted to the Earl of Tullibardine, and the horse on the left wing were commanded by Sir James Scott of Rossie, a somewhat eccentric individual who had served in the Venetian army. As with the foot a reduction of about 50 per cent in their alleged strength might be prudent.

For their part the rebels' right wing comprised 500 Athollmen, Robertsons and Stewarts mainly, under the personal command of Montrose. Drawn up in only three ranks, they were evidently very poorly armed. In the centre, and probably drawn up six deep, since Ruthven is quite emphatic that it was only the wings which were extended by reducing their depth, were the Irish regiments and the battalion from Badenoch,[8] all under the command of Alasdair MacColla. Most sources agree that they mustered in the region of 2,000 men. If we remove from this total the 500 Badenoch men—probably commanded by Ewan Og McPherson, Cluny's son—that leaves 1,500 Irish, which equates pretty well with the numbers originally landed two months before. The discrepancy is accounted for by garrisons being left in Kinlochaline and Mingarry Castles. The three regiments were not of equal size: Colonel O'Cahan's Regiment which had taken Kinlochaline was 400 strong, and both they and Colonel James McDonnell's Regiment had only half the number of companies as Lieutenant General Alexander McDonnell's Regiment, which would suggest that on landing it had numbered 800 men. Oddly enough, of the three regimental commanders only one, Colonel James McDonnell, was actually present at Tippermuir. Stevenson has advanced a number of reasons for supposing that Alexander McDonnell and Alasdair MacColla were not one and the same man, as has been assumed in the past, but that McDonnell was Antrim's brother and still in Ireland. In consequence the regiment was commanded by the Connaught man, Major Thomas Laghtman, since the Lieutenant Colonel, James McDonnell, was ill. O'Cahan for his part had been earlier sent to Ormonde with despatches, and cannot have rejoined his regiment by this time; it must have been led by the most senior officer, Lieutenant Colonel Donoghue O'Cahan.[9] The rebel left wing, again drawn up in three ranks instead of six, comprised the 500 men led by Lord Kilpont, sometimes described as highlanders though they were almost certainly lowlanders. For some reason modern commentators persist in describing them as bowmen, but while Kilpont himself may have been a keen archer in his youth there is, it would appear, no evidence that this battalion was so equipped. Wishart for example merely states that Montrose was joined at Buchanty by 500 'armed' men. Even allowing for the quirks of translating Latin into modern English the term 'armed' in the seventeenth century normally referred to armour rather than weapons, but in this instance it is probably used to distinguish them from the more poorly equipped Athollmen. Lacking evidence to the contrary it may be best to assume that they were conventionally armed, that is equipped with muskets and pikes. It is all too easily forgotten that this was the normal infantry equipment at this time, in Scotland as elsewhere, and unless clear evidence exists to the contrary it is a little illogical to assume that a certain body of troops was *not* so equipped. A small body of Keppoch MacDonalds was also on this wing, and the Irish officer who referred to bowmen on the left undoubtedly had them in mind rather than Kilpont's lowland militiamen.

The principal difference between the forces was that Elcho's army had something like 400–600 horse, and Montrose's army had none. It was only necessary for the rebels to extend their wings, not their entire army, to avoid being outflanked. Both the Athollmen and Kilpont's battalion each numbered about 500 men. One would normally expect them to be drawn up six ranks deep, but if for simplicity's sake a depth of five ranks is assumed, the frontage of each unit will have been 100 men. Therefore by doubling the files of these regiments and drawing them up only three ranks deep, Montrose can have added no more than 200 men to his frontage, yet this was, it seems, sufficient to avoid his being outflanked by Elcho's and Rossie's cavalry. Even if the two cavalry regiments mustered as many as 300 men apiece, they would each have had a frontage of only 50 troopers, which equates pretty well with the extent to which the rebels extended each wing of their army.

Upon careful examination the rebels do not appear to have been quite so dramatically outnumbered as has been supposed, and their victory was in consequence not quite so miraculous..

While the rebels were drawing up in order of battle, Montrose sent forward a messenger, David Drummond, the Master of Madderty, to announce his commission to the leaders of the government forces and demand their submission. He may have felt this to be necessary on entering the lists, as it were, and may have hoped to demonstrate the legitimacy of his taking up arms. Equally, since Kilpont and indeed young Madderty himself had just changed sides, he may have entertained some hopes of a larger scale defection. Madderty too may have thought this, else he might not have gone; for not surprisingly, notwithstanding his status as an envoy, he was unceremoniously slung into the tolbooth with the cheerful assurance that he would have his head cut off once the rest of the rebels were disposed of.

Battle Joined

As soon as the rebels came within cannon-shot, Tullibardine sent out some men to act as a forlorn hope, preceding his main assault, by skirmishing with the rebels. This body was commanded by Lord Drummond, and although identified as cavalry it is possible that he may also have had some musketeers with him as was the usual practice. At any rate, before they could inflict any damage, Montrose in turn sent out

52

a forlorn which drove Drummond's men back in confusion upon the main body, so swiftly that Drummond was afterwards accused of treachery. Observing that this repulse had thrown the government forces off balance, Montrose ordered his whole army to attack 'with a loud cheer'. Wishart's account asserts that the whole army charged, but he was not there, and Ruthven's narrative suggests that it was a little less straightforward. Establishing exactly what happened is important, for the real mechanics of the victory have been lost in the glorious vision of an exuberant 'highland charge'. Wishart says that it began as soon as the rebels were within cannon shot, but it is unlikely that they should have run or jogged more than a couple of hundred metres before coming into contact with Tullibardine's infantry. A salvo fired by the government artillery did, we are assured, very little execution at such a distance, but the gunners were overrun before they could discharge a second one, which strongly argues that although the rebels were clearly outside effective musket range they were close enough to be able to cover the intervening ground in something less than a minute (a modern infantryman, appropriately laden with rifle and ammunition, is reckoned to be able to cover 100 metres in 30 seconds during a 'run-down' on a firing range). As the rebels moved forward though, the government forces did likewise, and it is now necessary to look at events in the centre and on the wings separately.

In the centre something like 3,000 levies faced 2,000 Irish and highlanders. The rebels, we are told quite specifically, had few pikes or even swords, a fact which renders some of the more lurid modern accounts of hapless militiamen being cut to pieces quite literally in a blood-soaked orgy of killing a little hard to justify, if not quite impossible. Wishart and Ruthven, the two principal chroniclers, are very much at odds in describing what happened when they met. The former implies that only a single volley was discharged by the rebels, either because they then threw down their muskets, or else, as is usually asserted, because they possessed only a single round of ammunition apiece; then when they actually met Tullibardine's men they had perforce to throw stones at them. Ruthven on the other hand declares that they were 'at the first encounter with the Irishes played vpon with hotte alarums and continuall fyre', which clearly indicates a rather more sustained and conventional firefight, in which the Irish, being better trained, prevailed over Tullibardine's 'ontryed men and fresh water shouldiours'. The latter account is rather more convincing, particularly since Wishart obtained his story from Montrose who, as will be seen, was fully occupied elsewhere, but Ruthven by contrast based his account on conversations both with Montrose and with Alasdair MacColla and perhaps other veterans as well.[11] The Irish were certainly experienced soldiers, but if through inclination or a lack of ammunition they had indeed fired only a single volley it would most likely have been followed by a precipitate and unchecked charge. The notion of their stopping a few metres away to throw stones at Tullibardine's men, having wasted their ammunition at long range, is quite unworthy of serious consideration. Ruthven does mention the stone-throwing, but states that it took place on the high ground on the rebels' right wing[12] where Montrose was in charge, and also presumably where stones were rather easier to come by in quantity than in the low lying and probably wet ground in the centre.

Getting the worst of what was almost certainly a firefight between two bodies of conventionally equipped infantrymen, Tullibardine's men fell back. The normal manner of conducting a firefight in the mid seventeenth century was for a unit to discharge its muskets by ranks, the front rank firing and then falling to the rear of the formation to reload, being succeeded by the second rank and so on until, in theory at least, by the time the first rank found itself in the front again it had completed its reloading and was ready to start the process afresh. Such a proceeding was meant to be carried out in a steady and deliberate manner, but if the soldiers were frightened, as Tullibardine's clearly were, disaster could ensue all too easily. The volleys would be discharged wildly by soldiers more concerned with emptying their muskets and making for the illusory safety of the rear rank as quickly as possible, than with doing suitable execution upon the enemy. With this in mind it is easier to understand Ruthven's otherwise improbable claim that the Irish and highlanders fell on with such a desperate resolution 'as there first and second ranks ware fallin to the ground erre the third ranke resolued what to doe'. What is rather more likely to have occurred is that the first two ranks discharged their muskets in the general direction of the rebels and then retired with indecent haste, not improbably causing some confusion in the rearward ranks as they did so, whereupon the rebels, suitably encouraged by such obvious signs of distress, pressed home their advantage by falling on with the butt ends of their muskets. Wishart states not inconsistently that: 'the Irish and Highlanders in gallant rivallry behaved with the utmost courage and pressed so hard on their retreat that at last they broke and fled'.

In essence therefore there was perhaps little out of the ordinary in the fighting in the centre, save perhaps for the speed with which matters were resolved. Both sides engaged in a firefight which the rebels won in short order, and followed up with a physical assault on an already beaten and retreating enemy. Although the end was obviously swift, to assert that the government forces were swept away by a 'highland charge' is very much an over-simplification.

On the government forces' left wing Rossie faced a rather different situation. When Tullibardine's infantry moved forward Rossie also moved his regiment, probably a little obliquely, towards some higher ground. His intention may have been not merely to deny the rebels the advantage of the slope, but also to use it himself, and perhaps even attempt to roll up their line. Whatever his intentions, they were frustrated by Montrose, who got there first with his highlanders. Wishart claimed that the engagement lasted longer here, presumably because both sides had to make a slight detour to reach the high ground, for the actual fighting seems if anything to have been of shorter duration than in the centre. Ruthven's version is that Montrose placed his men on the high ground at the outset of the battle; but it seems unlikely, given the uncertain temperament of these undisciplined highlanders, evidently unprovided as they were with pikes, that they should have stood motionless awaiting Rossie's assault. What probably happened was that they too advanced but halted when Rossie's men came within musket-shot, say about 50 metres. As they stood in three ranks Montrose ordered the first to kneel, the second to stoop, and the third to fire over their heads, so that all three ranks might fire at once. However, comparatively few of them were actually armed with muskets and this volley failed to halt Rossie's troopers, but as these advanced further they came under a barrage of stones. Given the short range at which this phase of the encounter must have taken place, it would have been rather more frantic than the rebels afterwards admitted, but the stones were thrown with such spirit and energy that Rossie's advance was checked and the highlanders thereupon fell on them sword in hand, driving them from the field. Ruthven says that, having recovered their composure, they attempted to rally and renew the fight, but were swept away by the fugitives from Tullibardine's division. This is certainly possible, but the horsemen in question are more likely to have been Elcho's men on the right, for if Wishart is right about the clash between Montrose and Rossie taking place after the Irish had broken through in the centre, then the fugitives from this earlier encounter can hardly have interfered with any attempt made by Rossie to rally his regiment.

Other than this possible reference to Lord Elcho's men, the events on the right are shrouded in darkness, but an educated guess may be made that very little at all occurred until the centre had been routed. Elcho, it is suggested, was hesitant and uncertain, while on the other hand Kilpont and his officers had defected to the rebels only the previous day and may well have been equally hesitant and uncertain how to act. Although the defection may have been premeditated by some of the officers, it is impossible to judge just how much unanimity there was in the decision to go over to the rebels; but certainly the common soldiers will have had no say in the matter, and the battalion may have been rather reluctant to fight if not downright mutinous. Their unreliability is certainly evident from events a week later at

THE CAMPAIGNS OF MONTROSE

Collace, halfway between Perth and Coupar Angus. One of Kilpont's officers, Major James Stewart of Ardvorlich, murdered him and then rejoined the government forces, while the regiment disbanded itself on the plainly specious excuse that they wished to attend Kilpont's funeral. It is stated in the burgh records of Aberdeen that there were Strathearn men under Montrose at the Justice Mills on 13 September, but if so they must have represented the mere handful who had genuinely supported the defection to the rebel army in the first place. In the circumstances therefore it is likely that Kilpont's and Elcho's men simply stood uneasily watching each other, and it was Elcho's cavalry, who, having failed to engage Kilpont's Regiment, being suddenly left in the air by the rout of Tullibardine's men, 'strowe to rely and put themselves in better posture to renew the fight', but were eventually caught up in the rout.

   With the government forces now running hard for Perth there was no restraining the highlanders and the Irish, and they pursued them all the way back to the town. Depending upon the authority consulted anything between 1,300 and 2,000 were slain, although even the former figure, offered by John Spalding, is too high. Wishart says 2,000 men were slain 'and a larger number captured'. Ruthven also gives 2,000 dead but also adds 1,000 prisoners. Both Spalding and the author of *True Rehearsall* give 1,500 dead (most of them Fife men according to the latter), and Spalding also says that the rebels took 800 prisoners. All agree that the cavalry escaped virtually unscathed, for obvious reasons, and that these casualties therefore fell almost entirely amongst the foot. Only 400 infantry from Fife took part in the battle, therefore if most of the dead were indeed from that regiment (Lord Balfour of Burleigh's), the total number of dead is unlikely to have exceeded 500 men and may even have been rather less. Ruthven's and Spalding's figures of 1,000 and 800 prisoners respectively are not incompatible, and since we are told that the rebels forcibly enlisted these prisoners in their army then notwithstanding the fact that they promptly deserted en masse, the figure is likely to be fairly reliable, though once again the lower one is perhaps the correct one. If Wishart's claim that more were taken prisoner than killed is true—and there is no reason to doubt that it is— then this would again suggest a figure nearer 500 dead than 2,000. Rebel losses are unknown, though claims that they lost not a single man ought to be treated with some scepticism.[14]

POST MORTEM

The allegedly precipitate attack by the rebels, or at any rate some of them, upon the government forces at Tippermuir, has been hailed as a devastating new tactic devised by Alasdair MacColla in Ireland,

and introduced by him to the Scottish highlanders; but a detailed examination of this and other battles does not support such a contention. A key element according to Dr. David Stevenson in the execution of the seventeenth (and eighteenth) century 'highland charge' was the introduction of the musket into Ireland and the Scottish highlands, and the replacement of the two-handed sword and the mail coat with the single-handed broadsword and targe.

> The adoption of the single-handed sword and targe was one change in weapons essential to the development of the classic 'Highland Charge'. The other was the widespread use of the musket in the highlands, and this may well not have taken place until the early seventeenth century, though here again earlier Irish practice was probably influential; the Highlanders' single volley of musket fire before charging may well be derived from the kerne's use of bows and arrows (or sometimes the throwing of darts or javelins) before charging. The Highlanders might only use their muskets to fire one volley before abandoning their guns and charging but this one volley was nonetheless central to their tactics, both because of the casualties and disorganisation it caused among the enemy just before the highland charge hit them, and because such a volley frequently led the enemy to reply in kind instead of waiting until the highlanders were at point blank range. Thus the highlanders could make their charge with relative impunity, while the enemy musketeers were struggling to reload their guns. By throwing down their own muskets after firing only a single volley the Highlanders might be abandoning their most modern weapon in favour of ones which were basically centuries old, but given the limitations of the musket it was a decision which brought them great advantages at a critical moment in the battle.[15]

Attractive though this theory may at first appear, it is actually quite untenable. In the first place regular soldiers did not fire all their muskets at once but rather by successive ranks (and then by platoons in the eighteenth century); and moving forward some years, the highlanders did not charge with much impunity at Killiecrankie, for as many as a third were killed or wounded by the regulars' musketry. More pertinently, however, the theory expressed above is emphatically not supported by the evidence which does exist as to the relative numbers of the various types of weapons actually in the hands of highlanders immediately before the Civil War. A detailed survey which was carried out in five Atholl parishes in 1638 minutely lists the weapons held by individuals. Out of 451 armed men—and there were obviously a number besides not included in the survey because they had no arms—only 11 lacked 'swords', but only 100, that is slightly less than a quarter, also possessed muskets. Furthermore only 124, about a quarter of the 'swordsmen', also boasted targes, yet Atholl might be considered to be one of the most prosperous areas in the highlands with ready access to lowland markets. That this was not an exceptionally low figure is illustrated by a muster of the Laird of Glenorchy's men in the same year, of 117 men paraded before him in their 'best array'— and once again we do not know how many were not included because they were unarmed—only 31, again only a quarter, carried muskets.[16] The west coast and the Hebrides are known to have been very much poorer at this time, with ironwork of all kinds in short supply, and were in general very much more backward. The usage of a 'high technology' weapon such as a musket is therefore likely to have been even lower there than in Atholl. Given this shortage of muskets the inability of the Athollmen at Tippermuir to stop Rossie's charge by musket fire alone is at once apparent. Although the same individuals comprised within the 1638 census are unlikely all of them to have been present on this occasion, the figure of 451 men counted equates sufficiently closely to the number of men led by Montrose for the survey to be an accurate reflection of the armament of Montrose's battalion. It is likely that no more than 100 musketeers fired upon Rossie's 300 cavalry (and not all of these will have been armed with large calibre military muskets).

As further evidence of the planned nature of a 'classic highland charge', General Hawley's well known 1746 description of highland armies, and in particular his account of their forming columns as they charged forward, has been cited by Dr. Stevenson and others. Yet to form column from line as Hawley and other contemporaries describe would, if carried out deliberately, require a degree of discipline and training utterly lacking amongst highland levies. A rather likelier explanation for the phenomenon thus evidenced, is that the less fit and the less enthusiastic men and boys simply fell in behind their leaders, sticking close to their friends and obeying the herd instinct. Far from deliberately forming column from line, they were coalescing into large clumps simply because they were incapable of maintaining a linear formation on the move. Not all highlanders were fighting men, far less the blood-crazed warrior heroes of popular legend. A great many highlanders, the majority of them perhaps, were as terrified as most soldiers are in battle, but lacked the discipline which sustains the regular soldier in such times of stress. They were in short a half-armed, undisciplined mob, and behaved like one.

In any case, although the defeat at Tippermuir undoubtedly had an adverse effect upon government morale and this adverse effect was increased with each subsequent rebel victory, it may be questioned whether the 'highland charge', innovative or not, actually had the impact now claimed for it. The rebels in general were feared, and the Irish loathed, but in future battles the government troops were to fight very determinedly indeed, and except under the most adverse terms battle was never refused by them. If highlanders were such consummate soldiers as one is sometimes led to believe, it is odd that they should continue throughout the Civil War period and after to be treated with some contempt. Both Ruthven and Spalding, for example, neither of whom could be accused of having the regular soldier's contempt for irregulars, clearly regarded highlanders as second class soldiers, and were careful to distinguish between the rebel army's regulars and the clans.

The victory at Tippermuir led to the surrender of Perth that evening, though apparently the burgh militia were only restrained with some difficulty from setting their usual watches on the walls—which would argue rather against too many of them having been slain in the battle. In the short term the results of the battle were very favourable to the rebels. They were able to replenish their ammunition, those lacking swords doubtless took them from the dead and the prisoners, and in addition to clothing stripped from both, the Irish officers obtained £1,300 worth of cloth for their men from the Perth merchants. From the mid eighteenth century onwards much play was made of the Gael's attachment to his natural dress, but in the seventeenth century no great difficulties are recorded in persuading him, be he Scots or Irish, to adopt 'lowland' clothing. What the rebels failed to do, however, was attract recruits other than the impressed prisoners. On the contrary, just as the highlanders were slipping away to secure their plunder, the government was assembling another army at Stirling.

On 2 September orders were given for fencibles to assemble at Stirling, and a number of regiments, chiefly from the Earl of Callendar's army, were ordered home from England. This had been one of the primary objects of Montrose's rising in the first place, but too few Scots regiments were recalled to relieve the pressure upon the English Royalists appreciably, and in any case fatal damage had already been inflicted at Marston Moor on 2 July. By 4 September Argyle and his military adviser, the Earl of Lothian, were at Stirling, and the rebel advance was confidently awaited. They never came. Still chronically short of the cavalry and pikemen needed for an advance into the lowlands, and already weakened by a steady stream of deserters, the rebels marched away from Argyle's army and made instead for Dundee. Although he summoned the city on 6 September, Montrose had already lost too many men to risk an assault, and when his summons was rejected the rebels marched north in a desperate attempt to seek recruits from the North-East.

4

Aberdeen and Fyvie

Despite their fine victory at Tippermuir, the rebels' situation remained perilous and indeed might have been said to have been deteriorating daily. Some few recruits, including two badly needed troops of horse, were gathered in as they marched north, but Argyle's army soon left Stirling and was on their track. More seriously, although they may not at first have realised the danger—intelligence was not the rebels' strong point—the rebels were in fact moving into the concentration area of a third government army.

On 6 September the committee at Aberdeen ordered the fencibles from the Mearns, Aberdeenshire and Banffshire, to assemble at the burgh by the 9th or 10th of the month, and called for the Morayshire fencibles to come in by the 12th or 13th. Had they done so, the rebels would have been heavily outnumbered in the battle on the 13th, but the response to this call to arms was mixed. The Mearns men failed to turn up at all, probably because the northward advance of the rebels prevented their assembly. The Banff and Moray men, though, had rather less excuse for their almost total failure to comply with the summons. The distance involved may of course have had something to do with it, but the real problem was a dispute which had arisen between the Aberdeen committee and Huntly's son, Lord Gordon. At least the covenanting lairds of Aberdeenshire brought in their tenantry: the Earl of Erroll's men under James Hay of Muriefauld, some of the Earl Marischal's tenants under John Keith of Clackbreach, and a Formartine contingent led by John Udny of Udny, who with many of his men had fought for the Royalists in 1639. Lords Fraser and Crichton led their men in person as did a number of lesser lairds. Three regular troops of horse also obeyed the summons: Captain Alexander Keith's, Sir William Forbes of Craigievar's, and one of Lord Gordon's led by his brother Lord Lewis Gordon. Lord Gordon was not himself present. Spalding alleges that he had been offended by the fact that a second regiment of foot, which he had raised after the first marched into England, had been re-assigned by the committee to Lord Forbes instead; but other accounts cite a refusal by the lairds to serve under Lord Gordon. Both versions are likely to be correct. Lord Gordon had understandably been somewhat backward in opposing his father's rising in the spring; consequently he was rather distrusted by the others of the committee, despite the fact that they themselves had done even less, and for that reason his second regiment of foot was given to Lord Forbes.[2] At this stage however such suspicions were unfounded, and the only result of this dispute was to rob the government forces in Aberdeen of a regular cavalry regiment and an experienced officer, who would have been quite capable of leading the army rather more effectively than the committee's uninspired choice, Lord Balfour of Burleigh. Indeed despite the evident distrust of the committee, Lord Gordon proceeded with his recruiting, and according to Ruthven, having assembled a large force at Kildrummy Castle was on his way to Aberdeen, sending his brother, Lord Lewis Gordon, ahead as a token of his good faith.

In addition to these levies two other regiments of foot were available for the defence of the city. The first was a regular unit generally referred to as the 'Fyff Regiment'; this was Lord Elcho's, commanded by its Lieutenant Colonel, Sir Charles Arnott; Elcho himself was not of course present. The second regiment was the Aberdeen Militia commanded on this occasion by a professional soldier, Major Arthur Forbes. As in 1639 the soldiers were chiefly drawn from the New Toun but also included men from the surrounding area, especially from the Aultoun where one of the baillies, William Rait, had been organising them since the beginning of September, much to the disgust of John Spalding who may have been one of those serving with this contingent.[3] Both these regiments were 500 strong,[4] and Lord Forbes' Regiment 400 strong.[5] The remaining infantry levies seem to have amounted to about 1,000 men divided into three regiments, commanded by Muriefauld, Clackbreach and Udny.

The cavalry, regulars and levies alike, together mustered something like 300 troopers—which Wishart predictably doubles—and in total therefore the army was not much weaker than Lord Elcho's had been at Tippermuir, although there were rather more regulars at Aberdeen. The biggest problem which it suffered from, as indeed had been the case at Tippermuir, was the lack of a competent or even active leader.

ABERDEEN, 13 SEPTEMBER 1644

From Dundee the rebels moved northwards skirting the hills, and discovering at last that an army was assembling at Aberdeen and that the Bridge of Dee had been re-fortified against them, they crossed the Dee some way upstream at the Mills of Drum, and camped at Crathes Castle on the night of 11 September. Next day they marched down the north bank of the river, but probably on hearing that the government forces had occupied a position at Two Mile Cross, halted a few miles short of the city. That night however the government troops evacuated the position and retired into the city. Montrose then in turn occupied the position, and as at Tippermuir, opened the proceedings by sending a messenger to demand the surrender of the city and its garrison. This time both the commissioner and the drummer who accompanied him were treated courteously; Provost Leslie convened a meeting at Alexander Findlater's house by the Bow Brig, the western entrance to the town, and while their response was debated the commissioner and the drummer were liberally plied with drink. Notwithstanding the understandable nervousness which the rebels' approach inspired, the answer was never in doubt, and even as their reply was being composed (with much scratching out and amendment), the army began marching out to take up a position on a southward facing ridge astride the Hardgate, the main road into the town from the west. As the commissioner and his drummer returned with the answer, the latter was pistolled by one of the marching troopers, and on Montrose's discovering this he ordered that no quarter should be given. The act was universally condemned both at the time and afterwards, though intriguingly enough Wishart makes no mention of the incident. What no-one seems to have asked though is *why* the drummer was pistolled. Was there perhaps a drunken taunt addressed by a catholic Irishman to a protestant Scot?[7] When this news and the committee's answer to his summons reached him, Montrose furiously set his own forces in motion, and after securing the Bridge of Dee marched along the axis of the Hardgate towards the city. According to Spalding they then deployed with the wind at their backs, a strong one blowing out of the west sou' west, but at some stage they must have swung around to face north in order to cross the How Burn and assault the ridge. When this occurred is not clear, but it must have been fairly early on.

Only two accounts of the battle treat of it in any detail, Wishart's and Ruthven's. Spalding's account, although containing some extremely useful points, is surprisingly brief, but circumstantial details suggest that he himself took part in the battle, and as a militiaman his awareness of what was happening other than within the immediate area of the regiment will naturally have been a little limited. Wishart and Ruthven are greatly at variance in describing the battle, but while the latter is clearly familiar with the topography and takes pains to assure his readers that: 'what I wreat is from there relation who were actores on both sydes and those of the best sort, and who have ever reported worthie of credit', Wishart by contrast not only appears somewhat muddled, but was dependent largely upon Montrose's recollection of events some years later. Apart from this conflict, modern reconstructions of the battle have also been complicated by reliance upon Gardiner's map of the battlefield. Although satisfactorily delineating the lie of the land, Gardiner performs the marvellous feat of cramming the 1,600 men of the rebel army into a frontage of only 120 metres!

There was in fact insufficient room for the rebels to draw up evenly on either side of the Hardgate, and they must instead have been drawn up on Willowbank, a little to the south of the How Burn, and for the most part to the east of the Hardgate. The rebel left was commanded by Colonel James Hay, a professional soldier who had been with Huntly in the spring, and comprised about 30 light cavalry—moss-troopers— under Nathaniel Gordon, and 100 Irish musketeers led by Captain John Mortimer of O'Cahan's Regiment. The right wing was similarly organised under Sir William Rollo, with another troop of horse led by Sir Thomas Ogilvie, and again a party of about 100 infantry, this time including some archers. The centre, led by Montrose in person, comprised the three Irish regiments, less the detachment on the left. Major Laghtman's, the largest of the three, ought as the senior unit to have had the right, but as Colonel James McDonnell was the senior officer present his own regiment probably had the honour. O'Cahan's Regiment may have stood next to them, but as a substantial detachment from this regiment was on the left wing, it seems likeliest that Major Laghtman's Regiment stood in the centre flanked by the two smaller units. In total the rebels mustered little more than 1,500 or 1,600 foot and 60 to 80 horse. Their artillery, captured from the government forces at Tippermuir, appears to have been planted on the high ground by the Hardgate.[9]

The government forces were fairly conventional in their deployment, and although no formal order of battle survives, it is possible to plot the positions of the various units on the basis of their reported adventures in the battle. On the right wing overlooking the Justice Mills were two regular troops of horse, Alexander Keith's and Sir William Forbes of Craigievar's. The eighteen volunteers of Lord Lewis Gordon's 'Lifeguard' were also on this wing. Wishart places them on the left, but as will be seen there is clear evidence that he was indeed on the right. From the fact that they do not appear to have been caught up in the rout back to Aberdeen, it may be inferred that the northern

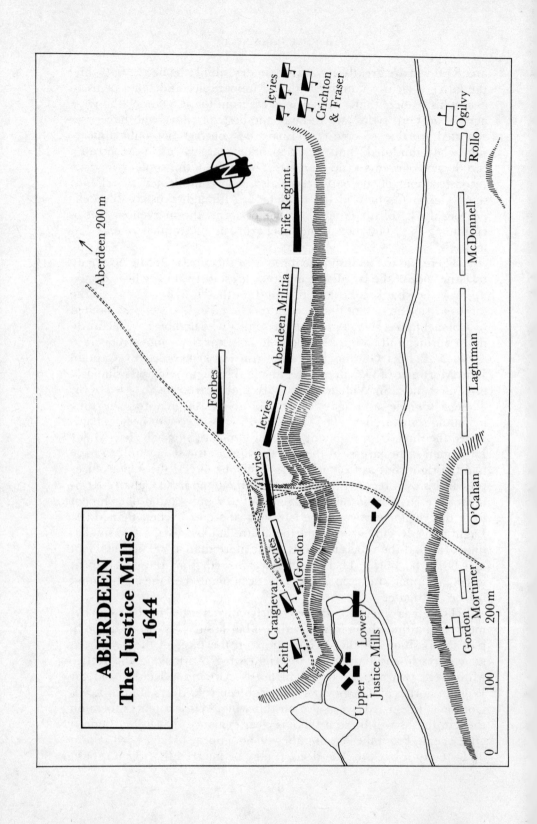

ABERDEEN
The Justice Mills
1644

Aberdeen 200 m

N

levies
Crichton
& Fraser
Fife Regimt.
Aberdeen Militia
Forbes
levies
levies
Craigievar
levies
Keith
Gordon
Upper
Lower
Justice Mills

Ogilvy
Rollo
McDonnell
Laghtman
O'Cahan
Gordon
Mortimer

0   100   200 m

levies stood on the right of the infantry, straddling the Hardgate. The Aberdeen Militia were more or less in the centre, and the Fife regiment on the left. Lord Forbes' Regiment must have been placed in reserve, probably fairly centrally. The left wing, deployed on rather flatter ground, comprised Lord Crichton's and Lord Fraser's troops of horse, and a fairly miscellaneous collection of mounted levies led by Abercrombie of Birkenbog and some minor Forbes lairds. The artillery was probably sited fairly centrally. Command of the army was theoretically exercised by Lord Balfour of Burleigh but in practice conduct of the fighting was left to the individual regimental officers.[10]

The Wings

The battle began with an attempt by Colonel Hay to drive a detachment of foot out of the Justice Mills, a collection of fairly solid buildings, yards and gardens, in the valley bottom on the rebels' left flank. In this they were successful, but checked by a troop of lancers, presumably Alexander Keith's. Although the rebel cavalry was outnumbered, the fire from Captain Mortimer's musketeers was sufficient to drive off Keith's men in some confusion, throwing their lances away as they went. Nothing daunted, Craigievar prepared a heavy counter-attack. First he ostentatiously moved forward with all his cavalry, gripping the rebels' attention, and at the same time had a battalion, which must have been Lord Forbes' Regiment, fetch a wide compass to the right, remaining behind the crest of the ridge for as long as possible before descending the road to the Upper Mills and suddenly appearing on the rebels' flank. At this point, unfortunately, their resolution failed them. They failed to realise that an immediate assault would not only overrun the rebels opposite, but also capture their artillery and allow them to break into the rear of the rebel centre. Instead a long-range firefight developed between them and Captain Mortimer's men, who may by this time have been esconced in the Lower Mill buildings. Realising that Forbes' men could not be held off for ever, a further 100 musketeers were fetched by Nathaniel Gordon, and with his small horse troop in support a successful assault was mounted driving off Forbes.[11]

This success may indeed be attributed, as Ruthven suggests, to a 'want of experience' on Forbes' part, but more immediately perhaps to a sudden lack of support from Craigievar's cavalry. They had been distracted by an altogether more urgent threat posed by the rebel centre, which was now advancing, forcing them to leave Forbes to his own devices. Before dealing with Craigievar's attempts to stop this advance, it is necessary to examine Wishart's version of the fighting on the flanks and to discuss the fighting on the government left wing.

The discrepancies between Ruthven's and Wishart's accounts of the battle of Tippermuir may be satisfactorily accounted for by the latter having relied heavily if not entirely upon Montrose's own reminiscences. These were necessarily limited by his role as commander, not of the army as a whole, but only of the right wing, notwithstanding which Wishart accepted his experiences there as being true of the army as a whole. The discrepancy in the two accounts of the Justice Mills battle is much more serious, but can be traced to a single though significant error on Wishart's part. Ruthven states that the rebels' left was commanded by Colonel Hay and the right wing by Sir William Rollo. His account of how these gentlemen conducted themselves is entirely intelligible. Wishart, on the other hand, not only places Rollo on the left and Hay on the right, but then introduces an entirely unconvincing set of adventures. The right wing under Hay is, we are assured, attacked by Lord Lewis Gordon with a strong body of horse. Seeing the danger, Montrose orders Rollo to march across the rear of the rebel centre, from west to east, to Hay's aid, and thus reinforced the rebels defeat Gordon. The now unprotected left is then attacked by Craigievar, so the whole body of the rebel horse (rather improbably numbering only 44 men in total) again traverses the battlefield, this time from east to west, in order to deal with this latest threat. These astonishing peregrinations only make sense if it is accepted that Wishart was first aware that Colonel Hay required to be reinforced by Sir William Rollo, and secondly that the government forces were decisively beaten by them on the left, but erroneously transposed the two officers, thus finding it necessary to make Rollo traverse the battlefield twice, in order to meet his destiny upon the left.[12]

Seeing the rebel right depleted—if not called away in its entirety—to the fighting around the Justice Mills, Lord Fraser and Lord Crichton twice led their troops of horse forward against the right flank of MacColla's infantry. Ruthven does not make it clear whether both troops attacked twice in concert, or whether they came forward singly one after the other, and although he says that they charged, it is more likely that they may only have fired their pistols and then retired; although Sir Thomas Ogilvy, the rebel cavalry commander on this wing, had his horse shot from under him, and Ogilvy of Inverquharity suffered a lance thrust in the thigh. It is of course possible that these and similar wounds were sustained on the left flank if Ogilvy accompanied Rollo to Hay's aid, but Ruthven only mentions infantry reinforcements, and it is most unlikely that all the troops covering the rebel right would have been called away. On balance it would seem likely that the rebels were strong enough to hold Fraser and Crichton at bay, and they retired lamenting the failure of the irregular cavalry to support them. It was here in Ruthven's opinion that the lack of an effective commander told against the government troops, for the rest of the horse stood off, 'not for want of good will to feght, but for want of experience, not knawing that it was there time to charge; and this errour came chiefly for want of a generall commander, whose ordours they should obey'.[13]

The Rout of the Infantry

The battle had probably been raging for about an hour when Montrose ordered a general advance up the hillside towards the main body of the government forces. Unaware as he was that Lord Forbes' Regiment was about to appear on his left, both flanks at this point must have seemed secure, and his as yet unengaged infantry were receiving a number of casualties from artillery fire to which his own gunners could make little effective reply. The ineffectiveness of the rebel artillery is sometimes attributed to their firing uphill, but in fact as they were planted at the top of a rise by the roadside there was not a great deal of difference in height, and in any case it is in fact more difficult to fire artillery effectively downhill. The true explanation is quite simply that the rebel gunners were enthusiastic but untrained. Whatever the reason, Montrose was well aware that as soon as his flanks were secure he must advance, and although once set in motion the proceedings may have been quite brisk, the slope must have prevented the attack from being quite so precipitate as Wishart suggests, and what really happened was no highland charge, classic or otherwise. Wishart quotes Montrose as ordering the Irish forward with some panache:

> We shall gain nothing, my men, by fighting at a distance. Who can distinguish the strong from the weak, the coward from the brave? Get to close quarters with yon craven feeble striplings; they will never withstand your valour. Fall on them with sword and musket butts. Crush them; drive them off the field, and take vengeance on the traitor rebels.[14]

If Montrose did indeed deliver such a speech it must have been at the commencement of the battle, not in the midst of it; notwithstanding Wishart's claim that on hearing these words they instantly hurled themselves upon the government forces and routed them, the fight was stiffer and of somewhat longer duration than this. Another propaganda tract has Montrose simply ordering Laghtman's men to 'lay aside their Muskets and Pikes, and fall on with Sword and Durk'. This is sufficiently brief to be rather more convincing than the oration which Wishart recounts, but both the rather more reliable Ruthven and the participant, John Spalding, emphatically state that the ensuing fighting was prolonged. We may therefore dismiss Wishart's wild charge up the slope as simplistic propaganda and look instead to a rather steadier push up the slope by the Irish. In any case this advance was checked

almost at once by a fierce cavalry attack initiated by Forbes of Craigievar, the senior officer on that wing of the government forces.

Craigievar took advantage of the fact that Colonel Hay's men
were fully occupied in fighting off Lord Forbes' Regiment and Keith's
cavalry, to launch a two phase attack on the flank of O'Cahan's
Regiment. First to go forward was Lord Lewis Gordon with his own
eighteen troopers, and they trotted up firing their pistols and then
falling away. Although subsequently criticised as being obsolescent, this
mode of proceeding was in fact the normal means of delivering a cavalry
attack against formed bodies of men, and in any case with only eighteen
men it is hard to see what else he could have done. Although he may
not have inflicted any real damage on the 300 rebel infantry, what
Gordon very probably did achieve was to halt the battalion and draw
some of its fire just before Sir William Forbes of Craigievar charged
home with his rather stronger squadron. Once again Ruthven's and
Wishart's accounts of Craigievar's charge differ, but if taken together
provide a rather satisfactory explanation of what actually happened.

According to Ruthven, Lord Lewis Gordon and his men blazed
away, and were then followed up by Craigievar's men jealously wishing
to emulate the Gordons' valour. Craigievar disdains popping away
with pistols and goes straight in, but instead of resisting, O'Cahan's men
open their ranks—actually they must on the contrary have bunched
together tightly in companies leaving big gaps in their line—Craigievar's men ride through the gaps and then the Irish turn upon them
inflicting heavy casualties. Wishart for his part makes no mention of
Lord Lewis Gordon, having already (erroneously) described his defeat
on the opposite wing, and makes no mention of the Irish either. Instead
he describes a purely cavalry encounter, with the outnumbered rebels
avoiding the first onrush and then falling on the flank of Craigievar's
squadron, routing them. Taking the two accounts together, however,
would suggest that the Irish 'being so well trained men as the world
could afford no better' (which hardly suggests an undisciplined gaelic
war-band) opened their lines to let the cavalry through, fired a volley
into their backs and then cheerfully stood back while Nathaniel Gordon's moss-troopers administered the *coup de grace*. Ruthven naturally
enough says that few or none of them got away, but since the troop
was active again shortly afterwards, one may draw the obvious conclusion that as in most cavalry encounters, the defeated party might
have been well scattered, but lost very few casualties. Craigievar himself
was taken prisoner, however, as was Forbes of Boyndlie, the Tutor of
Pitsligo.[15]

By the time Nathaniel Gordon had finished mopping up, the two
main bodies had joined in battle. The fact that this phase of the fighting
seems to have been of comparatively long duration clearly points to

there having been a heavy firefight. According to Ruthven 'it was disputed hard for a long space'; and Spalding, after relating that the battle continued for two hours, merely says 'At last we tak the flight', the implication obviously being that they were eventually beaten, not that they were overwhelmed in the first rush of a wild highland charge. Moreover he goes on to say that 'there wes littell slauchter in the fight, bot horribill wes the slauchter in the flight fleeing bak to the toune'.[16] The three battalions of Aberdeenshire levies under Muriefauld, Clackbreach and Udny, appear to have escaped virtually unscathed, probably retiring due north to the Aultoun and the bridge over the river Don at Balgownie. The Aberdeen Militia may have wished to follow their example, but Spalding declares that Provost Leslie ordered them to make for the town instead, and then, he indignantly declares, galloped off on his horse to safety. Presumably until this moment the militia were still holding their positions. What probably happened is that O'Cahan's men, having shaken off the attentions of Cragievar's cavalry, pushed up the Hardgate and routed one of the Aberdeenshire battalions, initiating a progressive collapse of the line. The Fife Regiment on the extreme left, 'lyke bold and well trained souldiouris', held together despite this crumbling, and with fugitives and rebels alike running over the cornfields behind them, took the only course open to them and began marching off in good order towards the river, no more than 500 metres away. MacColla, still in control of his men, 'takes furth foure hundreth Irishes'—presumably McDonnell's Regiment—and caught them before they got very far.[17]

The horrors of the rout and the subsequent sack of the burgh are harrowingly described by Spalding, but it is evident that only a small part of the rebel army was actually involved. Spalding, who of all people was probably best placed to know, says that Montrose in following up the chase left most of the army standing 'closs vnbrokin upon the field'. Presumably therefore it was only O'Cahan's men who chased the militia into the town. Nathaniel Gordon's cavalry were probably keeping an eye on the retreating right wing, while MacColla and the remainder of the Irish remained on the field. Laghtman's Regiment certainly engaged the militia in a firefight, but as the largest regiment present, their absence from that army 'standing closs vnbrokin' would have been commented upon had they joined in the pursuit.

The author of *True Rehearsall* appears to be the only one to put a figure on the government's losses: 520 slain, besides the Aberdeen men, whom Spalding listing by name puts at 118, not all of whom had actually been serving in the militia. Nearly all the accounts agree that apart from the Aberdeen men most of the dead belonged to the Fife Regiment, but as usual reports of its demise are exaggerated and it turns up again a few months later serving under General Baillie in

Perthshire. Neither the cavalry nor the Aberdeenshire levies will have escaped unscathed, but it seems obvious from their sudden collapse and the absence of pursuit that the latter escaped lightly.[18] It is quite possible that Udny's men, many of whom were former Royalists, may have run without firing a shot as the Irish approached.

Royalist casualties are harder to assess. Wishart alludes to the cannon making 'no small havoc of our men', but advances no figures. Ruthven gives seven dead, and MacColla, in a despatch to Ormonde, four. Both figures are far too low. The fight lasted for two hours and involved a great deal of shooting. Moreover in September 1645 a James Reid penitently explained to the town council that he had buried his father and uncle, both slain in the battle, in the grave of a former Provost, Reid of Pitfodels: 'not intending to wrong any thairby; quahairas any of the strangeris Irishes, or wthers who wer at that tyme killed micht have beine buried thair'. Both this and Wishart's statement strongly suggest that rather more than seven rebels were slain, although obviously their casualties must have been less than those sustained by the government forces.[19]

The rout of the army was followed by four days of rape and pillage in and around Aberdeen. Montrose had ordered his men to give no quarter after his drummer was slain, and having unleashed at least one of the Irish regiments on the town he was quite unable or unwilling to control them. Characteristically Wishart makes no mention whatever of the city being sacked, and indeed blandly states that Montrose allowed his men two days rest there.[20] While the atrocities were being committed in the city, most of the rebel army, commanded by MacColla, in fact moved north-westwards to Kintore and Inverurie on the 14th, and were rejoined there by Montrose on the 16th after hearing that Argyle was approaching fast. Laden down with the plunder which, in Alasdair MacColla's own words, 'hath made all our soldiers cavalliers',[21] they were only three days ahead of Argyle as they withdrew westwards towards Rothiemurchus.

Argyle meanwhile had reached Aberdeen on the afternoon of 19 September. He had with him rather more men than the rebels, some of them regular soldiers recalled from England. There were three foot regiments from Argyllshire, most of them probably highlanders, and stiffening these rather unreliable levies were two good foot regiments, the Earl of Lothian's and Sir Mungo Campbell of Lawers'. Neither regiment mustered more than 500 men, making around 4,000 foot in total, and in addition there was the Earl of Dalhousie's regular regiment of horse and ten other troops. Dalhousie's Regiment is unlikely to have mustered more than 400 troopers at this stage, and if a rather generous 50 men are assigned to each of the other troops, Argyle would have had 900 cavalry, though not improbably a couple of hundred less. On

21 September Craigievar's Troop (he himself was still a prisoner) was detached and sent southwards as escort to Lord Spynie, who had just been captured, but this loss was more than compensated for by the addition of the Laird of Buchanan's Regiment of foot, 500 strong, which passed through Aberdeen on 23 September on its way to join Argyle.[22]

The rebels meanwhile had quite literally commenced marching round in circles. As Argyle continued moving westwards, they found their way into Moray blocked on Speyside by local levies, stiffened by Lord Gordon's Regiment, and instead turned south into Atholl. There Alasdair MacColla departed with at least 500 men to relieve his garrisons on the west coast. Argyle was resting his army at Ruthven in Badenoch when he heard of this split on 9 October, and at once took the opportunity to place a strong garrison in Inverness. This comprised Campbell of Lawers' Regiment and the Laird of Buchanan's. Mindful of the fact that both Perth and Aberdeen had been lost when their garrisons had perforce to march out and encounter the rebels in the field, orders were given for the fortification of the highland capital. These fortifications apparently comprised an earthwork wall and ditch, with palisades and four fortified gates: one to the east, one to the south at the top of Castle Street, one by the bridge over the River Ness, and the fourth 'low at the church'.[23] Every parish, it is related, came into the town one after the other until the works were completed. The same method was to be used a year later for the rather belated fortification of Glasgow, when all the fencible men were ordered to come in by parishes to labour for a week at a time, and their ministers enjoined to attend also 'to encourage them'.

From Inverness Argyle rejoined the rest of his army in Badenoch, and after plundering and burning the area in reprisal for the earlier provision of recruits for the rebel forces, he moved into Atholl in pursuit of Montrose. The rebels were still on the move, however: having picked up enough recruits in Badenoch and Atholl to replace the missing Irish, Montrose embarked upon another circular tour, bypassing Perth and Dundee and heading north again to Aberdeen. The Earl Marischal meanwhile had stirred himself to organise a muster at the Bridge of Dee for 14 October, but word of the rebels' approach inspired a wild panic amongst the citizens, and despite drums being sent through the streets, none turned out. Instead, the newly appointed local commander, Sir James Ramsay, could only muster seven troops of horse, all of them happily regulars, comprising three troops of his own regiment, three of Lord Gordon's, and Captain Alexander Keith's. Next day reinforcements arrived, comprising a further eight troops under a Lieutenant Colonel Hamilton. This at least is how Spalding describes them, but it in fact seems likely that it was Sir Frederick

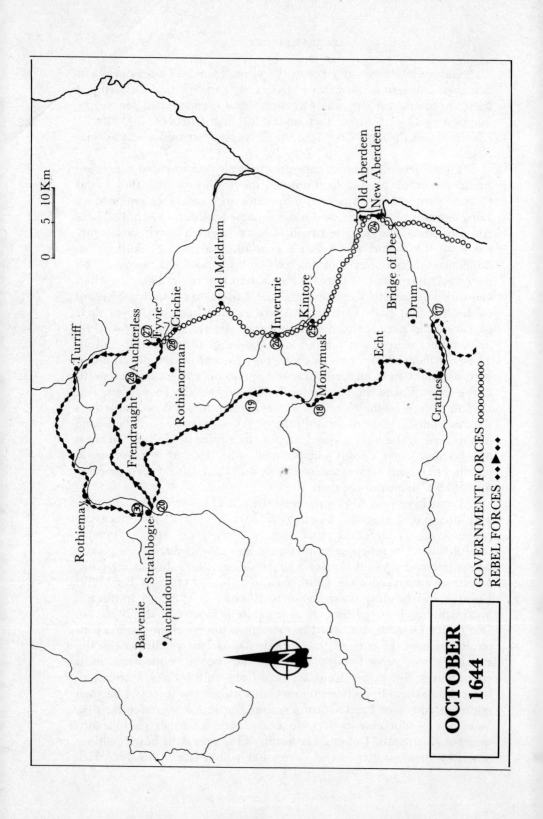

OCTOBER
1644

GOVERNMENT FORCES oooooooooo
REBEL FORCES ◆◆▶◆◆

Old Aberdeen
New Aberdeen
24
Bridge of Dee
Drum
17
Old Meldrum
Inverurie
Kintore
23
22 Fyvie
27 Crichie
26
Monymusk
Turriff
Auchterless
28
29
Rothienorman
Echt
19
18
Frendraught
Crathes
Rothiemay
Strathbogie
30
20
Balvenie
Auchindoun

N

Hamilton's and Sir James Hackett's regiments of horse, under Hamilton's Lieutenant Colonel, Sir Patrick McGhie.[24]

Confirmation that Montrose intended to force the Bridge of Dee seems to have been obtained from one of the rebel Scoutmasters, Captain Aleiss, who was captured by Ramsay's men somewhere on lower Deeside (he afterwards escaped); but while Ramsay guarded the bridge, the rebels forded the river once more at the Mills of Drum on Thursday 17 October, and promptly embarked upon an orgy of destruction and plundering, in particular burning corn yards, as they made their way to Strathbogie. Ramsay made no further attempt to intercept them, but instead awaited the arrival of Argyle on the 24th with 2,000 foot and seven troops of horse. Argyle had been pressing Montrose hard, and was in no mood to let up now. Next day, 25 October, he marched on to Kintore taking Ramsay and seven of his troops with him, leaving McGhie's and Hackett's regiments to garrison Aberdeen.[25]

FYVIE, 28 OCTOBER 1644

The discrepancies previously discussed between Ruthven's and Wishart's accounts of the rebellion may be attributed to Ruthven's drawing upon a variety of sources, while Wishart relied upon Montrose alone. In their differing treatment of the engagement at Fyvie, however, a sinister element emerges, and it is evident that any alleged animus which Huntly may have borne towards Montrose was more than repaid by the bitter animus which Montrose bore towards the whole house of Gordon. Wishart alleges that Montrose's attempts to enlist the aid of the Gordons was absolutely thwarted by Huntly's orders, and that the Gordon lairds, although secretly wishing to join with Montrose, were instead constrained to hide themselves from him on their Chief's insistence.[26] This is plainly nonsense, and if the Gordons did hide from Montrose it was because they feared his rapacious soldiers. Ruthven admits that Huntly's absence was a hindrance to recruiting, but not his orders, and goes on to enumerate 200 lowland foot from Strathbogie, 200 highlanders from Braemar and 100 from Strathavan as having joined the rebel army at this time, all either of the name of Gordon, or Huntly's vassals.[27] It is true that, save for a few recruits, cavalry was not forthcoming, but it is quite unfair to blame Huntly alone for any reluctance to join the rebels. Quite apart from the fact that many of the gentry are likely to have felt the same sense of betrayal by Montrose as their chief, Huntly's sons had to be considered. Huntly was far away in Strathnaver, but two of his sons, Lord Gordon and Lord Lewis Gordon, were close at hand with a regular cavalry regiment very largely officered by their friends and relations, and recruited from amongst their tenantry, and this regiment was fighting for the government. Contrary to Wishart's assertions, few of the Gordons had any love for Montrose, and although it evidently dates from about a year or so later, a short catch recorded by Pennant is somewhat revealing:

> If ye with Montrose gae, ye'll get sick and wae enough.
> If with Lord Lewis gae, ye'll get rob an reave enough.[28]

Besides the Gordons, Montrose had by Ruthven's account 800 or 900 Irish infantry and a fresh contingent of 200 Athollmen. Added to the Gordons, this gives a total of 1,500 or 1,600 infantry, which tallies pretty well with the 1,500 given by Wishart. On the night of 25 October 1644, the rebels moved eastwards from Strathbogie to Auchterless, and from there the next day to Fyvie, where on the 28th they discovered that Argyle's army was almost upon them.

Fyvie was the first in a series of major failures in the rebels' intelligence gathering. Wishart avers that Montrose was unaware that Argyle was north of the Grampian Mountains, and that the move was undertaken because he had given up on the Gordons. Ruthven says it was because he wished to avoid eating Strathbogie bare. Neither version is in fact very satisfactory, although Ruthven's does at least make sense, but both accounts fail to explain why a night march was necessary. Even at the present day, night marches can be fraught with problems; in the seventeenth century they were quite literally a nightmare, and never undertaken without very good reason. Spalding, on the other hand, although a little out on his dates, states that Montrose evacuated Strathbogie on hearing of Argyle's having marched from Aberdeen, and this is much more likely. Argyle's intelligence gathering was much better than the rebels', however; he knew of the move almost at once, and accordingly marched from Inverurie northwards on the 28th, presumably by way of Old Meldrum, and then along what is now the A947.[29] Montrose, having as he thought shaken off Argyle, was rudely surprised by his appearance, which caught most of his cavalry away foraging; and Wishart is quick to blame Argyle's unexpected arrival on false intelligence from Montrose's spies. Although this may be correct, Montrose was to make a habit of being crept up upon unawares, and must himself ultimately take the blame for the inefficiency of his intelligence service. Be that as it may, once the rebels realised they were about to be attacked they stood to arms and awaited the onslaught.

Happily for the rebels, Montrose had chosen an excellent defensive position, and before proceeding further it is necessary to look closely at the battlefield. Ruthven helpfully states that the rebels had the river Ythan on their right and a wood on their left, with what he describes as a 'hollow bruick' to their front. Wishart says that Montrose, disdaining to shut himself up in the castle—which would in any case have proved fatal—instead led the rebels on to higher ground on a hill overlooking the castle. The Fraser *Chronicles* specify a 'craggy hill', the author of *True Rehearsall* simply states that the rebels were esconced in the wood of Fyvie, and Spalding likewise.[30] Ruthven's version implies that the rebels were facing southwards, but as Argyle's cavalry was apparently quartered around Rothienorman and Auchterless to the west of Fyvie, it seems rather more likely that although Montrose at first chose the position described by Ruthven, he ended up on the high ground facing west across the Ythan valley. Even so, he was still able to make use of Ruthven's 'hollow bruick': this was obviously the stream which emerges from a prominent re-entrant in the hillside about 300 metres south of the castle, and now feeds a small thin loch; but in 1644 it must have continued south-westwards, diagonally across the rebels' front, to the river. Immediately to the north of this stream, and between the castle and the hillside, is a low rise creating an area of dead ground at the foot of the main slope which Montrose was to make use of. This low rise and perhaps even the lower slopes of the hill were covered with a number of earthen walled agricultural enclosures, giving the ground an 'appearance like a [fortified] camp'.

Because the ground was so constricted, the fighting never developed into a general engagement, and instead comprised three separate probing attacks. These were quite distinct, and may conveniently be dealt with in turn. Before the fighting began, though, the rebels suffered a bit of a blow when the entire Strathbogie regiment deserted. Ruthven naturally makes no mention of this, but is uncharacteristically reticent as to any part they may have played in the fight; and the report may be accepted as being true, although it is quite unlike their usual conduct.

Perhaps as a result of this desertion a regiment of foot, presumably Lothian's, in mounting the first assault by the government forces broke into the enclosures, killing about fifteen or sixteen of the rebels. The survivors fled, and esconced behind the dykes Lothian's men commenced firing upon the rebels' main body. Montrose, realising the danger, ordered an immediate counter-attack, but in describing this phase there is a direct conflict between Ruthven's and Wishart's versions. The former declares unhesitatingly that the counter-attack was led by Donald Farquharson of Monaltrie, at the head of Huntly's highlanders from Braemar and Strathavan, whilst the latter credits Colonel O'Cahan with leading the assault, and adds by way of circumstantial detail that bags of powder were left behind by the government soldiers. The immediate difficulty with Wishart's version is that O'Cahan had been sent to Dublin in mid-August and had almost certainly not yet returned to the army (he probably did not rejoin it until the third rendezvous at Blair Atholl in November), but the officer

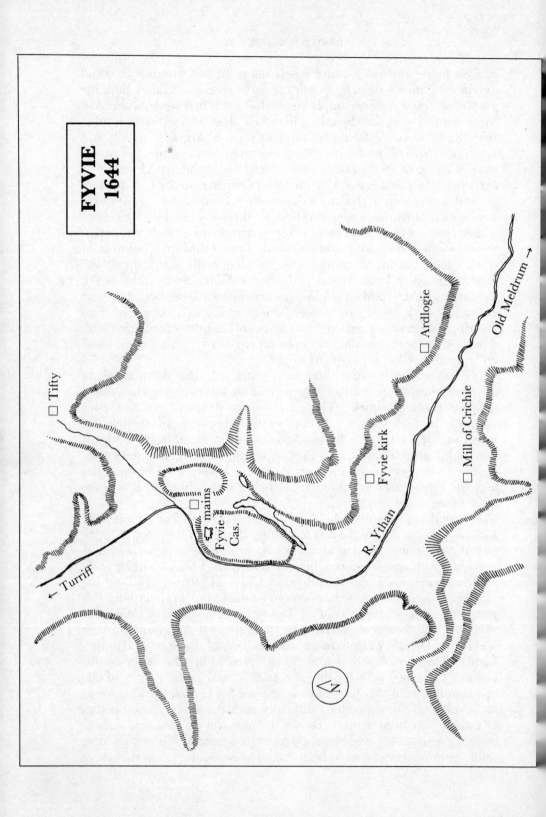

FYVIE
1644

Tifty

mains
Fyvie
Cas.

← Turriff

R. Ythan

Fyvie kirk

Ardlogie

Mill of Crichie

Old Meldrum →

N

in question may well have been his second in command, Lieutenant Colonel Donoghue O'Cahan. Although Ruthven is normally the more reliable of the two, Wishart only says that O'Cahan was directed to take those soldiers nearest to him, and they may well have been not his own men but Huntly's under Monaltrie. A hint that it may well have been highlanders who rushed the enclosures lies in the fact that cavalry were employed in Argyle's second attempt. Lothian's men at any rate fled without fighting.[31]

The second attack was carried out by a 'regiment' of horse, or more accurately five troops, and this time it was the rebels who fell back without offering resistance. The reasons for this were two-fold. In the first place, if they were indeed highlanders rather than Irish regulars, they were poorly equipped to face horsemen; but in the second place Montrose wished to ambush the cavalry. The main body of the rebels was concealed in dead ground, ready to fall on the horsemen once they had crossed the 'hollow bruick' and had it at their backs; but the Athollmen, still concealed in the trees on the southern flank, fired too soon and at too great a distance to cause any casualties. The cavalry, realising their danger, immediately halted and started to retire, and their retreat became precipitate when the rebels, anxious not to be baulked of their prey, rushed upon them with a loud cheer. Captain Alexander Keith counter-attacked in turn, but was slain, and a number of his men with him. He had succeeded though in effectively covering the retreat of the other four troops, and as with the first assault it seems that although many were frightened into running away, there was little if any actual fighting.

The third attack was even more abortive. This time another regiment of foot (Lord Forbes'?), supported this time by some troops of horse, came forward but they were again driven off. 'Bravely encountered' is Ruthven's phrase describing the affair, but it seems most likely from the absence of other details that this brave encounter consisted of the rebels standing their ground in the enclosures and blazing away at the government forces, who fired back and then retired.

After this Argyle was reluctant to mount another assault: the position was strong, the rebels actually outnumbered him in foot, for his 1,000 remaining highlanders seem to have been regarded as useless, and the ground was unsuitable for cavalry. Accordingly for the next two days there was some skirmishing, and a steady stream of wounded sent by Argyle for treatment in Aberdeen, but on the 30th, finding that his cavalry had eaten their quarters bare, Argyle was forced to move a couple of miles south to Crichie.[32] Montrose, who may by this time have been wondering how he was to get out of what was looking increasingly like a trap, immediately seized the opportunity to decamp northwards to Turriff, which he plundered; and then went along what is now the B9025 and B9117 to Rothiemay, the home of one of Lord Gordon's officers, which was also plundered, and so to Strathbogie again. On the 31st Argyle marched in pursuit again to Tullochbeg, and resumed skirmishing with the rebels again. Although said by the Royalist chroniclers to be getting the best of the skirmishing, the rebels were at the end of their tether, and the government forces had effectively run them into the ground. On 3 November Nathaniel Gordon, for one, decided to call it a day, and taking Sir William Forbes of Craigievar with him by way of insurance, rode into Argyle's camp to surrender.[33]

On the 6th Montrose realised that his position was untenable, and withdrew up the river Deveron and past Auchindoun to Balvenie Castle. Argyle at once occupied Strathbogie; and with Lord Gordon lower down Speyside and his army melting away, Montrose fled southwards to Blair Atholl. Apart from the Earl of Airlie and his sons, all the lowlanders and the Gordons left him, and most followed Nathaniel Gordon's example by surrendering and accepting Argyle's offer of safe conduct. Satisfied with the apparent destruction of the rebel army, Argyle returned to Aberdeen where he dismissed his highlanders on 14 November, and magnanimously arranged to have Nathaniel Gordon's excommunication lifted, before returning to Edinburgh and laying down his commission.

Despite their victories at Tippermuir and Aberdeen, the rebels had effectively been contained, and had been so closely harried by Argyle as to prevent any significant recruiting; their campaign, in short, had been a complete failure, and the government may well have felt justified in trusting to the winter to complete their destruction.

5

The Winter Campaign

Argyle left Aberdeen on 21 November having first settled his army in its winter quarters. Lord Forbes' Regiment seems to have disintegrated, for on March 1645 reference was made to the 'remnants' of the Aberdeenshire forces and the question of who was to command them.[1] Lothian's Regiment, bereft of their Colonel, who like Argyle wished to lay down his commission as Major General, was quartered in Aberdeen, while Campbell of Lawers' Regiment and the Laird of Buchanan's Regiment continued to garrison Inverness. Unpopular though these soldiers may have been with their involuntary hosts, the cavalry were even more unwelcome, since the horse of course required to be fed as well as the man; and to alleviate the problems caused thereby, the cavalry were quartered in small groups over a wide area. There were estimated to be a thousand troopers in all quartered in the north; Lord Gordon's Regiment was in Banffshire and Moray, while in Aberdeenshire were Sir James Hackett's, Sir Patrick McGhie's and the Earl of Dalhousie's Regiments, the last under its Lieutenant Colonel, John Innes. In addition there was Sir James Ramsay's Brigade, comprising his own regiment of three troops and four independent troops—Craigicvar's, Keith's, Crichton's and Fraser's. In total they may have mustered about twenty troops, each with an average strength of fifty men, though some of the regular units are likely to have had more than three troops apiece, in which case the average strength of each will obviously have been lower. Hackett's Regiment was quartered around Aberdeen itself, but the others were somewhat scattered, particularly through the presbyteries of Aberdeen, Deer and Ellon. The two latter were almost certainly chosen because they had escaped the worst effects of the campaign. Argyle's own troop naturally enough escorted him south.[2]

In Edinburgh, triumphantly returned from the storming of Newcastle Upon Tyne on 19 October, the Earl of Leven was assembling an

79

army intended to be used to finish off the rebels in the spring. He himself would shortly have to return to England to lead the army there, and since neither Argyle nor Lothian, who was heartily sick of soldiering, nor the Earl of Callendar, whose loyalties may have been a little equivocal, could be persuaded to take command of this force, it was resolved by the Estates to send for William Baillie of Letham. Baillie was a professional soldier who like most of his colleagues had been in the Swedish service. In 1632 he was Colonel of a German regiment and had been amongst the first to return to Scotland in 1638 and offer his sword to the Covenanters. More recently he had been serving as Leven's Lieutenant General of the Foot, and had distinguished himself in the chaos of Marston Moor. Like Leven, he had after the fall of Newcastle returned to Edinburgh on private business, but was on his way back to the army and at Belsay Castle, within twelve miles of Newcastle, when a messenger from the Estates overtook him with a summons to Edinburgh which he at once, if no doubt a little wearily, obeyed. Arriving back in Edinburgh he consented to take command of the Scots army, but immediately and ultimately disastrously fell out with the Marquis of Argyle:

> because I would not consent to receive orders from the Marquis of Argyle, (if casuallie we should have mett together,) after I had received commission to command in chieff over all the forces within the Kingdome, my Lord seemed to be displeased, and expressed himselfe so unto some, that if he lived, he should remember it; wherein his lordship indeed hath superabundantly been alse good as his word.[3]

Perhaps as a consequence of this refusal to bow to Argyle's authority, Baillie did not actually receive his commission as commander in chief until 8 March, but in the meantime was directed to march to Argyllshire where the rebels had unexpectedly appeared.[4]

The revival in the rebels' fortunes had been brought about by Alasdair MacColla. Rejoining Montrose as arranged at Blair Atholl in late November, he brought back not only a few hundred Irish soldiers, but also perhaps as many as 1,000 men of the western clans. With this very welcome accession of strength, Montrose was soon persuaded to abandon his original plan of wintering in the lowlands in favour of a rather more daring large scale raid into Argyllshire. Although a winter campaign in the mountains was obviously extremely risky, there were a number of excellent advantages to be considered. Not the least of these was the very unexpectedness of such an undertaking, and politically the resulting humiliation of Argyle was obviously very desirable. The arguments and the accruing advantages to the rebels have previously been well discussed by most writers, but not the fact that the rebels really had little other option but to remain in the field no matter what the weather. If Montrose genuinely intended to winter in the lowlands, the only place where he could realistically have expected to do so was in Strathbogie. Yet Strathbogie had already been repeatedly plundered by both the rebels and, rather more systematically, by the government forces, and a winter there would have been a hungry one. Moreover it was rather vulnerable to attack by the numerous government forces still in the area. They might not, it is true, have been strong enough or indeed resolute enough to meet the rebels in open battle, but they could certainly have made life very uncomfortable for them by harrying them constantly, interfering with foraging parties, destroying food stocks and beating up any isolated quarter. Furthermore, inactivity would have proved just as fatal to the rebel cause as a lost battle. The highlanders who had joined MacColla and come to the rendezvous at Blair Atholl had not joined simply to sit around grubbing for food and squabbling with patrols and each other, far away from home through the winter. The rising, arguably, was already faltering, and a winter of inactivity could easily have led to its extinction. Montrose, in short, although he may have entertained serious misgivings about the choice of target, had no real option but to embark upon a winter campaign if his army was to be held together until the spring.

The result of the decision to march westwards was everything which the highland chiefs could have hoped for. Unusually mild weather kept the mountain passes clear of snow, and by 13 December 1644 the rebels, having met no resistance worthy of the name, were in Argyllshire, and spreading death and destruction throughout the Campbell lands. They captured Inverary, though not the castle, and narrowly missed capturing Argyle himself, but he escaped in his galley down Loch Fyne. Back in the lowlands he not surprisingly demanded immediate action to deal with this upsurge in rebel activity, and Baillie was ordered to march the army westwards on 20 December, but at Rosneath, or more likely Gairlochhead, he met Argyle, who decided to assert his authority. However, since Baillie refused to take orders from Argyle, he advanced the not inconsequential argument that the country was in any case incapable of supporting all of Baillie's army at that time of year, and so prevailed upon him, through the committee, to give him instead a contingent of regular infantry to stiffen his own local levies. This was readily assented to by the committee and just as quickly expedited by Baillie, whereupon he gratefully turned the army eastwards again and made for Perth, leaving Argyle to go after the rebels who by this time were heading northwards through Lorne and Lochaber.[5] Although no real opposition had so far been encountered by the rebels, neither had they gained many recruits, and indeed more had deserted, anxious to secure their plunder, than had come in. Prominent amongst these were the Gordons under Donald Farquharson of Monaltrie, and by the time the rebels had reached Kilchummin (now Fort Augustus) at the foot of Loch Ness, they were down to rather less than 2,000 men. There on 31 January 1645 they learned that Argyle was not too far behind them (how familiar this news must have sounded), at Inverlochy (near modern Fort William).

It is quite ridiculous to suggest, as many writers have done, that the rebels were trapped thus between Argyle's army at the foot of the Great Glen and the Inverness garrison stiffened by northern levies at the top. Had the rebels been unwilling to face either, they could have marched up Glen Tarff and then over the Corrieyairack Pass into Speyside, or, as in fact they did after the battle, marched up Stratherrick and down Strathnairn across Drummossie Moor. Montrose may indeed have been considering an attack on Inverness, but with so few men and no artillery it seems rather unlikely. An attack on Argyle's army at Inverlochy was a different matter altogether, though.

Having taken the decision to fight Argyle, the rebels were all too aware of the difficulty of forcing a passage along the narrow lochside roads in the Great Glen, and in any case recognised the need to use surprise to offset their numerical inferiority. Therefore they resolved instead of simply marching straight down the glen to go over the mountains. Their precise route has sometimes been a matter of some contention, and one traditional school, perhaps misinterpreting James Fraser's account of their movements after the battle of Inverlochy, has suggested that the rebels marched up Glen Tarff, over the Corrieyairack and then along the headwaters of the Spey into Glen Roy. It is possible that the rebel cavalry may have followed this route, but as Alasdair MacColla himself categorically states that the rebels came over the hills 'the nearest way',[6] a slightly shorter and more direct route is indicated, and was followed in 1980 by members of English Civil War Society retracing the march laden down with muskets, swords, and other seventeenth century impedimenta.

From Kilchummin the rebels marched due south up Glen Tarff as far as Culachy, and then marched parallel to the Great Glen for five kilometres to Glen Buck, shielded by the long ridges of Meall a Cholumain and Drium Laragan. Up to this point the march will have been fairly easy, although the climb up Glen Tarff is a fairly stiff one, but now the rebels will have been faced with the gorge of the Calder Burn. In good weather it is, without too much difficulty, negotiable by musketeers or more lightly equipped infantrymen; but in winter it will have been a much more formidable obstacle, and the rebels may have stuck to the eastern side, although they would thereby have foregone the convenience of the drove road on the west side. In either case there was probably a short halt at the head of the glen by a small farmstead near the present Glen Buck Lodge, at which point they were about

1,000 feet above sea level; and they now had a further 1,000 feet to climb up to reach the col below Carn na Larach, and pass out on to the windswept Teanga Plateau. The climb however is relatively easy, although clearly more difficult in the winter snows, and an army of 1,500 men is capable of trampling a quite adequate path for itself. The descent into Glen Turret off the Teanga which followed, although at first deceptively gradual, soon turns into a very steep slope indeed. Given the likely difficulty in crossing the Calder Burn and getting down this mountainside, the possibility must be considered that although the infantry, or at least most of them, came by 'the nearest way', the cavalry may instead have taken the longer but easier route further up Glen Tarff and over the Corrieyairack. Once in Glen Turret, however, the worst of the journey is over and the march will have been much easier. In marching down Glen Roy the rebels will have been able to make use of the parallel roads—a geological feature—before reaching Glen Spean at Keppoch. There was a brief and violent encounter with a government patrol, and after killing them or chasing them off, the rebel army halted for three hours at the farm—the barn in which many of them slept is still standing[7]—to let stragglers catch up. How many there were does not seem to have been counted, though there may have been quite a number, and they could well have included the cavalry if they had indeed taken the long way round, crossing the Corrieyairack. Having re-assembled, the rebels then forded the River Spean at Corriechoille, and pushed on through the Leanachan Woods around the base of Ben Nevis. By this time night had long since fallen, although it was apparently a clear moonlit one, and they threw themselves down exhausted near Torlundy, overlooking Inverlochy. In thirty-six hours they had marched over 50 kilometres through the hills in midwinter, and were about to fight an army twice their number.

Spalding says that the rest of the night was spent in skirmishing with some of Argyle's patrols, lest his army should steal away rather than fight; but there was little fear of this, and with his men cold, wet and hungry, and badly in need of rest, Montrose had nothing to gain by initiating such skirmishing.[8] On the contrary the skirmishing is much more likely to have been initiated by the government forces. They obviously required information as to exactly where the rebels were, and as to how many of them there were, whilst by the same token the rebels needed fighting patrols out, not to harass the government troops, but to prevent their patrols from obtaining this vital information. Both armies waited shivering for the dawn, drawn up in order of battle, and at sunrise on Candlemas Day the battle began.[9]

INVERLOCHY, 2 FEBRUARY 1645

Both sides adopted similar dispositions. The rebels had, it seems, only 1,500 men divided into four 'divisions' or battalions; Alasdair MacColla took command of the right wing at the head of Major Thomas Laghtman's Regiment, which would appear by this time to have only been about 400 strong. There are strong indications that although few had so far been killed, desertion was a big problem amongst the Irish regiments. In the centre was largish body of high-landers, perhaps a little more than 500 of them, MacDonalds, Mac-Leans, Appin Stewarts and Athollmen, and on the left wing Colonel Manus O'Cahan's Regiment. In reserve behind the centre was Colonel James McDonnell's Regiment and some other highlanders. These latter were probably those too exhausted to stand in the front line, although it is known that at least some Gordons were present under Captain John Gordon of Littlemill, a Strathbogie man. Neither O'Cahan's nor McDonnell's Irish regiments can have mustered more than 300 men, and very likely a lot less. Finally also, somewhere in the rear, was a small troop of horse led by Sir Thomas Ogilvy. This was probably fifty strong, and Gordon of Littlemill may have served with it rather than with the infantry.[10]

Establishing the composition of the government forces is to a certain extent quite straightforward, although there is a frustrating gap in our knowledge. Like the rebels they posted their regulars on the wings and the highlanders in the centre. According to Ruthven there was a strong battalion of highlanders posted a little way in front of the main body, armed he tells us with guns, bows and axes.[11] Such a particular description rather implies that the levies behind them were much less well armed. If so it is likely that this battalion was in fact Argyle's own regiment of foot recalled from Ulster. It was certainly present at the battle, and indeed Argyle watched the battle from the safety of his galley while the army was actually led by the regiment's commanding officer, Lieutenant Colonel Sir Duncan Campbell of Auchinbreck. Argyle's Regiment, to judge from the strength of other Scots units recalled from Ulster, will have been something like 500 strong or thereabouts, and they were backed up by about 1,000 high-land levies, not improbably the same men who had pursued Montrose and the rebels widdershins round Scotland in September and October. The two wings of the government army comprised sixteen companies of regular soldiers detached from Baillie's army and formed into two provisional battalions under Lieutenant Colonel Lachlan Roughe and Lieutenant Colonel John Cockburn. Although usually described as lowlanders, some of them may themselves have been highlanders, for Lieutenant Colonel Roughe and at least two other of the officers later captured by the rebels, Captain William Murray and Captain Thomas Stewart, belonged to the Earl of Tullibardine's Regiment which contained a sizeable highland contingent, and may have been selected for that very reason.[12] None of the other contributing regiments can be identified, though as Sir John Wauchope of Niddrie was with Argyle at this time, it is possible that companies from his regiment were also present. James Fraser, curiously enough, identifies the lowland soldiers as being militia from the Mearns and from Moray, but although he adds the circumstantial detail that many of them readily enlisted with Montrose after the battle, none of Baillie's regiments appears to have been raised in the north. It is possible that Fraser was confusing their recruitment with the subsequent defection of many of the Morayshire levies.[13]

Set back a little from the main body, two cannon, probably fframes, were set upon a slight eminence, and the left wing of the army was anchored on Inverlochy Castle, which was itself garrisoned by fifty musketeers.

At first sight the battle of Inverlochy would appear to have been a classic example of the vaunted 'highland charge' in action, but as with other examples, such a simplistic view does not stand up under close examination, and a slightly more complex series of events culminated in the rout of the government forces. Nevertheless the battle was brief but bloody.

The rebels having spent a cold and hungry night had no reason to hang about, and immediately some of them set off down the hillside towards the government forces. Since the Irish moved off before the highlanders under Montrose's personal command, the MacDonalds afterwards claimed that Alasdair MacColla had begun the attack without orders and that in consequence the success was due to his direction and not Montrose's, but this is rather unlikely. What Mac-Colla did do before he set off, almost certainly as ordered by Montrose, was impress upon his regimental commanders the absolute necessity of holding their fire until the very last moment, enjoining them to fire into the enemies' breasts.[14] Although it is not mentioned in any of the rather sketchy accounts of the battle, they are likely to have been drawn up only three deep as was done with the wings at Tippermuir, in order to avoid being outflanked by the two 500 man battalions opposite them.

In short it was a test of nerve: the Irish declined to engage in a firefight which they were unlikely to win, being so heavily outnumbered, and instead 'patiently endured' the regulars' fire, delivered as was normally the case by each rank in turn. O'Cahan's and Laghtman's men, instead of firing by Extraduction, were committed to firing by Salvee. Normally the battalion which fired first, although naturally reducing the number of musketeers able to return their fire, could

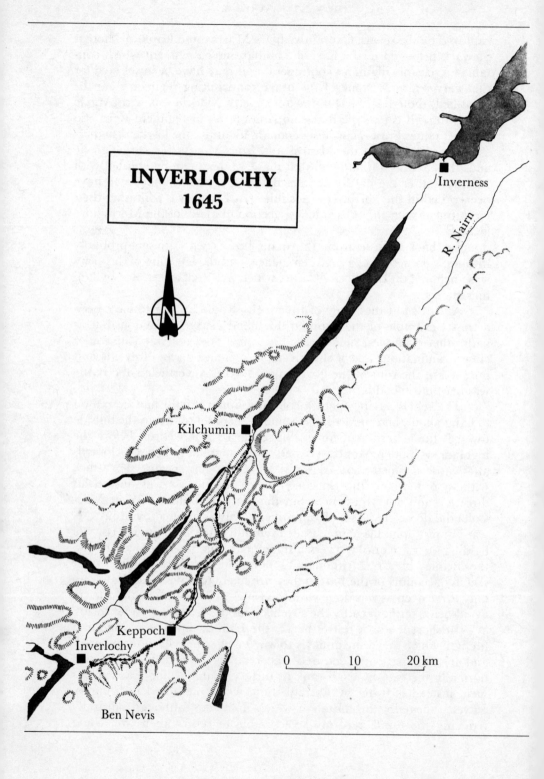

INVERLOCHY
1645

Inverness

R. Nairn

N

Kilchumin

Keppoch
Inverlochy

Ben Nevis

0   10   20 km

expect to receive a deadlier volley in return fired from much closer range. In this instance though, Colonel O'Cahan delayed firing until his soldiers could not merely see the whites of their enemies' eyes but actually 'fyred there beards'. While one need not necessarily take this statement too literally, the meaning is clear that they held their fire until they were only a few feet away from government soldiers. Fired at such a range, the Irish volley ensured a deadly effect, and was followed up by a physical assault so promptly as to prevent any volley being fired in reply. Ruthven says that the Irish fell on with sword and targe, but given their close proximity to the government troops it is unlikely that there would have been time to discard muskets, unsling targes and draw swords, otherwise there would have been time for a return volley. Montrose, in his own despatch describing the battle, interestingly enough mentions fighting with swords and pikes, but whether he was referring to the fighting on the wings or in the centre is not clear. There is evidence that many of the Irish were by this time equipped with pikes, but as will be seen it is equally possible that many of the rebel highlanders were so equipped as well. On the government left MacColla and Laghtman duplicated O'Cahan's success, and set upon violently before they had had a chance to recover from the rebel volleys, the regulars panicked and ran.

Now, suitably encouraged by this success, Montrose and the high-landers comprising the rebel centre also moved forward. As was done at Aberdeen it seems likely that the advance of the centre was delayed until the flanks were secure and success already very largely assured. The highlanders met even less resistance than the Irish. Argyle's Regi-ment, understandably unnerved by the collapse of the flanking battalions, fired a single volley at long range—and almost certainly fired too high—then broke and ran as the rebels came up with them, falling back on the levies behind. Almost at once the highlanders, both Argyle's and the levies, dissolved into a panic-stricken mob quite incapable of offering any serious resistance. There was indeed very little fighting at all in the accepted sense, but rather a ruthless butchery of the terrified rabble. About 200 of them retained only enough grim purpose to make for the safety of the castle, but Sir Thomas Ogilvy at the head of the rebel cavalry succeeded in driving them away from it, and they were massacred by some MacDonalds.[15] The fact that they were able to stick together so purposefully amidst the rout suggests that they may have been regulars, perhaps from Argyle's Regiment, or rather more likely from Tullibardine's companies under Lieutenant Colonel Roughe. Certainly they were capable of offering some resist-ance, for one of the few recorded rebel casualties, Sir Thomas Ogilvy, was shot through the thigh—a wound which subsequently killed him.

As with previous battles the majority of casualties were inflicted by the rebels not in the brief fighting but in the excited slaughter of helpless fugitives. There seems to be a general agreement that the pursuit was continued for eight to ten miles through the hills, but Spalding rather realistically qualifies this by pointing out that the pursuit was not so relentless as it might otherwise have been since the rebels had marched eighteen miles the day before on little food and were cold and wet and weary, 'quhairby they war the moir unhable to follow the flight'. Since an eight mile pursuit by infantrymen would be regarded as exceptional at the best of times it is questionable whether the rebels were up to it at this moment, and there may be rather more heroic legend than truth in this version. Similar doubts ought to be cast on the remarkably consistent figure of 1,500 dead quoted by all the chroniclers. Allowing Auchinbreck, (who was himself slain in the battle, perhaps after being granted quarter), 3,000 men, 1,500 casualties therefore represents half of them. Over a third of Auchinbreck's forces were lowland regulars who, while obviously suffering a number of casualties when set upon by O'Cahan's and Laghtman's men, seem to have readily been granted quarter (since the Irish do not appear to have participated in the pursuit they may have been securing—and robbing—the prisoners), and indeed according to Fraser many afterwards enlisted with the rebels. If a generous 200 casualties are allocated amongst them, then if the chroniclers are to be believed, no fewer than 1,300 of, at the most, 1,900 highlanders were slain, which is plainly too many. Nevertheless it is obvious that the Clan Campbell suffered severely in the battle, if only in the disproportionate number of its leaders killed or taken. The raising of strong Campbell regiments subsequently should be enough to dispose of any thoughts of the clan losing an entire generation of fighting men at Inverlochy, no matter what the MacDonald bards might boast. Royalist casualties were predictably light, only three dead according to Wishart, although the Irish must have sustained more in their advance to contact.

POST MORTEM

As far as the battle of Inverlochy is concerned, the most intriguing question is why the highlanders under Auchinbreck performed so badly by comparison with the far more exhausted highlanders led by Montrose. Many writers have over the years invested highlanders with the qualities of Caledonian supermen, and very largely accepted uncritically highland folklore extolling the bravery of their warrior heroes. Yet the paradox posed by Inverlochy has gone unanswered. There is no reason whatever why a highlander named MacDonald or Cameron or Stewart should be a better fighter, even when tired and outnumbered, than one named Campbell, just because he was a Mac-Donald and the other a Campbell.

The principal drawback of a warrior society, wherever it is encountered, be it Homeric Greece or seventeenth century Scotland, is that it is not, as is sometimes mistakenly thought, a society in which every adult male is a warrior: quite the contrary. There are in fact comparatively few warriors, comprising a threadbare aristocracy, with the bulk of the population being made up of impoverished peasants. In Homer's Greece the warriors were called 'Heroes', and in seventeenth century Scotland 'Gentlemen', and it is vital in understanding the effectiveness of a highland 'regiment' to observe this distinction between the warrior 'Gentleman' and the peasant levies called out to make up the numbers. Hawley's 1746 description is well worth quoting upon this point:

> They commonly form their Front rank of what they call their best men, or True Highlanders the number of which being always but few, when they form in battalions they commonly form four deep, & these Highlanders form the front of the four, the rest being lowlanders & arrant scum.[16]

As to how well or how badly armed these 'arrant scum' who made up the greater part of highland units were, one might profitably return to the Atholl census alluded to earlier, the findings of which may be summarised as follows.

Of the 451 men whose arms are described, all but eleven had 'swords'. The type of these swords is not stated, but as two or three two-handed swords are specifically mentioned besides, it may fairly be assumed that they were all of them single-handed weapons. Whether or not they were all broadswords is a very different matter. Dirks are not separately mentioned in the lists of arms, and since only 124, that is approximately a quarter of those surveyed, also had targes, it may not be unreasonable to suppose that the 315 swordsmen without targes were armed not with broadswords but with dirks. This is certainly suggested by the distribution of other weapons. All but eight of the one hundred muskets were carried by men who also possessed both sword and targe. It is quite clear therefore that slightly less than a quarter of those men surveyed actually conformed to the conventional picture of the highlander as being armed with musket, broadsword and targe. It also tallies remarkably well with General Hawley's description quoted above. Eleven of those armed with sword and targe were also armed with bows, and seventy-eight of the others had bows, but up to three quarters of the Athollmen were effectively unarmed.[17] It might also be added that by the time the rebellion broke out in 1644, some efforts had been made by Argyle's forces to disarm the Athollmen, and whilst this may not, judging by later efforts, have been too successful, it will hardly have improved matters. The possibility must therefore seriously be considered that those highland units, maintained as Monaltrie's Gordons were as a 'standing regiment', were conventionally armed with musket and pike, since the broadswords so commonly associated with highlanders were simply not available in any quantity. Indeed it is significant in this regard to note that in 1639 Monaltrie obtained muskets and pikes from Huntly with this purpose in mind, and would have equipped his highlanders with them had the arms not been seized. Since he was himself a highlander he can hardly be accused of not understanding highland warfare. Pikes and muskets were also issued by Huntly in 1644; and Lord Seaforth's Regiment in 1645, although it too must have been a highland formation, received 150 muskets and 150 pikes.[18]

All of this evidence reinforces the belief that highlanders were not after all very good soldiers, they were no better equipped (and frequently worse equipped) than lowland troops, and devoid of discipline. Lowland peasants could be turned into soldiers, highland peasants remained an undisciplined rabble. The victory at Inverlochy therefore was won, not because the highlanders in Montrose's centre were innately superior to those opposed to them (who were if anything more experienced and probably rather better equipped), but simply because the regular troops on Auchinbreck's flanks were defeated by Montrose's Irish regulars, and Argyle's Regiment, posted in front of Auchinbreck's main body as a forlorn hope, found itself with both flanks 'in the air' just as it was about to receive the rebel attack. Not surprisingly they gave way and were driven in among the main body. In short the rebels won because they were better handled.

The Campbell 'Gentlemen', the warrior 'Heroes', evidently fought well enough, as is attested by their death or capture; but the peasant levies, the 'arrant scum', fled in their hundreds offering little or no resistance. This pattern is repeated in all of Montrose's battles. The brunt of the fighting was first borne by Irish or lowland infantry, and, increasingly, by lowland cavalry, after which the highlanders were led forward against an already shaken foe to reinforce a victory already half won.

After the battle, Montrose, still unable to contemplate an assault on the fortifications of Inverness, marched up Stratherrick and Strathnairn along what is now the B851 and then turned south-east down Strathdearn and over the Slochd pass into Speyside, where at Ballachestell (now Grantown on Spey) the rebels were joined by James Grant of Freuchie and 300 men. Suitably encouraged by this accession of strength, the rebels then marched further down Speyside to a rendezvous with Donald Farquharson of Monaltrie at Balvenie Castle. From there they marched down the Glen of Rothes to take Elgin without any resistance.

The reason they were able to take the city without any resistance was quite simple. Most of Lord Gordon's Regiment, the regular cavalry unit which had for so long been the mainstay of the Moray forces, actually defected to the rebels led by its Colonel! This quite catastrophic turn of events was, as Spalding indicates, totally unexpected:

> Mony mervallit at the Lord Gordoun's going in efter sic manner being vpone the countrie service, and collonell to tua foot regimentis and to ane horss regiment. Sum alledgit the Estaits oversaw him in diverss poyntis touching his honour, quhilk he could not digest. Vtheris said he wes liklie to loiss his father for following the countrie causs, if he sould contynew, and the countrie happin to be borne doune. Vtheris againe said it wes a plot devysit betuixt Montrose and Nathaniell Gordon when he wes with him and when he cam fra him with Craigievar ... Howsoever it was, in he went; bot how or vpone what ressone, I can not tell.[19]

It was undoubtedly this defection and the consequent capture of Elgin, rather than the victory at Inverlochy, which inspired the indecent scramble by the northern gentry to submit to Montrose, for most of them had still been meeting in Elgin trying to arrange for its defence as late as 17 February. After Elgin fell, the Earl of Seaforth, Thomas MacKenzie of Pluscardine, Sir Robert Gordon of Gordonstoun and others all came in, though they declined to follow Lord Gordon's example by actually raising men for the rebel army. Not all followed this craven path: the Laird of Innes and his followers esconced themselves in Spynie Castle and declined to surrender; but for the moment there was no effective opposition in the north to the rebels, and the defection of Lord Gordon had not only brought to them a regular cavalry unit but at last made possible large scale recruitment amongst the Gordons, and in particular recruitment of the cavalry and lowland foot which the rebels so badly needed. The war was about to enter a new and altogether more dangerous phase for the government.

6

Alarums and Excursions

The rebels took Elgin on 19 February and remained there for two weeks. Why they did so is not very clear in contemporary accounts, but after a winter campaign in the mountains the army must have badly needed a rest. Most seventeenth century armies suffered dreadfully during the winter at the best of times, and Montrose's son, Lord Graham, who died on 5 March, is unlikely to have been the only one who succumbed to the hardships of the campaign. While the army was recovering and Montrose was receiving the unconvincing submissions of Seaforth and others of the northern gentry, some of the Gordons took the field with an alacrity which suggests that Lord Gordon's defection had been resolved upon some time before. On 20 February, only the day after Lord Gordon went over to the rebels, young Gight and Leith of Harthill intercepted a messanger named Alexander Forbes and relieved him of despatches intended for the now defunct shire committee of Moray. Three days later they then staged an audacious raid on Inverurie, surprising ten of Craigievar's troopers 'in thair naikit beds'. Having appropriated everything they possessed, the rebels then turned them loose. Craigievar not surprisingly was 'heighlie offendit',[1] but although these attacks were in themselves inconsequential they encouraged an excess of confidence amongst the rebels at the very time when the government, alarmed at the resurgence in the rebellion, was taking effective steps to deal with it.

The counter-offensive, however, got off to a bad start. On 26 February, only a week after the rebels took Elgin, the Earl of Balcarres rode into Aberdeen at the head of his veteran cavalry regiment. His orders were to rendezvous with Sir James Hackett's Regiment and the rest of the forces in the area, and secure Aberdeen against the arrival of General Baillie, who was marching north from Perth with six regiments. Unfortunately all was not well with the garrison. Hackett's Regiment seems to have been a poor one, and was rather unreliable, whilst

Lothian's foot regiment was downright mutinous. Hearing in early March that the rebels were on the move again, Balcarres decided that he would be unable to hold the town against them and evacuated Aberdeen rather precipitately, retiring southwards. So hasty was the retreat that a considerable quantity of arms had to be left behind in Torry, then a fishing village on the south side of Aberdeen harbour. Nevertheless, given that Balcarres was reckoned to be a brave and determined officer, he must have had good reason for considering such a swift retreat to be necessary, and it is hard over three hundred years later to be too critical of his decision even though the rebels were a little slow in following it up.

On 9 March, while an unhappy deputation from the Burgh was waiting upon Montrose at Turriff, pleading with him to spare them another visit by the barbarous Irish, a party of rebel cavalry led by Nathaniel Gordon clattered into Aberdeen and accepted its surrender. His first act was to release all the prisoners from the Tolbooth, but on being joined the next day by 100 Irish dragooners he pushed south, and in a vicious little fight at the Bridge of Dee he killed and captured some of the late Alexander Keith's troop of horse, routing the rest. His orders were to patrol southwards as far as Cowie, at the foot of Megray Hill, but his reconnaissance was rather cursory, and instead, transferring his prisoners and the precious arms left behind in Torry—1,800 muskets and pikes—into Aberdeen's Tolbooth, he rejoined Montrose, who by this time had leisurely moved to Frendraught, plundering as he went.[2]

Part of the reason for the slow progress was that the rebels were capitalising upon their recent successes, and Lord Gordon's defection, by some fairly large scale recruiting for once. At Turriff Montrose had agreed to keep the Irish out of Aberdeen, conveniently ignoring the dragooners, but insisted in return that the militia be mustered for his service, and at the same time issued instructions for the Aberdeenshire fencibles to muster at Inverurie on 15 March. This muster was by all accounts well attended, even if many turned up out of fear rather than choice, although the 500 men of the reconstituted Strathbogie Regiment will have been particularly welcome. Any elation which this accession of strength may have occasioned was abruptly dispelled that very night, however, for the government forces at last struck back.

On 12 March Nathaniel Gordon had again ridden into Aberdeen, and although accompanied by about 80 troopers was seemingly intent only on some 'mirryment'. Amongst the party were Donald Farquharson of Monaltrie and Captain John Mortimer of O'Cahan's Regiment, the latter being a particular friend of Gordon who shared the same mistress with him. No thought was given to security, and as they scattered carelessly through the town word was sent to Sir John

Hurry, the commander of Baillie's cavalry, urging him to strike. Hurry, lying at North Water Bridge on the North Esk, eagerly accepted the invitation, and at once marched northwards with eight score horse and foot. The cavalry were drawn from the Earl of Balcarres' Regiment, half of which had originally been raised in Aberdeenshire and the Mearns, and were presumably picked for the operation for their local knowledge. The foot were commanded musketeers drawn from various regiments, though they will presumably have included members of Lothian's Regiment since it had spent the winter in Aberdeen.

Hurry was himself an Aberdeen man—he had indeed been General Drill Master of its militia in 1627—as well as a thoroughly competent professional soldier, and he used both his familiarity with the town and his skill to execute a flawless raid. It was in fact a textbook operation and easily bears comparison with the procedure recommended in John Cruso's 1632 *Militarie Instructions for the Cavallrie*. Arriving outside the town unchallenged at about 8 o'clock on the evening of Friday 15 March, he first secured the gates, presumably with parties of musketeers, before galloping into the streets as noisily as possible. The rebels, dispersed to their lodgings and given over to carousing, were taken completely by surprise, and sufficiently intimidated by the sound and fury of the incursion to offer little or no resistance. Ruthven says that Nathaniel Gordon and some others made off at once, though whether they evaded Hurry's musketeers at the gates or went to ground somewhere in the town is unclear; they probably escaped over the back yards. Most, prudently, simply remained indoors and kept their heads down, which is usually the safest course in such circumstances, but others made the fatal mistake of pulling their boots on and rushing into the streets. Among them were Farquharson of Monaltrie and some of his men, and as soon as they appeared on the causeway they were surrounded by horsemen who demanded their names. Monaltrie stoutly answered at once, but then tried to draw his sword, whereupon, not surprisingly, he was pistolled by one of the troopers and his body afterwards stripped. His cousin was wounded and captured at the same time, but otherwise only two or three other rebels shared his fate, for Hurry, well aware that time was of the essence, concentrated on capturing their horses. Most of the troopers' horses were seized from the Court de Guard, a timber guardhouse constructed some time before in the Castlegate, while the officers' horses were brought from their stables by townspeople. Captain John Forbes, Craigevar's brother, was particularly fortunate in that he fell heir to Huntly's best horse, which had been borrowed by Nathaniel Gordon. Having secured the horses— and one hopes released the prisoners from the Tolbooth—Hurry did not waste time by trying to round up the rebels, but instead prudently

94

retired southwards again while the shaken rebels fled on foot to Kintore.[3]

Montrose naturally enough was furious at this totally unnecessary reverse, but there was no help for it. By the time word reached Kintore, Hurry had too strong a start, and escaped safely back across the North Esk where he added insult to injury by snatching Montrose's second son and his tutor and sending them off to Edinburgh. After this incident, plead as they might their innocence, the citizens of Aberdeen had to endure another visit from the rebels. A fine was levied upon the town, and Monaltrie was given a soldier's funeral in St. Machar's cathedral. Alasdair MacColla supervised the arrangements, and none of the courtesies were omitted, as the Irish saw him into his grave with 'the trailling of pickes and thundring vollie of muskets'.[4]

Afterwards the rebels moved southwards into the Mearns, although, as earlier, any sense of urgency seems to have been subordinated to a lust for plundering and destruction. The Earl Marischal once more shut himself up in his impregnable fastness at Dunottar, and refused rebel blandishments to join them. Like Seaforth he was essentially a neutralist. He raised men in obedience to the government's command, but would not lead them in battle against his King's forces. Although seemingly at heart a Royalist he was equally unwilling to rebel against the government. Such a dilemma was a common one, but although it has received some considerable attention from historians of the war in England, commentators on events north of the border are a little too prone to see things in black and white. Consequently Seaforth's attempts to avoid becoming actively involved in the internecine struggle have in particular attracted considerable adverse comment. At any rate, although the Earl Marischal's brother George Keith (who was himself to lead regiments at Preston and at Worcester) held discussions with Montrose and Lord Gordon, nothing came of them, and after burning everything in sight the rebels pushed southwards again.

With their recent recruiting in Aberdeenshire the rebel army now numbered about 3,000 infantry. Most of them were lowland Scots, and rather less than a third were Irish. Grant's men had remained behind in Elgin and the only highlanders still with the army were a few Athollmen and Monaltrie's battalion, now commanded by James Farquharson of Inverey. They and the Irish together can have amounted to no more than 1,500 men. Of the remainder, the 500 men of the Strathbogie Regiment might be considered reliable and were, certainly, given the quantity of arms captured in Aberdeen, well armed; but the remaining 1,000 or so were Aberdeenshire levies, lacking both enthusiasm and training. The cavalry, on the other hand, promised to be effective. There were 300 of them now, and although some obviously were the survivors of Ogilvie's Troop, most of them were regulars belonging to Lord Gordon's Regiment.[5]

By 22 March, however, a full week after the debacle in which Monaltrie had been slain, the rebels were still only at Fettercairn when their cavalry clashed with Sir John Hurry again at Halkerton Wood close by Laurencekirk. This encounter took place some six or seven kilometres due east of Fettercairn, so Hurry was presumably only carrying out a reconnaissance and trying to work around the rebel flank; and although seemingly worsted in the fight and forced as a result to evacuate North Water Bridge and Brechin, it is not unlikely that he made an important discovery which in some measure explains Baillie's strategy. The fight with Hurry seems to have awakened no sense of urgency amongst the rebels, for they only occupied (and partly burnt) Brechin on the 25th, but they were soon aware that Baillie's army was close at hand.

Baillie had about the same number of infantry as the rebels, comprising Crawford-Lindsay's, Cassillis', Lauderdale's, Lothian's, Loudon's and Callendar's regiments, but twice as many cavalry; Balcarres' and Hackett's regiments, and perhaps a few unregimented troops as well.[6] Notwithstanding this superiority in cavalry and the fact that all his infantry were experienced regulars, Baillie was reluctant to engage in battle and instead concentrated on blocking the river crossings. Having got across the North Esk without any difficulty after Hurry's retreat, the rebels marched southwest, crossing the South Esk at Inverquharity, pushing south to Kirriemuir, and then west through the Kirkton of Airlie to Ruthven on the river Isla, where they found Baillie's army drawn up waiting for them, blocking their advance on Coupar Angus. Montrose was keen to bring Baillie to battle as quickly as possible, but not so keen as to fight his way across the river against a better army; so instead both armies faced each other throughout the night of 29 to 30 March, and next morning Montrose formally challenged Baillie to fight. He first asked Baillie to draw back a mile from the river in order that the rebels might cross and fight him on a plain field, but Baillie, although subject to acute paranoia, was no fool and not surprisingly refused. Montrose then offered to draw back from the river two miles to allow Baillie to cross. This he consented to, but as soon as the rebels withdrew he did likewise, and given such a lead marched unmolested back to Perth. Some biographers of Montrose have presented this as a triumph, as evidence that Baillie dared not face him, but in fact the reverse was the case. Montrose was forced to march westwards to Dunkeld, where the army fell apart. What Baillie, almost certainly as a result of Hurry's reconnaissance reports, had realised, was that the rebel army was already in trouble. His reluctance to fight the rebels was occasioned not by fear of the consequences should Montrose defeat the only army between him and Edinburgh, but by the knowledge that the rebel army was disintegrating and that time was on his side. The Aberdeenshire levies who made up such a large part of the rebel forces were deserting in their hundreds. Perhaps as many as 500 had deserted at Durris as soon as the rebels crossed the Dee, and now the Athollmen too were slipping away to their homes. Dunkeld was in effect the end of the road. The rebel offensive had run out of steam and Montrose has to be held responsible. Far too much valuable time had been wasted in pottering around, plundering and burning, with inevitable results; and now, misled by a report that Baillie had crossed the Tay at Perth, Montrose, far from curbing his over-confidence, made a near fatal mistake.

Since the remaining highlanders were anxious to be gone he made a virtue of necessity by dismissing them to their homes, and sending all but 300 of the Irish to Blair Atholl with the baggage train. Retaining another 300 of the lowland foot—nearly all of them presumably mus-keteers, for pikemen will have been too slow—and the 200 troopers of Lord Gordon's Horse, the remainder of the army was sent on to Brechin. Dunkeld was evacuated at midnight on 3 April, and at Blairgowrie the 600 commanded musketeers and 200 cavalrymen turned south-east along the line of the A923, crossing the Sidlaw Hills and arriving outside Dundee before dawn. They must have paused then for some rest, for Lieutenant John Gordon in Captain Innes' Troop of Lord Gordon's Regiment was lying half asleep when he was ordered to take in a summons at 10 o'clock. He afterwards testified that the attack began before he was able to return with a reply, but it is likely that in any case the militia were determined to fight.[7]

Although Dundee had no regular garrison, the militia's readiness to fight may have been encouraged by word that relief was at hand. Baillie had already been informed of the rebel move, either by his spies or by cavalry patrols in the Coupar Angus area, and it is not unlikely that he may have been able to warn the townspeople and reassure them that he was marching to their assistance. The defence was organised by a Lieutenant Cockburn, although it is unlikely that he was in fact a junior officer. Lieutenant is frequently used in seventeenth century sources as a contraction for Lieutenant Colonel or even Lieutenant General, and the gouty Lieutenant Cockburn was almost certainly a half-colonel, not improbably the same Lieutenant Colonel Cockburn captured and paroled at Inverlochy. At any rate, although the militia under his direction made a fight of it, Montrose and the Irish forced their way in by the West Port while Lord Gordon and his men got in by the north. Once through the gates they then pushed up the streets into the market place, and there, although some resistance may have continued through the afternoon, the rebels began to disperse in the customary orgy of plundering which followed the storming of any town. By Ruthven's account, just as they reached the market-place, word came that Baillie's army was approaching. Some Royalist accounts suggest that his arrival was rather later in the day, but since most of the burgh seems to have remained in the hands of its garrison, and John Gordon had not been released from the tolbooth when the rebels hastily evacuated the burgh, Ruthven's version must be the correct one. Either way, the news that Baillie was not on the other side of Perth as had been thought but a bare two miles away and coming on fast, came as a rude shock. There could be no question now of fighting him, and it was all the rebel officers could do to re-assemble the infantry and escape by the East Port as Baillie entered by the West.[8]

The conduct of the ensuing pursuit led to furious recriminations at the time, and the rebels' eventual escape has been hailed by some as one of Montrose's greatest exploits. It therefore justifies some close examination, and while it cannot be denied that breaking contact and retreating by night is a difficult operation, and one which Montrose nevertheless carried out extremely successfully, it is also true to say that the difficulties under which the government troops were labouring have not fully been appreciated; nor the fact that the pursuit was, once initial contact had been broken, not quite as close as is sometimes represented. It is indeed hard to escape the conclusion that the significance of the episode has been rather inflated, in order to avoid discussion of why Montrose was so nearly captured in the first place.

At the outset it has to be said that although much is made of the fact that at the commencement of the retreat the rebels had already marched 46 kilometres from Dunkeld and of course fought their way into the town, they had been rested before the assault, and so close on their heels was Baillie, that having done so they fled before they had much chance to set about sacking it. The British soldier's capacity for getting drunk remarkably quickly should never be underestimated, but nonetheless it is unlikely that the rebels' marching capacity can have been much impaired in the little time which was available to them. By contrast it is all too frequently forgotten that the government forces had marched 35 kilometres from Perth to Dundee, and presumably at a rather harder pace than the rebels; indeed so desperate had been their attempt to save Dundee that the infantry were left behind on the road. This necessitated a halt, and the rebels were allowed to break contact from the tired government cavalry. By the time the pursuit got under way again, darkness had fallen, and Hurry, sent along the coast road, clashed with the rebel rearguard some way short of Arbroath. There was a brief fight and then Hurry, having inflicted some casualties, drew off.[9] Had there been light he might have clung on to the rebels with rather more determination, but with no infantry he was either unable or unwilling to launch another attack until daylight. As a result he lost contact with the rebels for a time and missed their turning north-westwards. Until now they had been hurrying along what is now the A92 towards Arbroath, but at midnight they headed north west, presumably at Muirdrum. By this means they will have regained the present B961 and a clear road to Brechin. Hurry, missing them at the crossroads, continued on probably as far as Arbroath. There he will have discovered that the rebels had not preceded him, and himself turned north towards Brechin. The rebels are next heard of at Guthrie Castle, from where they headed due north to Careston. This can only have been because they discovered that Hurry, pushing up the present A933, was astride the Brechin road at Froickheim.

Baillie meanwhile had been perfectly aware that sooner or later the rebels would have to turn inland, and if Ruthven was correct as to the efficiency of his spies, he will have known of the intended rendezvous at Brechin. Therefore while Hurry was, he hoped, maintaining contact with the rebels, Baillie marched hard due north with the infantry up the road which is now the A929 from Dundee to Forfar. He reached Forfar at dawn, but by that time the rebels were across the South Esk at Careston, about 10 kilometres away, and out of his reach. Baillie had evidently been relying upon Hurry to force them westward—as indeed he succeeded in doing to a limited degree at Froickheim—and afterwards complained bitterly that Hurry had not heeded his repeated orders to attack the rebels in flank, orders which would have made no sense had Hurry merely been following after them.[10] At any rate with the coming of daylight Hurry's tenacity re-asserted itself, and regaining contact with the rebels he pursued them northwards into Glen Esk, abandoning the chase only after inflicting further casualties on them in a skirmish at Edzell.

Writers from Wishart onwards have hailed the episode as heroic, though more recent ones have had the grace to point out that Montrose was over-confident and took a foolish chance in attacking Dundee. Furthermore, although the exertions of the rebel officers from Montrose downwards were considerable, and the endurance of their men even more so, there was little genius displayed in the conduct of the retreat, and the rebels had no energy to waste in some of the more fanciful manoeuvres attributed to them by some. Part of the problem apparently lies in a misreading of Wishart's Latin, which led some to believe that Montrose doubled back from Arbroath to Panbride and then turned north to Guthrie, and this error has subsequently been embellished with all manner of even more fanciful detail.[11] However, since he is unlikely to have tried to move across unfamiliar country in the dark (and there is no suggestion that he did), Montrose will have been

99

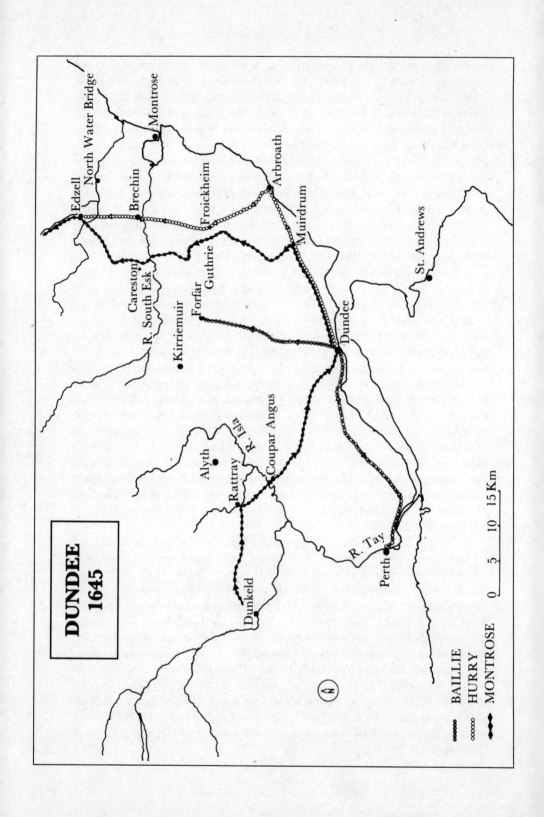

DUNDEE
1645

Edzell
North Water Bridge
Montrose
Brechin
Arbroath
Froickheim
Guthrie
Muirdrum
Careston
R. South Esk
Kirriemuir
Forfar
Dundee
St. Andrews
Alyth
R. Isla
Coupar Angus
Rattray
R. Tay
Dunkeld
Perth

0   5   10   15 Km

N

BAILLIE
HURRY
MONTROSE

sticking to the roads, and the doubling back aside, such a move will have entailed some very extensive detours and an excellent chance of getting lost. Moreover, such a theory also seems to rest upon the extraordinary assumption that Baillie's infantry was marching eastwards, parallel to the coast, since otherwise there would be no reason for such a doubling back which might otherwise have taken the rebels straight into Hurry's arms. A glance at a map will show furthermore that if, as seems most likely, Montrose was retreating along the present A92, there is no road running parallel to it further inland until the A94 is reached at Forfar. Rogers, in his *Battles and Generals*, goes so far as to have Baillie marching along the A92 to Arbroath, and expecting there to be ahead of the rebels; while they for their part, having hugged the coastline, hid in Panbride until Baillie's army cleared the Muirdrum crossroads, before striking northwards *behind* him.[12] It is surprising indeed how much attention appears to have been lavished upon this episode without resorting to a map and some commonsense.

Having abandoned hope of catching the rebels, Baillie moved on to Brechin later on the 5th, where he met some of the Aberdeenshire gentry and reluctantly agreed to Sir John Hurry's moving north with two regiments of infantry, the Earl of Loudon's and the long-suffering Earl of Lothian's, and 160 cavalry, comprising most of Sir James Hackett's Regiment.[13] With the rest of his army Baillie then returned to Perth.

The rebels, not surprisingly, were in a pretty sorry state after this. Although their casualties are unlikely to have been anything near the 500 or so claimed by the government, quite a number must have been killed or otherwise lost, and it is hardly surprising that the Gordons long afterwards were to remember Montrose's service as being productive of sickness and woe. Bitter recrimination may well have followed, unless the rebel officers were unusually forbearing, after what was the rebels first serious defeat, gloss over though Montrose's biographers might. Lord Gordon took his remaining men northwards back to Strathbogie, Alasdair MacColla took most of his men up into the Braemer area, and Montrose was left with only a single battalion of foot (said by some to be 500 strong, but probably only the survivors of the 300 Irish who had been on the Dundee raid) and 50 cavalry. Montrose's movements for the next week or so are obscure, but on 17 April Baillie attacked him at Crieff, forcing another undignified flight up Strathearn and into the hills. Montrose was hoping to meet with Lord Aboyne who had earlier broken out of Carlisle with 16 horse and was known to be heading north. In his anxiety to make contact, Montrose even pushed as far south as Doune Castle near Dunblane, where on 20 April he managed to get a dispatch away to the King;[14] but as soon as Aboyne was picked up he retired quickly into Atholl. In this the rebels were aided by a raid on Coupar Angus mounted by Alasdair MacColla and, of all people, Forbes of Skellater, whom Lord Gordon had 'persuaded' to change sides.

Notwithstanding the fact that Aboyne had badly injured his shoulder when his horse fell down a hole during the ride north, he and Montrose pressed on rapidly to meet Lord Gordon and MacColla on Deeside, for the government counter-offensive was threatening the rebel power-base.

Hurry's arrival in the north had greatly improved the situation and not only curtailed rebel recruiting but forced them on to the defensive. Reaching Aberdeen on 11 April he had rested there for a couple of days, but on the 15th a mutiny broke out which delayed his march until the 17th. Lothian's Regiment had been upset by the fact that Loudon's Regiment and the cavalry had been paid and reclothed, but not they, and they finally decided that enough was enough. Only after further supplies of clothing arrived on the 17th were they reduced to obedience.[15]

Hurry had decided that the best plan was to undertake a sweep through the whole of the north-east lowlands, westwards to Inverness, where he sent orders for the Earl of Seaforth and Lord Sutherland to assemble their men. On the way he picked up Lord Findlater's Banffshire regiment and recruited a number of dragooners, together with other levies, all eager to avenge the rebel depredations of March. Lord Gordon prudently retired into the hills at Auchindoun, and then rode to meet Montrose and MacColla.

Once re-united the rebels were agreed that their first priority must be the defeat of Hurry's army, and so they set off in pursuit, which was exactly what Hurry hoped would happen. He crossed the Spey on 3 May, and at a meeting with Seaforth and the Laird of Innes at Elgin resolved to turn and fight as soon as he could pick up Seaforth's men and the Inverness garrison. Confident of victory, the last thing Hurry wished to do was scare the rebels off from this concentration, and so he remained in Elgin until the rebels crossed the Spey and then retired slowly through Forres. In his retreat Hurry once again showed his professionalism to advantage. Covered by his cavalry his infantry retreated in two or three mile bounds, halting to cover the retiral of the cavalry and then moving off on the next bound. As with his raid on Aberdeen in mid-March it was very much a textbook operation and for the rebels a slow and frustrating business. Montrose afterwards wrote that he had beaten up Hurry's rear for 14 miles and chased him into Inverness, but although 15 or 16 of Hurry's troopers were lost, none of his infantry fell, and it was he who held the initiative all that day. Rebel losses are not known, but Hurry presumably inflicted enough to keep them at a respectful distance. One was James Gordon of Rhynie, wounded as the rebels crossed the Spey and afterwards murdered in his bed by some of the Laird of Innes' men, presumably sallying out of Spynie Castle.[16]

At this point there are some serious discrepancies both in contemporary accounts and in modern reconstructions as to what happened where and when. Montrose's own account has been interpreted by Dr. Stevenson as meaning that he pursued Hurry all the way to Inverness on the 7th, then retired to Auldearn on the 8th, and was attacked there by Hurry on the 9th. This however is most unlikely. In the first place Montrose declares that his running fight with Hurry's rearguard stretched over 14 miles, yet since we know from Ruthven's account it only began in earnest at Forres, then 14 miles on from there will have taken the rebels only as far as Cawdor. Ruthven, on the other hand, simply has Montrose halting for the night at Auldearn while Hurry carries on to Inverness without further interference. Both versions become compatible if one assumes that Montrose pursued Hurry as far as Cawdor with his cavalry, and then retired to Auldearn to rendezvous with his slower moving infantry.[17]

The timings of these and subsequent movements present however a number of problems. Fraser, who as the only local chronicler ought to be reliable, gives the date of Hurry's meeting with Seaforth as the 3rd, which is likely, but places it at Kessock, which is unlikely, despite the circumstantial detail which he adds; but as he spoils the effect completely by putting the battle of Auldearn as the next day, 4 May, he rather destroys his credibility.[18] There may have however been two meetings, one at Elgin on the 3rd and a subsequent one just before the battle, although as will be seen the Kessock meeting-place still seems unlikely. More important is the date on which the rebels crossed the Spey. Spalding puts it at the 5th, but this seems a bit early and is quite incompatible with Ruthven's account. It probably did not take place until the 6th or more likely the 7th if Ruthven's version is correct. It may not indeed have been until the 8th (in which case Spalding's manuscript '8' may have been misread as a '5'), for Ruthven suggests that Hurry turned about the same night to attack the rebels at Auldearn. As Dr. Stevenson has pointed out, there simply would not have been time for Hurry to march all the way to Inverness, take command of the garrison and the northern levies, and march out again to Auldearn, in the space of a single day and a night. However it is clear that the Inverness rendezvous had been arranged much earlier, almost certainly on the 3rd if not before, and Spalding goes so far as to state that Hurry drew his army together not at Inverness but 'be wast Olderne'.[19] This clearly suggests that Hurry rendezvoused with the Inverness forces, not in the town, but somewhere to the east of it. Such a hypothesis fits in well with the known facts (excepting Fraser's muddled and unreliable version); if Montrose broke off contact with Hurry at Cawdor at nightfall he may well have assumed that Hurry was pressing on to Inverness but would have been unaware of a closer rendezvous. Moreover, although differing in detail, all the accounts are apparently in agreement that Hurry did in fact attack the rebels the next morning; but if, as Dr. Stevenson suggests, Hurry spent the day in Inverness, then the rebels must in turn have spent a day sitting idly in Auldearn, which was certainly not the case. Montrose's failure to realise that Hurry may not in fact have gone as far as Inverness, but may well have been much closer altogether, may also explain if not excuse the near fatal lapse in security which followed.[20]

7

The Battle of Auldearn, 9 May 1645

It is probably true to say that the battle of Auldearn has excited more attention than any other of Montrose's battles. This is very largely due to the celebrated reconstruction of the affair by Samuel Rawston Gardiner in his *History of the Great Civil War*, published in 1893–4, which first postulated the admired flank attack by the rebels said to have won them the battle. Recently, however, this reconstruction has been sharply challenged and the existence of the flank attack rejected by Dr. Stevenson.[1] His own reconstruction of the battle, relying very heavily upon Gordon of Ruthven's account (rejected rather short-sightedly by Gardiner), and a thorough study of the topography of the battle area as existing in the seventeenth century, presents a very different picture to the accepted version. Although Gardiner was clearly wrong in presenting the battle as a carefully arranged ambush, his interpretation of the sources was very nearly right. The battle was, as Dr. Stevenson is at some pains to demonstrate, a very messy and unsophisticated affair in which the rebels were very nearly beaten, but in the end they were saved not just by the tenacity of the rebels holding Auldearn itself, but by Montrose's decisive leadership and by his perfectly timed counter-attack.

On the night of 8 May 1645 the rebels were camped around the village of Auldearn. From subsequent events it would appear that one of Lord Gordon's units, probably Gordon of Minimore's battalion, was camped in Auldearn itself, while the rest of the army bivouacked in the open to the east of it. Spalding says that they camped 'commodiously', which rather suggests that they spread themselves around seeking shelter in cottages and barns over a fairly wide area; certainly this might be indicated by the obvious difficulties which the rebels encountered in drawing the army together, on realising that they were under attack. When they last saw the government forces at dusk they had been marching away from them towards Inverness, and it will have been

105

this as much as any other factor which lulled the rebels into a false sense of security. Ruthven freely criticises the rebels for their poor security that night:

> Above all things they should have bein carefull of intelligence, either by disguysed espyeles, as some choose subtill and darring men in beggeres wied or womenes apparell, or a pairtie send forth to catch ane centrie or bring in a prisoner; for want of which intelligence, if God had not prevented it beyond all expectation all ther throats had bein cutt.[2]

Instead a strong 'watch' or picquet was set, together with sentries 'on all quarters', after which the army settled down to gain what sleep it might in pouring rain. Some of the Irish evidently crammed into the village with the Strathavan men, and it seems likely that they will have been the members of the picquet, thoroughly demoralised by the rain and the apparent pointlessness of their task. As a result of their taking shelter, such warning as the rebels did receive came from five or six scouts sent out by Alasdair MacColla shortly before dawn 'as God would have it'. It is possible that they were sent out by MacColla when he discovered the picquet asleep in the village instead of at their posts, but the attribution of the act to divine intervention rather than earthly wrath suggests that he was perfectly aware of their dereliction and had casually ordered a routine clearance patrol. Whatever the circumstances it was these men who, as Ruthven says, saved the rebels from having their throats cut, for, borne on the wind, they heard a 'thundring report' as the government troops cleared their muskets.

Somewhere between Cawdor and Inverness Hurry had picked up the garrison and the northern levies, and swinging around was marching back up the road hoping (not unreasonably) to surprise the rebels in their beds. In this they would probably have been successful, had they not halted about four miles off to discharge their muskets, since they feared that the rain had dampened their powder. Although they apparently turned to seaward to fire them off, hoping that the noise of the discharge would be carried away from the rebels, it seems a remarkably stupid action. Loaded muskets were not generally considered necessary for dawn attacks on sleeping men, and indeed some commanders insisted on going into action on such occasions with *unloaded* muskets. Be that as it may, MacColla's scouts ran back to rouse the sleeping soldiers in the village, and as they stood to, Nathaniel Gordon warned Montrose that they were about to be attacked.

THE ARMIES

The government forces hastening up the road and deploying as they heard the drums beating frantically to arms were considerably stronger than the rebels. Hurry had no fewer than five regiments of regular

106

infantry at his disposal: three of his own, Lothian's, Loudon's and the Earl of Findlater's, and two from the Inverness garrison, Sir Mungo Campbell of Lawers' and the Laird of Buchanan's. These units were variously described as being well trained and the best troops in the kingdom, though this is of course something of an exaggeration. Lawers', Lothian's and Loudon's were certainly veteran units, but Buchanan's, although raised in 1644, had never seen action, and the Earl of Findlater's Regiment was only commissioned at the beginning of March 1645.[3] If each of these regiments had mustered 500 men, Hurry would have had 2,500 regulars at his disposal, but this is almost certainly too high, and no more than 400 men apiece for the 'old' regiments might not be unreasonable. However Buchanan's (confused by Fraser with Lothian's Regiment) provided only a detachment, and most of the regiment was left guarding Inverness.[4] How successful Findlater's recruiting had been is impossible to say, but given the short time available to him and the very unsettled conditions, he will have been lucky to have brought 300 men to Auldearn. Allowing 100 men for the detachment from Buchanan's Regiment, Hurry might therefore have had something in the region of 1,600 regulars. Seaforth had around 300 men in July 1645,[5] and allowing for losses at Auldearn and the inevitable attrition afterwards, he is likely to have had around 500 men at Auldearn. If the same number is allocated to Sutherland's Strathnaver men, the total then rises to 2,600 men or thereabouts. Besides these regiments there were also several hundred local levies, both highland and lowland, Frasers from Beuly and the Morayshire fencibles, both horse and foot; and in total Hurry's infantry will indeed have mustered something over 3,000 men, although the 4,000 quoted by Ruthven is probably too high and the 4 to 5,000 claimed by Montrose is certainly too high.

Hurry's cavalry is rather more difficult to reconstruct. Some estimates give him as many as 600 to 700, but this is certainly too high. Campbell of Lawers had a troop of horse and Abercrombie of Birkenbog (mentioned by Spalding as being present)[6] had led a troop at the Justice Mills fight in 1644. Some Morayshire cavalry, under the Laird of Innes' son and a Major Drummond, may have represented that part of Lord Gordon's Regiment which had not gone over to the rebels in February; but other than Hackett's 160 troopers,[7] these are the only cavalry who can be identified, and it is unlikely that Hurry could in fact muster much more than 300 cavalry—many of them rather seedy at that—a point of some considerable importance as will be seen.

The rebel army was nothing like as strong, except in cavalry, and its weakness emphasises the point that Hurry had lured Montrose into a trap. He seems to have believed that the rebels had 2,000 foot, although Montrose himself claims to have had only 1,400 men, both horse and foot. Although this seems rather low, it may not have been very far from the truth.[8] Fraser credits Lord Gordon with having brought 1,000 foot in addition to his 200 regular cavalry[9] (Spalding agrees and adds 400 dragooners). This is perhaps a little on the high side, though not inconsistent with the 800 foot said to have fought at Kilsyth or in the 1646 campaign. Ruthven, oddly enough, gives no figure either for the Gordon contingent or for the rebel army as a whole, save to quote Hurry's estimate, but makes it clear that there was more than one Gordon infantry regiment. One of these will of course have been the Strathbogie Regiment (mentioned by Fraser), and the other Minimore's men.[10] 200 of the Strathavan battalion were to fight at Alford and there are unlikely to have been many more of them at Auldearn. The Strathbogie Regiment may therefore have accounted for as many as 600 of the Gordons, though 500 is probably more realistic. There is no real reason to suppose that there was a third battalion, though it is not impossible. The Irish probably also mustered around 700 to 800 men. McMuirich cites MacColla's detachment in the village as being 140 strong, although he credits the Gordons with being rather stronger—as many as 300 or more of them. As MacColla's detachment included some highlanders, it was evidently drawn at least in part from Laghtman's Regiment. Other than these, and of course the majority of Minimore's men, no other highlanders were present. The Athollmen had returned home shortly before, on hearing that Baillie was threatening Blair, and no mention is made in any of the accounts of the Deeside men under Farquharson of Inverey. With the cavalry we are on surer ground, and there is ample confirmation that Lord Gordon had 200 good cavalry, and that there were perhaps another 50 under Montrose. The rebel cavalry was very nearly as strong as Hurry's, and moreover rather better at that.

THE BATTLESITE

In 1644 the main road from Inverness to Forres was much further inland than the present A96, and passed through Cawdor rather than Nairn on the line now followed by the B9090 and B9101. Consequently the village, a typical straggle of cottages, ran southwards from St. Colm's Church along what is now the Boath road. About 200 metres due east of the church was the Castle Hill, the double mound of a now vanished motte and bailey castle. The village itself is not built on a ridge as is sometimes said, but upon the side of a westward facing slope descending into a marshy 'bottom' formed by the Auldearn burn and its feeders. These streams and the associated marshy ground formed a sort of horseshoe (or more accurately perhaps a circle), with the toe at the village and the heels enclosing a small hill lying west sou' west of

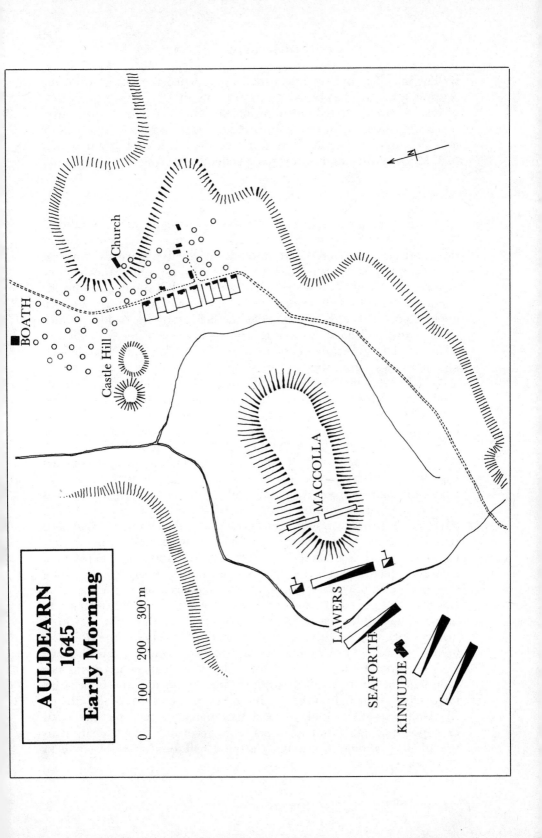

**AULDEARN
1645
Early Morning**

0   100   200   300 m

BOATH

Castle Hill

Church

MACCOLLA

LAWERS

SEAFORTH

KINNUDIE

N

it. The fact that the Inverness road approached the village from the southwest in 1645 has been known for some time, but the significance of this has been inflated out of proportion,[11] for the fact of the matter is that the government forces in their final approach to Auldearn were *not* following the road at all, and indeed the battle itself began rather further to the west than seems to be generally accepted.

OPENING MOVES

Although Alasdair MacColla had only the two units actually billeted in Auldearn at his disposal, he did not remain in the village once they had been mustered but instead led them westwards 'towards a marishe and som bushes, which was a strong ground and fencible against horsemen'. This was obviously the low hill surrounded by the Auldearn burn and its feeders described above; and Hurry in turn deployed his army at Kinnudie,[12] facing them across the Auldearn burn itself, which will have made a pretty passable start line on which to form up. The government forces were thus facing due east about a kilometre away from the village, not pressing close up against it from the southwest. Montrose meanwhile busied himself in drawing up the remainder of the foot to the east of the village, while Lord Gordon assembled his cavalry regiment, dividing it into two squadrons: one commanded by himself and Alexander Gordon of Cairnburgh, and the other under Aboyne and William Gordon of Arradoul.[13]

For the moment though, MacColla was on his own; and attacked by one of Hurry's regiments, probably Lawers', supported by two troops of horse, was forced to retire after a brief firefight. The rebels opened fire first, according to Fraser, but quickly got the worst of it. MacColla's Ensign was slain, and though his yellow banner was at once raised again, no fewer than three or four men were shot down one after the other keeping it aloft: 'So efter a brave and long maintained resistance, he is forced a reteir to som yards of the town'.[14] In so doing the rebels will have fallen back almost due east, closely followed by Lawers' Regiment and some of Seaforth's who came up on the flank to support them. The rest of Hurry's army also followed, but at a little distance behind, for although Hurry was very properly intent on the fight immediately to his front, he cannot have been unaware that the two weak battalions being driven in by his advance-guard did not represent the entire rebel strength. Prudently he kept the bulk of his forces clear of the fight. Once in amongst the back yards of the village, MacColla was able to make a stand once more, and this time succeeded in stopping the government forces with, according to Ruthven, 'continuall shot', though the marshy ground will also have slowed them down somewhat.

Having thus checked the government forces, MacColla then mounted a hasty counter-attack, which quickly came to grief in the marshy bottom. He has been pretty universally condemned for this move, generally attributed either to his rashness, or less charitably, stupidity; but in reality he probably had very little choice in the matter. Even one regiment had been enough to win the firefight against him on the high ground, and now he was faced by two, one of them comprised of experienced regulars and well supplied with ammunition. His own force, by contrast, although including some Irish regulars, contained a high proportion of highlanders, temperamentally unsuited to fighting on the defensive, ill-supplied with muskets, and not improbably short of ammunition. Furthermore, although it will not have been too difficult to control them in the open, once scattered amongst the yards and outbuildings of the village, this control will very largely have been lost. The importance of an officer being able actually to see the troops under his command (and for him to be seen by them), in the days before the advent of wireless telegraphy, cannot be over-emphasised. Floundering about in the marshy bottom, however, they presented the government forces with an irresistible opportunity, and they also counter-attacked in turn before MacColla's push had even properly got under way, driving the rebels back into the village again.

It is unlikely that there was much blood-red, tooth and claw, physical combat at this stage, and the rebel retreat may well have begun as soon as they saw Lawers' and Seaforth's men coming down the slope towards them. As they fell back up the slope into the yards though, resistance once again stiffened. It would still be wrong or at least an overstatement to imagine a vicious mêlée. MacColla, we are told, had a number of pikes stuck fast in his targe, which he chopped off with his broadsword. Since pikes were generally 16 feet long (or sometimes 14 feet long), both sides were hardly therefore treading on each others' toes, and indeed Ruthven says as much, declaring that none dared approach within range of MacColla's sword. What may therefore realistically be postulated is that the pikeman of Lawers' Regiment were literally herding the rebels back like recalcitrant cattle, at a pike's length. Although most men in the regiment were musketeers, they may well have been hanging back in order to provide fire-support, shooting the pikemen in, as it were, although their fire and the archery of some Lewismen belonging to Seaforth's Regiment seems to have been rather ineffective, if McMuirich's anecdotes are reliable. Firing uphill is of course notoriously inaccurate, since there is always a tendency to shoot too high. Once they got in amongst the back yards, the government soldiers soon got bogged down, but MacColla was under no illusions that his men could take the pressure for long:

111

then for griefe was he ready to burst, seeing non to second him, and saw no hope of victorie, but all the simptoms of a disasterous and dreadful overthrow. Wherefor he called to those that wer about him, 'Ach, messoures,' said he, 'sall our enemies by this on dayes work be able to wreast out of our handes all the glorie that we have formerly gained. Let it never he said that a basse flight shall bear witness of it, or that our actiones should seem to confesse so much; but let us die bravely; let it never be thought that they have triumphed over our courage, nor the loyaltie we ow to our soveraigne lord, and let us hope the best. God is stronge enough'.

And whill he whispered these words for he would not speak aloud, least the enemies might imagine of yielding, behold how gratious Heavin and the Devyne Power did assist him.[15]

THE REBEL COUNTER-ATTACK

The crisis of the battle had now been reached, and particularly in view of the recent controversy attending it, it requires to be looked at in some detail. The generally accepted version of what happened derives from Gardiner. Knowing that, while MacColla was defending the village against Hurry's leading brigade, which was directing its attack due eastwards from Kinudie, Montrose was assembling the rest of the rebel army in a hollow, Gardiner located that hollow behind the crest of the high ground overlooking the Inverness road (B9101). Montrose was thus ideally placed to fall upon the right flank of the government forces, and so ideally placed that all his dispositions must have been carefully thought out with that object in mind. The later realisation that the old Inverness road approached the village from the south west (the modern A96 did not exist in 1645) has led to the position of the celebrated hollow being moved by subsequent historians, and the rebel counter-attack directed due westward instead of northwards, but otherwise the essentials have remained unaltered. Dr. Stevenson, however, relying heavily upon Gordon of Ruthven's account and the red herring created by the old Inverness road, has proposed a radically different version of events. In Stevenson's reconstruction, the rebels were taken by surprise by Hurry and had no time to prepare a trap or ambush as claimed by Gardiner. Instead Stevenson sees MacColla holding on grimly to the village while Montrose assembles the army behind it. Once the rebels are all mustered Montrose reinforces MacColla in the village and sends his cavalry round the flanks. There is no large scale attack on Hurry's right flank, but instead a strong push in the centre.

His mistaken belief that Hurry marched straight up the road against Auldearn aside (Fraser, it will be recalled, specifically states that he deployed his forces at Kinnudie), Stevenson begins well and is undoubtedly correct as to the confusion inspired by Hurry's assault. His account of the rebel counter-attack is, on the other hand, unconvincing. The course of action proposed is quite impractical, and he fails to realise that Ruthven's, Fraser's and Montrose's accounts of the battle are entirely compatible and complement each other quite well.

According to Montrose, in what was a rather brief letter to the King:

> they being confident both of their men and their number fell hotly on, but being beat back, seimd to coole of their fury, and only intended to blocke us up (as it wer) till more number should come which perceiving I divided myselfe in two wings (which was all the ground would suffer) and marched upon them most unexpectedly.[16]

Now, it will soon be clear that in this extract he and Gordon of Ruthven are describing the same battle. Hurry's advance guard, Lawers' Regiment and a couple of troops of horse (and later Seaforth's men), 'fell hotly on', only to be beaten back by Aboyne's cavalry charge. Meanwhile Montrose, having gathered the rest of the foot and brought them up to make 'on body' with MacColla, not by throwing them into the village—for that would have been disastrous—but by extending the main fighting line to the south, MacColla's men forming one wing and Montrose's the other. Had Montrose's men been fed into MacColla's position they would have achieved little beyond adding to the congestion, and would certainly have been incapable of mounting a successful attack from that position. After all, when MacColla earlier attempted a counter-attack it came to grief as much because of that marshy 'bottom' as anything else. Extending the main fighting line to the south, forming two wings, not only made excellent sense but is explicitly confirmed by Fraser, who describes the Strathbogie Regiment as setting forth to the south of MacColla's men.[17]

The counter-attack itself comprised three fairly distinct phases. In the first, Aboyne launched a successful spoiling attack against the right flank of Lawers' brigade. This was followed shortly afterwards by Lord Gordon's attack on the opposite flank, which was followed in turn by the rebel infantry's assault on Hurry's main battle.

Aboyne's squadron having saddled up, he led them in a circle around to the south, and seeing that MacColla, whom we are picturesquely told had 'brak two swords', was in considerable difficulty, he at once charged Lawers' right flank. Ruthven implies that at first they were met by a tremendous fire: 'They receive his charge with such a continuall gieving of fire, as he seemed, by the thick smok throw which he went, to asalt a terrible cloud of thunder and lightening'; but powder smoke tends to hang around in damp weather, and the smoke described by Ruthven will more likely have come from the musketry directed at MacColla's men. In any case, other accounts show that it was not the infantry who were first attacked by Aboyne, but a troop

113

of cavalry led by an officer named Drummond. Seeing Aboyne's men approaching, Drummond panicked, and instead of turning his troop to the right to face them, he turned them to the left, which they took to be an order to shift for themselves. The poor man may, it is possible, have been unable to tell his right from his left, or there may have been treachery; but as the rebels were charging downhill upon his flank and almost certainly outnumbered him, it is equally possible that he was intent on running away from them. In any case the move was disastrous, for his men ploughed into the flank of Lawers' Regiment, scattering the infantry in disorder. As a result Aboyne was able to keep his men together and mount what virtually amounted to a second charge, not giving the hapless infantry time to rally. They evidently broke in amongst the pikemen as well as the musketeers, for four or five colours were taken in the charge or the pursuit. This attack at once relieved the pressure on MacColla, but the fight was by no means over. The remnants of Lawers' and Seaforth's regiments scrambled back up on to the high ground behind them, and called for reinforcements.

The fact that Aboyne's attack was carried out in advance of the main rebel counter-attack is of considerable importance in reconstructing what happened, for while it is evident that his single squadron did indeed fall upon the flank of Lawers' brigade, there is, as will be seen, no evidence that the rest of the rebels did so, quite the contrary in fact; and it is the failure to distinguish between Aboyne's attack and the main counter-attack which has led to the erroneous belief that Montrose fell upon Hurry's flank rather than meeting him head on as was actually the case.[18]

Now it was Lord Gordon's turn. It is possible that he had been intended by Montrose to have attacked at the same time as Aboyne, but having perhaps further to go in order to clear the Castle Hill, he arrived in position after Aboyne's attack had gone in. Lord Gordon's attack was evidently more successful than Aboyne's, partly of course because Lawers' brigade had already been softened up by Aboyne (and further discouraged by the sudden appearance of the Strathbogie Regiment to the south of Auldearn at the same time), and partly because the attack was pressed home with unusual vigour. Ruthven's account of it is worth quoting in full, and it should be remembered that Lord Gordon's Regiment was not the rude multitude of 'bonnet lairds on cart-horses' imagined by John Buchan, but a regular cavalry regiment:

> My lord Gordon by this time charges the left winge, and that with a new form of fight, for he discharges all shootting of pistoles and carrabines, only with ther swords to charge quhyt throwgh ther enemies, who wer so many in number, and so stronge and weell horsed [they were probably Lawers' own Troop] as if by a desperat charge they had got them not broken, it

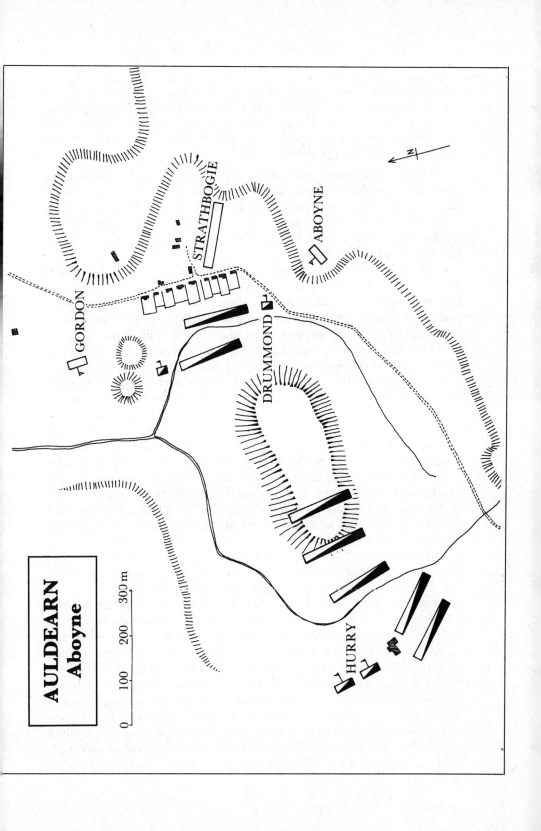

AULDEARN
Aboyne

0   100   200   300 m

GORDON

STRATHBOGIE

ABOYNE

DRUMMOND

HURRY

N

was too apparent that they might recover the day. But Aboyn having overthrowen the right winge, and the main battell left bair on that syd, and seeing Montrose and McDonell joyned to give a new charge, the great body began to stagger, all their hopes being in ther left winge; and that my lord Gordon charges so soundly with swords only, as if they scorned to be resisted; they had all sworn to go throw or dye.[19]

Having summarily chased off the cavalry, Lord Gordon, still keeping his regulars in hand, wheeled into the flank or rear of Lawers' and Seaforth's regiments (or perhaps Lothian's and Loudon's who were evidently hurrying up in support), routing them and chasing them southwards, where, according to Fraser, many were killed around Kinsteary and Brightmony.[20]

After these attacks, the main body of the government forces was ill-prepared to face the counter-attack by the rebel infantry which was now developing. To make matters worse, it is unlikely that they were even at this stage properly deployed, for Ruthven described them as standing 'on regiment still secunding ane other'.[21] This rather suggests that far from believing that MacColla's men represented the rebels' main body, Hurry was perfectly aware that they represented only a part of the rebel army, and was delaying the deployment of his own forces until he could ascertain more precisely where the rebels in fact were. The trouble was he left it too late, and could well have been taken by surprise by the speed with which the rebel counter-attack developed. The result was that Hurry was unable to use his superior numbers to any effect, for the Strathbogie Regiment, sweeping around the south side of Auldearn and then driving westwards in concert with MacColla's men, engaged Lothian's and Loudon's regiments. Accounts of this phase of the battle are tantalisingly brief, but Montrose perhaps gives the best picture when he relates that ther were 'some hot salvyes of musket and a litell dealing with sword and pike',[22] which indicates a certain amount of resistance as might be expected from these veteran regiments, a brief firefight and then an advance to contact by the rebels. For once there was some prolonged hand to hand fighting before the government forces finally broke, a phenomenon which can perhaps be explained by the government forces' refusal to be intimidated and by the rebels' determination to close with them. This determination may partly be explained by the ferocity which frequently animates men newly delivered from the threat of having their throats cut, and partly from a desire for revenge for the murder, the previous day, of James Gordon of Rhynie. The result was an extremely vicious fight, and a high death toll amongst the leading government regiments. The ferocity was clearly regarded as remarkable even by contemporaries; Spalding relates that they were 'for the most part cut af, fighting to the death most valiauntlie'. Fraser describes how the rebels 'run throw them,

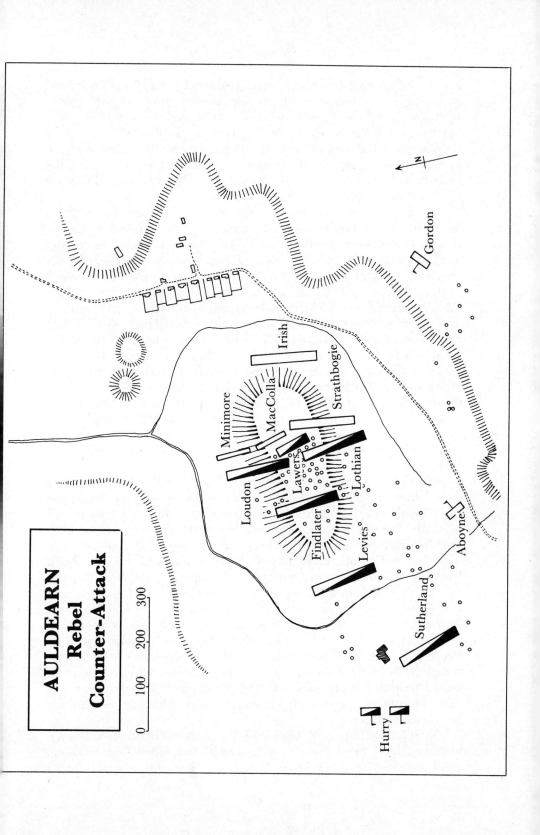

AULDEARN
Rebel
Counter-Attack

0   100   200   300

N

Gordon

Irish

Minimore

MacColla

Strathbogie

Loudon

Lawers

Findlater

Lothian

Levies

Aboyne

Sutherland

Hurry

killing and goaring under foot. . . . .Lairs and Lothians regiment stood in their ranks and files, and were so killed as they stood'; while Ruthven, with the air of an eyewitness, says 'you should have sein how the infantrie of the Royalists, keiping together and following the charge of the horsemen, did tear and cut them in pieces, even in rankes and fyles, as they stood, so great was the execution which they made efter the horse had shanken and quyt astonished them, by perseing rudly throw them, as it was very lamentable to behold'.[23]

Seeing his infantry thus overwhelmed, Hurry saw no profit in intervening and turned away for Inverness. Lord Gordon, having returned from the pursuit of those routed earlier, prepared to go after him, but halted on seeing a body of cavalry appearing bearing the government's distinctive colours. They were, as it turned out, Aboyne's men, still displaying the colours they had taken; but by the time the mistake was discovered Hurry had successfully broken contact, and was away, riding hard for Inverness. Fraser says that Hurry got his men away across the River Nairn by Howford, 3·5 kilometres from Kinnudie, without being pursued. Curiously, he declares that he crossed by night, which is the only corroboration for a report recorded by Sir James Hope, the Lord Advocate, that the fighting raged for twelve hours.[24] Other than the fact that it began about or shortly after dawn, there is no real indication as to how long the battle lasted. Military operations frequently take rather more time than expected, but the general impression obtained from the other accounts is that it lasted only a few hours.

There is no disagreement about the high death toll amongst the government soldiers. The usual scatter of figures between 2,000 and 3,000 dead are given, although 2,000 may perhaps be a little on the high side. On this occasion it is possible to a certain extent to establish the losses suffered by individual regiments. Campbell of Lawers' Regiment lost its Colonel, Lieutenant Colonel (William Campbell) and at least four of the company commanders: Captain Campbell, Captain William Bruce, Captain Cashore and Captain Shaw. They, together with five Lieutenants and 200 men, all presumably from the regiment, were afterwards buried at Cawdor. As many though are likely to have escaped, and while 1,200 recruits were ordered for the regiment from Perthshire in August 1645, the fact that the regiment's officers were complaining in February 1646 that they had been in Inverness for sixteen months (i.e. since October 1644), but received in that time only half a months' pay, is strongly indicative of its not having been entirely destroyed at Auldearn.[25]

The Earl of Lothian's Regiment's losses are not so easy to ascertain, but must have been similar, for they again included four company commanders: Captain William Douglas (presumably one of the nine nephews of Douglas of Cavers said to have been slain there), Captain Alexander Drummond, Captain Gideon Murray and Captain Sir John Murray. All four had led their companies since the regiment was raised in 1642. Although no recruits were allocated to the regiment in August, the survivors were sent into England to serve alongside Lothian's second regiment, raised in 1643.[26]

The Earl of Loudon's Regiment may actually have suffered the heaviest losses of all, for only 100 survived to fight at Kilsyth in August.[27]

A Captain Crichton buried at Auldearn is most likely to have belonged to the Earl of Findlater's Regiment. Both Findlater and his Lieutenant Colonel, Walter Ogilvy of Boyne, escaped, but nothing more is heard of the regiment and it may simply have disintegrated. As to Seaforth's Regiment and the other northern levies, there is little other than anecdotal evidence to go by. A Captain Bernard McKenzie was killed together with most of his company from the Chanonry of Ross, while Fraser records that Lovat was left with 87 Fraser widows to support. Most of the cavalry escaped, of course, but Lawers' Troop was allocated 20 recruits from Peebles in August, which suggests that they were the troopers ridden over by Lord Gordon. A final casualty was the cavalry officer Major Drummond, shot by Hurry 'at the post uppon the high rodde as yow go to Tomnihurich', for his accidental riding down of Lawers' men.[28]

Rebel losses were of course much lighter. Ruthven gives only 16 dead, 14 of whom were MacColla's men, while Spalding gives '24 gentlemen hurt to Montross, and sum few Irishes killit, whiche is miraculous'. Gordon of Sallagh, on the other hand, gives 22 gentlemen slain, which is consistent with Spalding's figure, but he also states that 200 common soldiers were killed, which is altogether more realistic in view of the prolonged and vicious nature of the fighting. After all, if four men were shot down one after the other within a short space of time, while holding MacColla's yellow banner when he bumped Lawers' Regiment at the start of the battle, one should expect to find rather more than the 14 dead quoted by Ruthven.[29]

Hurry's army had been destroyed, but Inverness was still too strong for the rebels, and instead they were forced to turn eastwards to face Baillie.

8

The Battle of Alford,
2 July 1645

Baillie meanwhile had been engaged in what he later described as 'ane unneccessarie voyage into Athole by order of the Committee'. This had begun on 3 May, and although the systematic harrying and burning of the area had caused the withdrawal of the Atholl battalion from the rebel army just before Auldearn, there was little real point to the expedition, and even the rebel garrison in Blair Castle, commanded by Robertson of Inver, had seen Baillie off. Capture of the castle would have been a considerable blow to the rebels, since it formed their main permanent base, and in addition to serving as a field hospital it was stuffed full of prisoners and plunder. Baillie, however, had evidently been unable to get any artillery through the Pass of Killiecrankie, and as soon as he decently could he withdrew to the lowlands, and then set off northwards with his 2,000 foot and 100 horse, intending to join Hurry.

However on 9 May the Committee travelling with the army were seized with cold feet, and just as Baillie was about to ascend the Cairn o' Mount pass, they decided that the lowlands should not be left unprotected, and that he should detach the best part of his army under the Earl of Crawford-Lindsay, comprising the Earl's own regiment, The Earl of Cassillis' and the Earl of Lauderdale's regiments. This left Baillie only with Glencairn's and Callendar's regiments, and the 100 or so troopers of Hackett's cavalry regiment not earlier detached to serve with Hurry.[1]

Having camped at Birse on the 10th, Baillie then crossed the Dee and encamped between Tarland and Coull on the 11th. Here he seems to have had word of Hurry's defeat, for not surprisingly he took the view that 800 foot and 100 cavalry was a totally inadequate force with which to face the victorious rebels, and refused to budge until he received reinforcements. For want of sufficient men at a time when the rebels were, as will be seen, extremely vulnerable, Baillie was immobilised for over a week, until the arrival of the Earl of Balcarres at the head of his cavalry regiment, and two battalions of 'redcoats' led by Colonel Robert Home. These had been drawn from all six of the Scots regiments still serving in Ulster under Robert Monro, representing something over 200 men from each of the regiments. This considerably weakened the army there, and reports that they actually included both Irish and English recruits may well be true. Furthermore, as Baillie was shortly to discover, they were not as reliable as he would have wished. Nevertheless they more than doubled the size of his army, and he at once made up for lost time by marching with all speed for the wood of Cocklarochy, just south of Strathbogie, where he went to ground.

Why he should have done so there rather than Strathbogie itself is not clear from contemporary sources. There was probably a rebel garrison in the castle—there certainly was a short time afterwards—but it may be conjectured that he was hoping to hide his army until such time as he could gain reliable intelligence of the rebels' whereabouts. As it was, he obtained the information not from his scouts but from Sir John Hurry himself. He had broken out of Inverness with the 100 or so remaining troopers of Hackett's Regiment, and slipped through the rebel outposts by claiming to be a detachment of Lord Gordon's Regiment (Hurry's Aberdeen accent must have come in useful here).

The rebels, never strong to begin with, had despite their victory at Auldearn been so roughly handled by Hurry there as to be quite incapable of attempting the capture of Inverness, despite its importance, and instead had given themselves over to their old habits of plundering everything movable and burning anything which was not. Instead of continuing the advance on Inverness they retired to Elgin on 11 May, and in revenge for the murder of James Gordon of Rhynie (or the pretext of it), plundered and burnt the houses of some of those believed to be responsible for the deed.[2] As usual, though, things got rather out of hand. Ruthven gives the impression that the rebels were moving eastwards with the express intention of meeting Baillie, but it is hard to escape the conclusion from the leisurely pace of the chevauchée that there was no urgency or enthusiasm to fight another battle so soon. The baggage train was passed over the Spey on the 12th and secured at the Bog o' Gight, one of Huntly's castles, held by 100 men under a professional soldier, Captain James Gordon of Leicheston.[3] Montrose himself crossed on Wednesday the 14th, and based himself at Birkenbog near Cullen for the next few days, sending out parties to plunder and burn all along the Banffshire coast. He must himself have been at the burning of Cullen, for his dispatch to the King announcing his victory at Auldearn was written there on the 17th. There too he must have had some word of Baillie's lying on Deeside, for he told the King that he was about to march upon him. First though he had to re-assemble his own by now rather scattered army and return to Birkenbog (only about 4 kilometres away), where he remained for a further four days before receiving on the 21st 'haistie advertesment' that Baillie was lying at Cocklarochy, and then marched hard for Strathbogie, arriving there just before evening. There he must have had a rude shock.

According to Spalding, as soon as he arrived he immediately set his army to digging in around the castle with every indication of determination to stay and fight; but as soon as it was dark he decamped briskly, westwards, to Balvenie Castle, covered by a cavalry rearguard which remained at Strathbogie until morning.[4] Ruthven says that this was done to spare the countryside around Strathbogie from the inevitable depredations of both armies, but Montrose had never been overly concerned on this account in the past, and a rather more plausible explanation for this extraordinary behaviour is that Montrose, whose scouting was never up to much at the best of times, was under the impression that Baillie had ventured north only with the troops with which he had crossed the Dee on 11 May. Only when he reached Strathbogie did Montrose realise that Baillie now had over 2,000 foot, and something in the region of 300 or more horse, where-upon, still lacking a good part of his army, he had little option but to beat a hasty retreat to Balvenie.

Baillie, discovering next morning that the rebels were gone, marched after them and came in sight of them again at Glenlivet, which argues for some hard work, but they kept ahead and shook him off again at nightfall. Next morning Baillie's scouts deduced by the trampling of the grass and heather that the rebels were making for Abernethy on Speyside. Following after again, Baillie eventually caught up with them 'in the entrie of Badzenoch, a very strait country, where, both for unaccessible rocks, woods, and the interposition of the river, it wes impossible for us to come at them'. This was probably somewhere near Aviemore, and here Baillie reluctantly had to admit defeat. His men, as on the march to Dundee and the subsequent pursuit of Montrose, had done all that could be asked of them and more in running the rebels to earth; but they were in an unassailable position, and his own men were exhausted and starving, the cavalry complaining that they had had no food for 48 hours. There was no help for it, he had to withdraw northwards to Inverness, leaving the rebels to slip away southwards. Had Inverness been taken after Auldearn he might have been in an even worse state, but as it was he was able there to feed and rest his army.

The rebels, having narrowly escaped his clutches, took advantage of his retreat to go after Crawford Lindsay. That worthy had embarked upon another 'voyage' into Atholl, but on being informed of the rebels' approach hurriedly retired down Strathardle and took up a strong position behind the river Isla at Newtyle. At this point Lord Gordon received word from his brother, Aboyne, that Baillie was loose in the north again, and insisted on returning with his men.[5] Left with only a couple of hundred Irish, Montrose in turn had to retreat northwards, taking refuge for a time at Corgarff Castle on the upper reaches of the river Don.

Having re-supplied his army and picked up the survivors of Lothian's and Loudon's regiments, Baillie marched east from Inverness, crossed the Spey, and marching past Strathbogie where his rear was beaten up by the garrison, he camped at Newton of Garioch near Old Rayne on 3 June. John Leith of Harthill, who had returned to the area and fortified his castle shortly after Auldearn, prudently kept indoors and made no attempt to molest Baillie when he rode past to try and obtain money and supplies from Aberdeen. Although he had an escort of only six troopers, he must have been convoyed past the castle by Lothian's and Loudon's regiments, for they arrived in Aberdeen that evening and were ferried south by sea shortly afterwards.[6] Nothing was to be had from Aberdeen. Hurry left the army shortly afterwards upon pleading indisposition, although as he and Baillie did not get on, his going cannot have disappointed the general; worse, though, was to follow. Baillie then had a letter from Crawford-Lindsay ordering him to meet him at Drum on Deeside. Arriving there with his army sometime beforehand, Baillie learned that Montrose was only a short distance upstream in Cromar, and seems to have decided to have a go at him before Crawford-Lindsay arrived. Having assembled his forces for the attempt, he then made an optimistic speech appropriate to such occasions, pointing out the undoubted wealth to be found in the rebel baggage train, but:

> when hee looked for a chearfull answer, the reid regiment, commonly called the reid cottes [Home's] with tuo old regiments more [Glencairn's and Callendar's] upon whose walour he most relyed, told him plainely that they saw no just quarrell, for Montrose and the Gordounes ware the Kinges subjects als well as they, and the Irishes, altho they were strangeres, ware the Kinges subjectes, professing to there obedience to his maiestie als well as they and all of them professed no other quarrell but the mantinance of the Kinges royall prerogatiue, which he was no good subject that wold refuse.

Not surprisingly 'this answer did mightelie perplex there generall', and thoughts of engaging the rebels had for the time being to be abandoned.[7] Although Home's men had (most of them) indeed been recruited originally for the King's service in Ireland, it is likely that they were simply being difficult and had no mind to go marching off into the mountains again—Montrose was not the only one to cause sickness and woe—for Home's men were to fight well enough at Kilsyth, and the others to do likewise at Alford.

When Crawford-Lindsay arrived he brought bad news for Baillie. The Committee was dissatisfied with his prosecution of the war and considered him insufficiently determined in his pursuit of the rebels (evidently none of them had actually accompanied him on his vigorous marches), and Argyle was again to take command of an army with the sole task of bringing the rebels to battle and destroying them. Baillie was to be relegated to a defensive role, protecting the lowlands from any rebel incursions in the meantime. Crawford-Lindsay's and Lauderdale's regiments, still lying in the Braes of Angus, were to provide the nucleus for this new army of Argyle's, and highlanders were also to be recruited, but more immediately Baillie was ordered to give up Home's 1,200 to 1,400 men and 100 of Balcarres' Horse, and in exchange he was given back Cassillis' Regiment, 400 strong.[8]

Needless to say the plan went wrong almost at once. Argyle for some reason refused command of the new army, and it was given instead to Crawford-Lindsay. He promptly vanished on another futile 'voyage' into Atholl, and Baillie was left to go after the rebels on his own after all, but with a greatly reduced force. Ignoring his weakness, the Committee ordered him to rendezvous with Seaforth, and he got as far as the Spey unmolested; whereupon, not meeting with Seaforth, commonsense re-asserted itself and he began to fall back, only to encounter the rebels at Keith on 24 June. Having some warning of their approach, he picked himself a good position by the church, and the rebels were reduced once more to challenging him to come down and fight them in the open. This as ever he sensibly refused, whereupon the rebels in turn started withdrawing southwards. Puzzled by this, Baillie sent his scouts after them, and discovering that MacColla and most of his men were not with the army (he was off recruiting in the west), he set off in pursuit and caught up with them at the foot of the Correen Hills on 1 July.

ALFORD, 2 JULY 1645

The fight at Alford was quite a straightforward affair. Baillie, marching in pursuit of the rebels, crossed the River Don by a ford at Mountgarrie, and found them drawn up awaiting him on the Gallowhill overlooking the village of Alford. He succeeded in deploying his army to face them, but after a stiff fight his cavalry were routed and his infantry overwhelmed. Unfortunately almost all the modern reconstructions of the battle, with the notable exception of Gardiner's, have wrongly assumed that the modern village of Alford did not exist in the seventeenth century, and so have quite unnecessarily complicated the affair by having Baillie cross the Don by the ford at the Boat of Forbes (now Bridge of Alford), right under the rebels' noses.

Wishart's account of the battle is for once quite clear. Baillie came in sight of the rebels at about noon on 1 July, at the foot of the Coreen Hills, some distance to the north of Alford. Montrose at once decided to turn and fight on some rising ground, which must have been at the Suie Foot or Knockespock (Gordon of Knockespock was with the rebel army), but Baillie failed to accept the challenge and instead 'turned aside about three miles to the left'.[9] This will have taken him to Leslie, where according to an important ballad tradition the government forces spent the night. Montrose for his part then continued down the Suie Road to Alford, where according to the same ballad he slept at Asloun Castle.

THE BATTLESITE

Early next morning Montrose ordered his men to stand to on the Gallowhill, a prominent eminence overlooking Alford, while he himself set off with a troop of horse to look for Baillie. The natural assumption for him to make, and which has unfortunately been made by most later historians, was that Baillie, if he was still pursuing the rebels, would come down the Suie Road and cross the river Don at Boat of Forbes, as the rebels had done the previous day. However while he was scouting the ford, word came to Montrose that Baillie was making for a different ford 'a mile distant from Alford'.[10] Montrose immediately jumped to the conclusion that Baillie was attempting to outflank him—which he can hardly have done if he was coming down the Suie Road straight at the rebels—and leaving the troop of horse to guard the ford he galloped off to 'order his battle' on the top of the Gallowhill. Baillie, far from following in the rebels' footsteps, had instead marched due south from Leslie, crossing the Correens between Knock Soul and Satter Hill, and coming down to cross the Don not at Boat of Forbes but further downstream at Mountgarrie.

Much unnecessary confusion has been caused by a curious assumption made by John Buchan, and followed by most subsequent writers, that the present village of Alford does not antedate the coming of the railway; and casting about for an Alford a mile distant from a ford, have fixed upon the small settlement now called Muir of Alford lying to the *west* of Gallowhill and within a mile of the ford at Boat of Forbes. Buchan was mistaken as to this however, and in any case Baillie's crossing of the ford at Mountgarrie is confirmed by the Aberdeenshire ballad already alluded to, which very helpfully states that his men had reached Mill Hill before being put in order of battle.[11] This farm lies about a kilometre north of Mountgarrie, on the road over the hills from

Leslie. The circumstantial evidence for Baillie crossing the Don there is also very strong. Had he come over the ford at the Boat of Forbes, as is usually stated to have been the case, then the other ford being reconnoitred by Montrose must have been the Mountgarrie one. This may be possible, but if it were so there would have been no need to leave the troop of horse there in what was shortly to become Baillie's rear area, while he prepared his army to meet the government forces at the Boat of Forbes.[12]

The whole episode indeed only makes sense if it is accepted that Baillie crossed the river at Mountgarrie. Montrose was under the impression, wrongly, that Baillie was trying to outflank him at this stage, which is hardly the impression he would have had if Baillie crossed at Boat of Forbes and was thus coming straight at the rebels on the Gallowhill. Crossing at Mountgarrie, some distance to the east, was however a different matter. Furthermore, Montrose, we are told, had already drawn his army up on the Gallowhill before setting off on his reconnaissance, and had Baillie come across at Boat of Forbes, there would have been no need for Montrose to have hastened back to draw them up again afresh, on hearing of Baillie's approach. Indeed had Baillie been rash enough to come straight across there and along a narrow causeway through boggy ground before deploying at the foot of the Gallowhill—and we know that if anything Baillie was inclined to be over-cautious—the rebels would most assuredly have fallen upon him before he could properly deploy, as Moray and Wallace did at Stirling Bridge in 1297. Crossing at Mountgarrie, however, Baillie was not only far enough away to deploy in safety, but was thus in a position to attack the Gallowhill position from the north-east or even the east; thus forcing Montrose to draw his own army up anew, no longer facing north, but north-east or east, to face Baillie, while leaving the troop of horse by the Boat of Forbes to cover the left flank of the army.

The rebel position was a very strong one; not only were they at the top of a hill, but their left flank and rear—about which Montrose seems to have been rather nervous, still perhaps expecting troops to appear down the Suie road—was well protected, not only by the detachment at Boat of Forbes, but in the rear by a marsh 'intersected by ditches and pools, which secured him . . . from cavalry'. This last can only be the Muir of Alford, and in order to place it in the rebels' rear, those writers who have supposed that Baillie crossed by the Boat of Forbes have made the extraordinary assumption that not only did Baillie get across unhindered, but then proceeded to edge his way around the foot of the Gallowhill. Far from doing so, Baillie was actually halted on flat, low-lying ground by the village. Neither side was at first willing to move; the rebels were unwilling to leave their strong position,

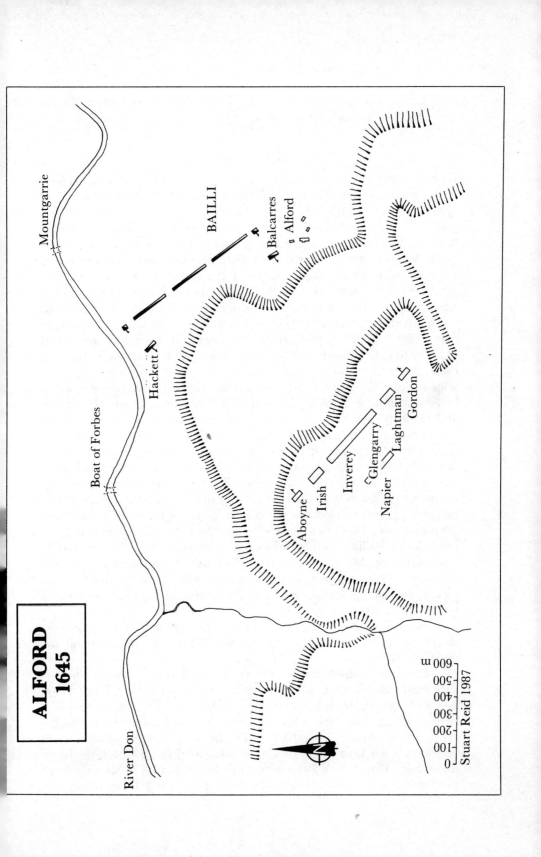

ALFORD
1645

Mountgarrie

River Don

Boat of Forbes

BAILLI

Balcarres

Alford

Hackett

Aboyne

Irish

Inverey

Glengarry

Napier

Laghtman

Gordon

0 100 200 300 400 500 600 m

Stuart Reid 1987

and Baillie, naturally enough since he may have been outnumbered, was equally unwilling to assault it.

THE ARMIES

Baillie's army can be reconstructed pretty well from his own account of the battle and from various official papers. He had six regiments of regular foot—Cassillis', Elcho's, Lanark's, Moray's, Glencairn's and Callendar's.[13] Some rebel accounts assume that they were raw levies, but in fact the reverse was the case. Cassillis' Regiment had been raised in 1643 and had fought at Boldon Hill, Marston Moor (where it had behaved with some distinction) and the siege of Newcastle, before returning to Scotland. Glencairn's and Callendar's regiments had both been raised in 1644 for service in England, and although they could not boast the experience of Cassillis' men they were still far from being raw recruits. Baillie gives Cassillis' Regiment 400 men, making a total of 1,400 to 1,800 infantry in all, which is not at all inconsistent with his estimate that he was outnumbered two to one by the rebel foot—for which reason his own were drawn up only three deep in order to avoid being outflanked.[14] As to his cavalry, Baillie mentions only Balcarres' and Hackett's regiments of horse, totalling 260[15] in all, though as the rebel accounts credit him with rather more than twice that number, it may well be that the diversion the previous day to Leslie had been made to rendezvous with some of the Aberdeenshire horse under Forbes of Craigievar. Baillie later states that Balcarres' horse were drawn up in three squadrons, but the normal practice in the Scots army was to use two squadrons and the third may actually have been an Aberdeenshire one. This is also suggested by the fact that it seems to have been under Baillie's command rather than Balcarres'. Unfortunately that part of Spalding's manuscript which might otherwise have settled the matter has been lost, but it would perhaps be surprising if Craigievar, at least, was not present, and Baillie should therefore be credited with at least 300 cavalry.

As to their dispositions, all that can be said is that the foot were drawn up in the centre three deep, with Hackett's regiment on the right and Balcarres' on the left.

The composition of the rebel army is not quite so clear. There is a general agreement that they had something in the region of 2,000 foot and 200 cavalry—Lord Gordon's Regiment, divided as usual into two squadrons: one, under his personal command, on the right and the other, led by Aboyne, on the left. The infantry bear some discussion. Ruthven states that the main battle comprised the Strathbogie Regiment and Huntly's highlanders—the latter being a rather elastic description which encompassed Badenoch men and Farquharsons as

128

well as 'the name of Gordon'—but Wishart states that the main battle was commanded by Angus MacDonald of Glengarry, which rather suggests the presence of a small MacDonald contingent. In addition to the Strathbogie Regiment, Ruthven helpfully mentions that Colonel William Gordon of Minimore had 200 men from Strathavăn. The centre may therefore have comprised 500 men of the Strathbogie Regiment, Minimore's 200 men, a further 200 from Deeside under Inverey, and say 100 MacDonalds under Glengarry, making 1,000 men in all. Laghtman's Irish regiment supported Lord Gordon's horse on the right, while O'Cahan's and McDonnell's Irish regiments supported Aboyne on the left. Allowing for some men from these units having gone off with MacColla, there were probably something like 300 Irish on each wing. Finally there was a reserve commanded by Lord Napier behind the centre. The composition of this reserve is obscure, but Baillie seems to have reckoned it to comprise the Irish who settled Balcarres.

There is some dispute as to who actually commanded the rebel main battle. According to Wishart it was Glengarry and Lieutenant Colonel George Drummond of Balloch (Napier's nephew), assisted by the Quartermaster General, George Graham; but Ruthven explicitly takes issue with this, declaring that it was not Balloch but Inverey who commanded the main battle. The likeliest explanation for this disagreement is that Montrose did indeed appoint Glengarry and Balloch to command, but the Gordons, who comprised all but a handful of this division, would have none of it, and took their orders from Inverey who, as the late Monaltrie's cousin, was regarded as one of their own.[16]

The Battle

All the sources agree that the battle began with a clash between Lord Gordon's and the Earl of Balcarres' horse. Baillie may not have been all that keen on fighting, for he says he was 'necessitate to buckle with the enemie, who were a little above our strength in horsemen and twyse als strong in foot'.[17] What necessitated him to 'buckle' or fight he does not say, but there seems to have been a pretty widespread rumour current that he had been led into the fight against his will by Balcarres' forwardness.[18] Since we know that the rebels were at first for the most part concealed behind the skyline on the Gallowhill, and that Balcarres was on the left of the government forces (that is, to the south), it may be that he had pushed across the river at Mountgarrie rather too hastily; when it was realised that the whole rebel army was on top of the hill, he was too far committed to be able to withdraw safely, and Baillie had little option but to support him where he stood and accept battle.

Both sides then watched each other for a time, but the rebels eventually decided to take the initiative. There is a story that Lord Gordon, seeing his father's cattle penned up behind Baillie's men, uttered some appropriate threats and dashed off anticipating the order to advance. It is not however explained just how he recognised them, and Ruthven makes no mention of the story; furthermore, although he was indeed a very determined officer, he was also cool enough in action to hold his men together for successive charges, and such an action is rather out of character. We may therefore accept Wishart's version that he moved forward on Montrose's orders. Balcarres at once accepted the challenge, and likewise moved forward to meet him with his three squadrons, two up and a third in reserve.

The ensuing fight clearly lasted for some time. Lord Gordon's single squadron with the slope in their favour at first threw Balcarres back, but his second squadron then engaged the rebels, giving him time to rally the first and then drive Lord Gordon back. He in turn rallied, and Baillie himself ordered the third squadron (which was probably an Aberdeenshire one) to charge Lord Gordon in flank, but instead they merely moved up into the rear of Balcarres' forward squadrons, and the chance to rout the rebels was lost. Nevertheless Balcarres' third charge put Lord Gordon under considerable pressure from sheer weight of numbers, and his second in command, Nathaniel Gordon, had to order up Laghtman's Regiment, standing in reserve. They responded with alacrity to his order to abandon their muskets and hamstring the horses with their dirks, and as soon as they began Balcarres' men panicked and ran, after only ten or twelve horses had been lamed. What happened on Baillie's right is less clear, although the collapse was equally dramatic. Baillie was evidently preoccupied with his left and says nothing about events on this flank, while Ruthven's and Wishart's accounts are at first sight contradictory. The ultimate fate of Hackett's Regiment, however, suggests the answer.

Ruthven simply states that Aboyne charged and overthrew Baillie's right with much less difficulty than his brother encountered. Wishart, by contrast, says that Aboyne contented himself with skirmishing in small parties (presumably popping away with their pistols), until Balcarres' men fled, whereupon Hackett's did likewise without further ado. Wishart's version sounds rather more convincing, and as Hackett's men wavered and ran, Aboyne will certainly have put a charge in to complete their discomfiture. That Hackett's men did indeed misbehave as Wishart suggests is strongly indicated by the fact that just over a week later, on 10 July, Hackett's Regiment was ordered to be 'brokin, and addit as a recruet to the Lord Balcarras regiment'.[19]

With Baillie's cavalry routed, Montrose ordered his reserve forward, and the rebel main battle closed with the government centre commanded by Baillie himself and Lieutenant Colonel John Kennedy of Cassillis' Regiment.[20] Until now they had either held back deliberately, or more probably perhaps been held at bay by Baillie's stout veterans, but as the rebel cavalry and the Irish broke in on their flanks and rear, the end came. 'The Foot' says Wishart 'for some time fought on doggedly, refusing quarter, and they were almost all of them cut down'; but it was Baillie who pronounced their epitaph: 'Our foot stood with myselfe and behaved themselves as became them, untill the enemies horse charged in our reare, and in front we were overcharged with their foot'.[21]

Baillie's army was substantially destroyed. His foot accepted no quarter and the Irish offered none. Most of the cavalry got away, of course, though Balcarres' men seem to have been roughly handled, but the infantry suffered terribly. Only 100 each of Cassillis' and Glencairn's men survived to fight at Kilsyth a month and a half later. Callendar's missed Kilsyth, but their losses at Alford may have been even greater, for although Cassillis' and Glencairn's were each allocated 800 reinforcements at the beginning of August, Callendar's were allocated 850.[22] Elcho's, Lanark's and Moray's regiments were also substantially destroyed. In total, therefore, Baillie must have lost about 1,000 men, including the usual crowd of wounded, sick and deserters.

Rebel losses are as usual dismissed as insignificant, but notwithstanding Wishart's predictably ludicrous claim that Montrose lost not a single common soldier, there is every reason to believe that they may have been quite high, since as at Auldearn the government troops fought back long and hard. Fraser, for example, says that 'Baily was overthrown with the loss of the greatest part of his army, and a considerable losse upon Montrosse his side also'.[23] Ruthven gives only seven, but normally refers only to gentlemen slain and makes no mention of common soldiers. Those named as having been slain included the Lairds of Balwholly and Milton of Keith, both serving in Lord Gordon's Regiment. Significantly, perhaps, Lord Gordon's own squadron, 100 strong at the outset of the battle, was afterwards, under Nathaniel Gordon, only 80 strong. Most serious of the losses, however, was Lord Gordon himself, shot in the back as he led his cavalry into Baillie's rear. His death was a considerable blow to Montrose, both personally and as commander of the rebel forces, for his relationship with Aboyne, against whom he had fought in 1639, was never as cordial and was soon to become acrimonious. The wounded included George Douglas, Montrose's standard-bearer, Hay of Delgatie—who had commanded the Covenanters at Turriff in 1639—young Gight, and Nathaniel Gordon.[24]

THE INVASION OF THE LOWLANDS

After the battle the rebels, trailing some way behind the remnants of Baillie's army, moved eastwards to Cluny Castle, and next day turned south again to camp at Craigton, below the Hill o' Fare; and from there Montrose, Aboyne and a substantial part of the army repaired to Aberdeen for Lord Gordon's funeral in St. Machar's cathedral. Solemn occasion though it was, Montrose took the opportunity to discuss future operations with Aboyne and impress upon him the necessity of moving south to exploit the victory and relieve pressure upon the King, who had been badly beaten at Naseby in Northamptonshire a couple of weeks earlier. Aboyne agreed to support Montrose in this, but first insisted on raising more men. Only Lord Gordon's squadron, now commanded by Nathaniel Gordon, would accompany the army to provide it with some cavalry support, while the rest of the Gordon contingent returned home to recruit and recuperate. Montrose for his part agreed not to fight until such time as he was reinforced either by MacColla or Aboyne. Since he had, apart from Nathaniel Gordon's 80 troopers, only a few hundred Irish left now, this stipulation may seem a little unnecessary; but it is perhaps indicative of his subordinates' fear, not without reason, that he was inclined to rashness.

MacColla rejoined Montrose at Fordoun in the Mearns with no fewer than 1,400 men of the western clans, and a couple of hundred Athollmen under Inchbrackie. With these Montrose felt strong enough to push on further south to menace Perth, for he knew that as a result of plague in the capital (probably typhus) the parliament planned to meet there on 24 July. With a view to disrupting its proceedings, therefore, the rebels marched to Dunkeld and then south to Methven Wood, a little to the east of the city, from where they mounted a series of demonstrations for about a week. Since he was so short of cavalry, Montrose, in an attempt to intimidate Balcarres' Regiment, resorted to mounting 100 picked infantrymen 'with such horses as they could come by', to serve as dragooners and make a respectable show.[25] On 2 or 3 August however, Baillie, having been prodded none too gently into action, assembled an army at Bridge of Earn to the south of Perth, and then went after the rebels, though with only a limited success. As soon as the rebels saw him coming they quite literally headed for the hills. In an effort to catch them, Baillie sent Hurry, with Balcarres' Regiment, ahead, but afterwards alleged that Hurry was so slow in crossing the river that he himself was just as soon at the ford of Almond with the infantry. The only real result of this wretched affair was the slaughter of some rebel camp-followers left behind in Methven Wood, and Baillie's exasperated resignation on his return to Perth on 4 August.[26] This will be further discussed in the next chapter, but for the moment it is necessary only to note that he was prevailed upon to remain in command until Robert Monro could be fetched back from Ireland to take his place. Montrose, for his part, having safely returned to Dunkeld, sent urgently to Aboyne for assistance. Aboyne had by this time assembled 400 cavalry and at least 800 infantry; on receiving Montrose's letter he left the infantry to come on through the hills, and rode ahead with the cavalry to join Montrose.[27] Thus reinforced, the rebels pushed southwards again, though their ultimate objective is a little obscure.

In the face of this offensive Baillie retired again to the Bridge of Earn, and dug in there awaiting the arrival of an infantry brigade from Fife. It had been with him in his abortive push against Montrose at the beginning of the month, but had afterwards disbanded itself. On 11 August the rebels appeared before his trenches, but judging them too strong to be forced, had drawn off and pushed further south towards the Mills of Forth. Baillie appears to have had another row with his political masters at this point, probably because they wanted him to sally out and fight, but common sense prevailed and Baillie marched off in the opposite direction trying to find the missing brigade. At Lindores he learned that they were still at Cupar, and sending Crawford-Lindsay off to bring them in, rendezvoused with them at Rossie on the 13th, after which he marched hard for Stirling, halting for the night near Tullibody. On the 14th, having had confirmation that the rebels had crossed the Forth, Baillie marched across Stirling Bridge in pursuit.[28]

9

The Battle of Kilsyth,
15 August 1645

It is a part of the accumulation of legends surrounding this battle that the government forces were the unhappy victims of the incompetent interference of a political committee who habitually disregarded the sage advice of the military commander, General Baillie. The actual situation was rather more complex, and in considering it, Baillie's own wilful behaviour and its consequences must be examined, and the plain fact borne in mind that having twice been utterly defeated, he quite naturally sought afterwards to vindicate himself and lay the blame for those failures elsewhere. An antipathy towards those upon whom he attempted to shift the blame, evidenced by the numerous hagiographers of the great Montrose, has led to Baillie's version of events being accepted without question or real examination, but in fact there is considerable room in reading between the lines for doubting that he was telling the whole story.

William Baillie was appointed Lieutenant General of the army in Scotland on 8 March 1645 (though he had in fact been exercising command for some time previously). Since then he had attempted, with little success, to crush the rebels, and had himself been defeated by them at Alford on 2 July. Although subsequently exonerated by the government, he then resolved to lay down his commission. What happened next requires careful consideration. His 'dimission' was accepted, with the rider that he should continue in service until 8 September 1645. Now, the meaning of this rider could not be clearer: his resignation was accepted, but would not be effective until the beginning of September, since time was needed to bring his successor, Robert Monro, over from Ireland. He had, in other words, to serve out his notice. Furthermore, on the following day, 5 August 1645, it was enacted that: 'the directing of the Warre shall be by the Parliament, or Committee of Parliament; and the actual managing and executing of the directions to be by the Commander-in-chiefe, as he will be answerable to the Parliament or ther Committee'.[1]

This was hardly remarkable, and although subject to the directions of parliament, Baillie was evidently still intended to command the army in the field; but he instead chose to interpret matters quite differently. At first he refused to continue his command, claiming that since he had now resigned he had no commission:

> I would have refused, alleadging that whereas I was so overcharged with aspersions while I served them with a commission, if anything should now miscarry, I wanting commission, and serving as it were at discretion, my enemies would undoubtedly take occaision to charge me far more. This wes not satisfactorie to the Parliament; and my best friends did advyse me to condescend to the Parliament's desyre: which I did, more for their satisfaction than my owne.[2]

Although petulantly agreeing to remain in command, only for a further fortnight and not until 8 September as requested, Baillie wilfully refused actually to exercise any command independently, and it seems more than likely that he was saddled with the famous committee precisely because of his own intransigence. He is rather too careful in his narratives to note that every march made by the army thereafter was carried out in strict regard to the express wishes of the committee. At Stirling, though on the day before the battle, a furious altercation took place, which, although we have only Baillie's version of it, sheds some light on the actual state of affairs:

> the Marques of Argyle, Earle of Crawford, and Lord Burghlie, and with them, if I mistake not, the Earl of Tullibardine, the Lords Elcho and Balcarras, with some others came up. My Lord Marquess asked me what wes to be done? I answered, The direction should come from his lordship, and these of the Committee. My Lord demanded what reason wes for that? I answered, I found myself so slighted in everything belonging to ane commander-in-chiefe, that for the short time I wes to stay with them, I would absolutely submitt to ther direction and follow it. The Marquess desired me to explain myself, which I did in three particulars, sufficiently known to my Lord Marquess, and the other Lords and gentlemen then present. I told his Lordship, Prisoners of all sorts were exchanged without my knowledge: the traffickers therein received passes from others; and sometymes passing within two myles of me, did neither aquaint me with their business, nor at their returne, where, or in what posture they had left the enemie. Secondlie. While I wes present, others did sometymes undertake the command of the army. Thirdly, Without either my order or knowledge, fyre wes raised and that destroyed which might have been of ane recompence to some good deserver; for which I could not be answerable to the publique. Which considered I should in everything freely give my own opinion, but follow the judgement of the Committee.[3]

Baillie was undoubtedly ill-used, and the interference in his conduct of affairs considerable, but the fact remains that he only had himself to blame for it. Since he refused to march a step but by the express command of the committee, and evidently then did so with a bad grace, it is little wonder that they were bypassing him. Baillie was quite clearly sulking, and perhaps the worst consequence of his behaviour was that having spent ten days stridently asserting that he was not in charge of the army, and not responsible for its conduct, some of his own officers may have been beginning to believe him. Leaving aside for a moment the question of the actual responsibility for bringing on a battle on 15 August, one of the causes of the defeat of the government forces might be considered to have been the indiscipline of certain field officers, notably Colonel Home, the commander of the 'Irish' regiment, and Major John Haldane, who led the musketeer battalion. Neither officer had previously served under Baillie for any length of time, and both were probably quite unaware of the acute paranoia to which Baillie's narratives reveal him to have been subject. It is hard to escape the conclusion that their disobedience may perhaps be directly linked to a very real belief that Baillie was *not* in command. Having publicly declared that he was not in command, it is hardly surprising that when he did stir himself to issue orders, they were disobeyed or disregarded by some of his regimental commanders.

APPROACH MARCH

From Stirling the government forces marched to Denny, and then to the farm of Hollandbush, where they spent the night, four or five kilometres away from the rebels who were encamped at Kilsyth, on a high meadow overlooking the road.

The next day, 15 August 1645, Argyle came to Baillie's quarters and enquired of him where the rebels now were. Baillie replied that they were still at Kilsyth, and on next being asked whether the army should march closer to them, said that they were near enough already if they were not going to fight them. Since Baillie's scouts were obviously in contact with the rebels, this was true enough, and he at least was under the impression at this stage that the government forces were simply to continue shadowing them until a favourable opportunity arose, or they disappeared into the hills again. Argyle, on the other hand, seems to have been in favour of fighting. It is possible that Baillie's outburst at Stirling the day before, and continual refusal to act other than strictly in accordance with their orders, was goading the committee into *doing* something rather than give him the satisfaction of seeing them at a loss how to act. Most historians ascribe their decision to perversity, and condemn their eagerness to fight before the arrival of the Earl of

Lanark with a further 1,500 men raised in Clydesdale. Lanark is said to have been only hours away, but perhaps one of the most remarkable aspects of Baillie's evidence is the total lack of any reference to this force. Baillie's excuses for the defeat are many and varied, but at no time does he suggest that it could have been avoided by waiting for these reinforcements. Indeed it is hard to escape the conclusion from his silence upon the matter, that on the morning of 15 August 1645, Baillie and the committee were ignorant of the proximity of Lanark's men, and at no time considered them in their deliberations.

At any rate the committee, mindful of the danger of the rebels falling upon them if they stuck to the road, agreed to leave the 'hie-way' (now the A803) and march across country towards Kilsyth; and so Baillie accordingly 'marched with the regiments through the corns and over the braes, untill the unpassable ground did hold us up. There I imbattled, where I doubt if on any quarter twenty men on a front could either have gone from us or attack us'.[4]

So far the government forces had not committed any major errors in their pursuit of the rebels. The correct decision, lacking as they did any positive information as to the whereabouts of Lanark's force, was undoubtedly to maintain contact with the rebels. Now, however, in the presence of the enemy, decisions were taken which have ever since been roundly condemned by historians, not infrequently in tones of deep derision. What must now be considered are the circumstances in which the decisions were taken, what was decided, and what the actual consequences of those decisions were.

The accepted version of events is that having occupied an excellent position overlooking the rebels in the meadow, Baillie wished to avoid fighting until Lanark arrived. Argyle and the committee over-ruled him, and insisted that the army should march off to the right in order to outflank the rebels. As a result the government forces committed the cardinal sin of embarking upon a flank march in full view of the enemy, were in turn attacked in flank by the rebels, and paid the inevitable price for their incompetence.

The actual circumstances and ensuing course of events were very different. Baillie had halted the army immediately to the east of the high ground, probably along the line of the present road running from the modern village of Banton to the A803 at Kelvinhead. Although he must obviously have had scouts out on the skyline, it is clear from Baillie's narrative that the army was halted on the reverse slope, for he states that after embattling he galloped over the brae to look at the rebels. Baillie is quite positive that it was impossible to advance further, and equally impossible to be attacked there, and even a cursory examination of the ground will bear out his opinion. Part of the meadow is now flooded by a reservoir (built in connection with the Forth and

Clyde canal), but the intervening ground, conveniently traversed now by a minor road running west from Banton to the A803, is extremely rough and broken by large hummocks. Presumably, before the reservoir was created, it also became much steeper towards the meadow. In short it was no place to fight a battle, and with the army halted behind it, the committee came up to Baillie and suggested that they should draw the army up 'on the hill on the right hand'.

In order to show what happened, one must again turn to Baillie's narrative:

> At the upcoming of the noblemen and others of the Committee, whom I dow not so weell remember, It was asked of me by the Lords, but by whom in particular I have forgott, If we could not draw up to the hill on our right hand? I shew them I did not conceive that ground to be good, and that the rebels (if they would) might possess themselves of it before us. Their Lordships then desired that some might be sent to visit the ground; which was done. In the meantime I went with my Lord Elcho and Burghlie to the right hand of the regiments. Not long after, I wes sent for by the other noblemen, and I desired the Lord Elcho and Burghlie to go with me, conjecturing they would press our removing; which at our coming they did, alleadging the advantage might be had of the enemies from that field, they being, as they supposed, allready upon their march westward. I liked not the motion: I told them, if the rebels should seek to engage us there I conceaved they should have great advantage of us; farder if we should beat them to the hill, it would be unto us no great advantage: But, as I had said upon like disputes near unto Methven and the Bridge of Earn to us the loss of the day would be the loss of the Kingdome. This wes not satisfactorie: and therefore I gathered the voices of such of the Committee as were there, namely the Marquess Argyle, the Earles of Crawford and Tullibardine, the Lords Elcho, Burghlie and Balcarras; who the rest were I remember not; but all agreed to draw unto the hill except Balcarras. This resolution wes immediately followed.[5]

It is clear therefore that although Baillie had serious misgivings about the move they centred around his concern that the rebels might get to the hill before them and so meet the government forces in a position of some strength. Baillie was not concerned about abandoning a perfectly good position, since he had not actually occupied one, and he was not keen to await the arrival of Lanark's men since he did not know of their approach. The choice was therefore both necessary and straightforward. The government forces could march no further upon their present course. The rebels had chosen an excellent position for their camp, the government forces would find it quite impractical to assault from the east and a southward move would expose them to the very attack from the high meadow which they had sought to avoid by moving across country. They might of course remain in their present position until the rebels decamped, and then follow after them at a safe

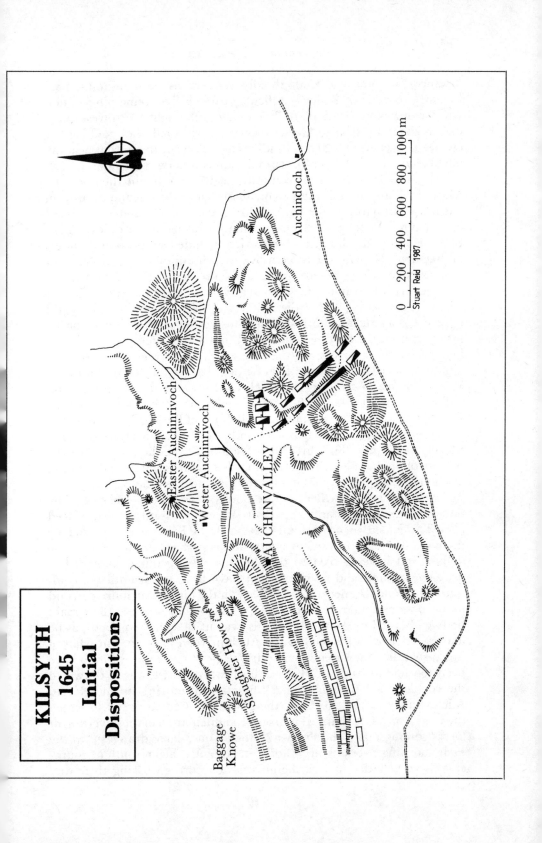

KILSYTH
1645
Initial
Dispositions

N

Easter Auchinrivoch

Wester Auchinrivoch

AUCHINVALLEY

Baggage
Knowe

Slaughter Howe

Auchindoch

0   200   400   600   800   1000 m

Stuart Reid 1987

THE CAMPAIGNS OF MONTROSE

distance, but this was undoubtedly rejected as pusillanimous, particularly in view of Baillie's difficult attitude. The remaining option was the one actually adopted. By moving to the right, northwest to the hill on which Easter and Wester Auchinrivoch stood, they could either engage the rebels at less of a disadvantage, prevent them from heading north again, or at the very least maintain contact with them.

In accordance with the committee's decision, Baillie then ordered Major Haldane and his musketeers to march to the hill and occupy an enclosure, probably at Wester Auchinrivoch, which he actually pointed out to him. As they were able to march rather more quickly than Baillie's other battalions, each of which included substantial numbers of pikemen, this was a sensible move, which afforded the government forces a good chance of seizing the hill before the rebels. Baillie himself, together with Balcarres and the cavalry, marched in support, having given orders for the rest of the infantry to follow them. This they did by every man turning to his right, thus converting the line of battle into a column. It must be emphasised that at this point they could *not* be seen by the rebels, since they were still on the reverse slope, but almost at once things started to go wrong. Baillie decided that it might be a good idea to see what the rebels were up to in the meantime, and telling Balcarres to stay with the musketeers, he left him and joined the Earl of Crawford-Lindsay and Lord Balfour of Burleigh, who together with some other gentlemen and a number of musketeers were standing higher up the hill. The three then 'galloped over the brae to see the posture of the enemie, who were embattled in the meadow and sundries of them disbanded were falling up the glen through the bushes'.[6]

Whatever their earlier intentions may have been the rebels had by now determined to stand and fight. Whether Montrose had indeed always intended to bring Baillie to battle at Kilsyth, or whether he merely found it a convenient camp-site, is perhaps a matter for some debate, but it seems likeliest that he was playing things by ear. The decision to stand and fight may not have been taken until the committee's reconnaissance party was seen on the hill by Auchinrivoch and its purpose correctly divined. Since Baillie could now see their main body embattled in the meadow, it is evident that they were not, as he had feared, racing his men to the Auchinrivoch position. But what of the 'disbanded' men seen moving up the glen? Since they seem to have been too few to frustrate Baillie's northward thrust, one is drawn to the conclusion that their primary function in moving up the glen to Auchinvalley was not to block the government advance but to screen the rebel army as it changed its front. In anticipation of the government forces coming down the 'hie-way', they would have drawn up in the early morning overlooking it and consequently facing south or southeast. Now in order to face the government forces working their way round to the north, it will have been necessary to turn their line through 90 degrees in order to face north-east. With an army very largely comprised of irregulars this is unlikely to have been a smooth operation, and although no rebel chronicler directly alludes to it, Ruthven does hint at a certain confusion. Furthermore it is probable that the bustle of this manoeuvre was what had led the committee to believe that the rebels were preparing to march off once more. At any rate, with the fighting about to begin, it is necessary to examine the dispositions of the two armies.

THE ARMIES

One of the most striking things revealed by Baillie's narratives is just how weak the government forces were. Baillie states quite categorically that he had but five regiments of regular infantry under his command. They can be identified as follows: the Marquis of Argyle's Regiment, the Earl of Crawford-Lindsay's, Colonel Robert Home's, the Earl of Lauderdale's and 'three that were joyned in one'. The last, 300 strong, comprised the remnants of three regiments earlier destroyed by the rebels: the Earl of Cassillis' Regiment and the Earl of Glencairn's, both of whom had served at Alford, and the Earl of Loudon's Regiment which had been at Auldearn. This battalion was probably commanded by Lieutenant Colonel John Kennedy of Cassillis' Regiment. Before the battle began a sixth was formed under Major John Haldane of the Earl of Loudon's Regiment, comprising musketeers commanded out of each of the others. With the exception of Home's, still over 1,000 strong, all had previously served in England—two of them at Marston Moor— and were by no means raw militia. In contrast to these veterans, however, the three regiments recovered in Fife can have inspired little confidence. They were commanded by Sir Thomas Morton of Cambo, Colonel James Arnott of Ferny and Colonel John Henderson of Fordell. The first had been raised in February 1645, and Henderson's Regiment may have been raised at the same time (if it were not that formerly commanded by Lord Elcho). Ruthven reckons this brigade to have totalled 2,000 men, but given that they had all run away only a short time before, something like half that number is probably more realistic. The average strength of Baillie's other regiments will have been around 400 men apiece, although Argyle's, mauled at Inverlochy, was a small regiment, and may have accounted for only 300.

In total therefore, on the morning of 15 August 1645, Baillie had something in the region of 3,000 to 3,500 infantry.

His cavalry was even weaker, and we have clear testimony that

141

only two units were present. The Earl of Balcarres' Regiment will have mustered no more than 300 troopers. Both his and Hackett's regiments had mustered a total of 260 men at Alford. If we take their combined losses there to have been in the region of 60 to all causes, then once the 100 men who had been with Crawford-Lindsay are added to the combined regiment, it will have totalled no more than 300. They were, it seems, divided into two troops, one armed with pistols, the other with lances. Colonel Harie Barclay's Regiment was newly commissioned and as yet incomplete. According to Baillie only 60 troopers were present under Lieutenant Colonel Mungo Murray, and there is indeed no evidence that Barclay was himself present. 360 troopers is very much less than Baillie is usually credited with; Ruthven, for example, blithely adds 500 horse to the Fife contingent, but Baillie himself makes no mention of them, and indeed is quite emphatic that only Balcarres' and Barclay's regiments were with him.

In addition Baillie also had three field pieces, including one, named 'Prince Robert', which had been captured from the cavaliers at Marston Moor, but he had no opportunity to use them.[8]

The rebel army was very much a mixed bag. Numbers are rather vague, since rebel chroniclers tend to speak in round figures, and a certain devaluation may therefore be prudent. There were three regiments of Irish regulars present: Thomas Laghtman's, Colonel Manus O'Cahan's and Colonel James McDonnell's. Shortly after the battle, MacColla took 120 of them off with him to the west coast to serve as his lifeguard, leaving Montrose with only 500 Irish in all, so given that they are unlikely to have suffered many casualties at Kilsyth it is evident that the entire brigade mustered not much more than 600 men on 15 August.[9] The rebels' main body was comprised of highlanders: 1,400 of the western clans and 200 Athollmen. This comes to a total of 2,200 men, which is rather lower than even the rebel chroniclers allow, and it is evident that sometime between 10 August and the 15th, the Gordon Foot had joined the army.[10] They may most probably be identified as the Strathbogie Regiment, accounting for half of them, and Inverey's and Minimore's highlanders accounting for the rest. As at Alford they were probably commanded in chief by Inverey.

The rebels therefore disposed of some 3,000 infantrymen, which was perhaps comparable with Baillie's army, although only a third of them were regulars. As to cavalry, however, the rebels considerably outnumbered the government forces. Most were Gordons, 400 by Ruthven's reckoning, but even if this total included the 120 dragooners mentioned by Wishart, then added to Nathaniel Gordon's 80 troopers they will alone have sufficed to match the government cavalry sword for sword—and at least a third of them were regulars, survivors of Lord Gordon's old regiment. In addition to these 360 troopers, however, the

THE BATTLE OF KILSYTH

Earl of Airlie brought in a further 80 troopers, giving the rebels a clear advantage in numbers—440, besides a body of dragooners. Aboyne, as mentioned, had brought 120, and there may in addition still have been the 100 Irish dragooners mounted by Montrose for his demonstrations against Perth, which could have given the rebels over 600 cavalry. This rebel superiority in cavalry was to have a crucial effect on the outcome of the battle, and indeed was clearly stated to have done so by Ruthven and admitted by Baillie; but Gardiner, and subsequent biographers of Montrose, mesmerised by the romantic vision of his noble Caledonian savages, have dismissed this claim, quite unjustly, as merely a piece of pro-Gordon propaganda.[11]

It is difficult to be precise as to how the rebels were drawn up, since a certain amount of confusion seems to have reigned. The government forces' thrust to the north may have caused a lot more problems for the rebels than they afterwards admitted. Baillie's own account seems to suggest that all or most of the front line was comprised of highlanders, and certainly as will be seen he was involved in some heavy fighting with elements of the western clans. The Gordon Foot and the Irish are not at all easy to place, and it seems likely that they were somewhere behind MacColla's highlanders. They were probably later responsible for the destruction of the Fife regiments. Indeed the main impression gained from the various accounts is that the rebels had not formed a main fighting line at all, but fed units into the fight as soon as they could be brought up. This was particularly true of the cavalry, and again tends to confirm that the rebels were indeed outflanked by Baillie.

Before commencing their march to the right the government forces were drawn up as follows: on the extreme right was Haldane's musketeer battalion and both the cavalry regiments under Balcarres. Next came the Earl of Lauderdale's Foot, then Colonel Home's and then Argyle's. Owing to lack of space Crawford-Lindsay's and the 'three joyned in one' were probably flanking the three Fife regiments placed in reserve, although they were soon to move forward into the main fighting line.

BATTLE JOINED

Baillie was afterwards in no doubt whatsoever that the responsibility for all that happened next lay squarely with Major John Haldane. Seeing the 'disbanded' highlanders, a party of Macleans under Captain Ewan Maclean of Treshnish (a deserter from Argyle's highland regiment), filtering into the enclosures at Auchinvalley, he suddenly chose to disregard his orders and instead of pressing on to Auchinrivoch he turned to his left and launched a hasty attack on the rebels. Why he did this has never been made clear. Most modern accounts of the battle

143

assume that Haldane and his men were a covering force protecting the flank of Baillie's army, but instead, as we have seen, Haldane was actually out in front leading the way, and this deviation is at first sight therefore all the more inexcusable. He had been given command of this battalion of lightly equipped musketeers with the express purpose of racing to Auchinrivoch and seizing that position before the rebels; yet, clear though his orders may have been on this point, one wonders if they were quite so unambiguous as Baillie implies. When he entrusted Haldane with his task, Baillie will certainly have impressed upon him the necessity of denying the position to the rebels, but now, seeing the weakness of Treshnish's party, Haldane may have decided that he could attain this primary objective better by turning aside and engaging the threat head on. He may also have been worried about the threat of a running fight developing, or even the rebels beating him to the hill, and preferred to take his chances there and then.

Baillie, whatever Haldane's reasoning, was horrified: 'we saw Major Halden leading up ane partie of musqueteers over the field, and towards a house near the glen, without any order from me; neither did they come off when I sent Colonel Arnott and thereafter Routmaster Blair, to Major Halden for that purpose.'[12]

In fairness to Haldane, disengagement under fire is never easy, particularly when the enemy is being reinforced: for Glengarry's men, and after him MacColla with the rest of the western clans, hurried up to Treshnish's aid. At the moment Major Haldane abruptly decided to attack Treshnish, neither side was really in much of a posture to begin the battle. The rest of the government forces were still standing on the reverse slope, still out of sight of the rebels, and before he could bring them into action Baillie had to move them clear of the 'unpassible ground'. That he did so, rather than ordering a frontal attack from their present position, clearly illustrates both the fact that the ridge was a bad position and that the government forces were not assailed in flank while on the march as popular legend has it. Once again Baillie's own narrative is instructive, not only in describing what happened next with a clarity lacking amongst most rebel chroniclers, but also in conveying a little of the excitement and confusion as the government forces moved into the attack. The resultant picture is a very different one from that generally accepted:

> seeing the rebels fall up strong I desired them (the Lords) to reteire, and the officers to goe to their charge. My Lord Balcarras and I galloped back to the regiments. He asked me what he should doe? I desired him to draw up his regiment on the right hand of the Earl of Lauderdale's. I gave order to Lauderdale's both by myselfe and my adjutant, to face to the right hand, and to march to the foot of the hill, then to face as they were; to Hume to follow their steps, halt when they halted, and keep distance and front with

them. The Marquess his Major, as I went toward him, asked what he should doe? I told him, he should draw up on Hume's left hand, as he had done before. I had not ridden farr from him, when looking back, I find Hume had left the way I put him in, and wes gone at a trott, right west, in among the dykes and toward the enemy.[13]

Baillie's feelings at this point may be imagined. First his attempt to seize the Auchinrivoch position as directed by the committee had been frustrated by the disobedience of one subordinate, now another was compounding the error by launching another unauthorised and uncoordinated attack, completely disrupting his planned orderly deployment. The reason for Home's attack has received even less attention than Haldane's, and most historians, taking their cue from Wishart, seem unaware that it took place at all and describe the subsequent fighting as taking place up on the ridge, claiming that MacColla's highlanders overran Haldane's battalion and then swept on and up to engage the main body. Baillie's account makes a nonsense of such a reconstruction. Home had under his command the strongest regiment on the field, amounting in numbers to a whole brigade. Although their political reliability may have been a little suspect, and they had not yet actually had the opportunity to fight against Scots rebels, they had long been accustomed to beating the Irish ones, and so undoubtedly held those now ranged against them in some contempt. Haldane, it hardly need be said, was in trouble, and it may have seemed to Home that his regiment was quite adequate for the purpose of extricating Haldane's men or even reinforcing them in a counter-attack. In this he was at first able to make some progress, and established a lodgement in the nearer enclosure, supported by two other regiments who had followed in his wake. As more and more rebels flooded into the top end of the enclosures, however, the advance was abruptly halted, and Baillie attempted to re-assert some control:

I followed alse fast as I could ride, and meeting the Adjutant on the way, desired him he should bring up the Earl of Crafurd's regiment to Lauderdale's left hand, and cause the Generall-Major Leslie draw up the regiments of Fyfe in reserve as of before; but before I could come to Hume, he and the other two regiments, to wit, the Marquess of Argyles and the three that were joyned in one, had taken in an enclosure, from whilk (the enemy being so neer) it wes impossible to bring them off. I rode down on the reere, and returned on their front.[14]

With the rebels fast approaching, the government army was now drawn up in three distinct bodies. Under Baillie's command amongst the enclosures by Auchinvalley were some 1,600 infantrymen, faced by a similar number of highlanders led by MacColla. Behind them and to the right were a further 800 infantry under Major General Holburn,

145

and Balcarres' 360 cavalry, while, probably somewhere to the left rear, were the Fife levies under Major General Leslie. Baillie's account of the ensuing events is somewhat telescoped, but it is necessary to introduce it now in order to clarify certain points:

> The rebels foot, by this time, were approached the next dyke, on whom our musqueteers made more fire than I could have wished; and therefore I did what I could, with the assistance of such of the officers as were known unto me, to make them spare their shott till the enemy should be at a nearer distance, and to keep up the musqueteers with their pickes and collors; but to no great purpose.[15]

Baillie then goes on to relate how the highlanders 'in the end' leaped over the dykes and fell upon his men, but it is evident both from that qualification and from the adventures which befell Aboyne, that the allegedly irresistible onrush of the highlanders was halted in its tracks by the enclosure walls, and by the heavy fire directed at them by the government forces. Had the highlanders been allowed a clear run at them, they might have come on sooner, but as it was they hesitated to climb the walls in the teeth of the storm of musketry directed at them by the soldiers. It is not unlikely that few of the highlanders were actually shot at this stage; they were behind a stone wall, and if the regulars were firing fast they were probably firing high; but is always difficult to resume an advance stalled behind solid cover, even when disciplined troops are involved. Not to put too fine a point on it, the famous highland charge had been stopped in its tracks, and the government forces were for the moment holding their ground.

On Baillie's right, on the other hand, fortunes were rather more mixed. Balcarres was it seems trying still to make for Auchinrivoch, but with his infantry trailing behind or distracted by the fighting below Auchinvalley, he was hit, and according to Ruthven driven back by a small body of rebel cavalry led by Captain Adjutant Gordon (possibly John Gordon of Littlemill).[16]

Initially Gordon was successful in driving Balcarres' cavalry back in amongst his infantry, but once there and unsupported by any of their own infantry, the rebels were surrounded and soon in trouble. Perceiving this, Aboyne, who had been left out of harm's way in the rear, resolved to go to his men's assistance. First sending to Nathaniel Gordon and to Montrose for support, he immediately, with his small lifeguard, rode towards the fighting. Although Baillie makes no mention of the incident, understandably being preoccupied with more serious matters, it is evident that Aboyne and his men actually rode between the highlanders in the enclosures and Baillie's men. Indeed, sheering away from Balcarres' lancer troop, they collided briefly with the pikemen of Home's Regiment, and then some of the flanking

146

musketeers. Ruthven was afterwards in no doubt that Home's was the regiment concerned, for he quite categorically refers to them as the 'reid regiment'.[17] This is extremely important, for it shows that, at the moment the Gordons on the rebel left were on the point of being overwhelmed, the highlanders in their centre still had not advanced into physical contact with Baillie's men. Battered by three successive discharges of musketry from the redcoats, Aboyne finally made contact with the Adjutant's men, rallied them, and doubtless after a suitable pause, renewed the fight. Ruthven loyally suggests that his efforts alone were sufficient to defeat Balcarres' men, but on the contrary, if place-names are to be relied upon, they were driven back up on to Slaughter Howe by Balcarres. The arrival of the rest of the rebel cavalry under Nathaniel Gordon and the Earl of Airlie was the decisive factor; Balcarres' cavalry were routed and the rebels swept on towards Holburn's infantry. The crisis was thus averted, and encouraged by this success the highlanders at last nerved themselves to climb the wall. Ironically they may also have been encouraged by a slackening off in fire, as Baillie and his officers brought it under control.

The end was evidently quite dramatic, for according to Baillie: 'In the end the rebells leapt over the dyke, and with downe heads fell on and broke these regiments'. There was but a short resistance, and afterwards Baillie recalled the end of these regiments:

> The present officers whom I remember were Home, his Lieutenant Colonel and Major of the Marquess's regiment, Lieutenant Colonel Campbell, and Major Menzies, Glencairne's sergeant Major, and Cassills's Lieutenant Colonell with sundry others who behaved themselves well, and whom I saw none carefull to save themselves before the routing of the regiments. Thereafter I rode to the brae, where I found Generall Major Hollburne alone, who shew me a squadron of the rebells horsemen, who had gone by and charged the horsemen with Lieutenant-Colonell Murray and, as I supposed, did afterward rowt the Earle of Crawfurd, and these with him.[18]

The reference to the Earl of Crawford-Lindsay 'and these with him' is interesting, for it indicates that his and Lauderdale's regiments may have been retiring in good order when the rebels—Airlie's troop, according to Ruthven—fell upon them. The remainder of the rebel cavalry meanwhile participated in the destruction of Home's regiment.

With all going to pot Baillie looked desperately around him for reinforcements: 'Hollburne and I galloped through the inclosures to have found the reserve; bot before we could come at them, they were in flight.'

The immediate implication is that the raw Fife levies simply ran away when they saw the front line broken, but as we have seen they may not have been quite so raw after all, and while we have a pretty good idea as to what the highlanders did, there is very little said as to

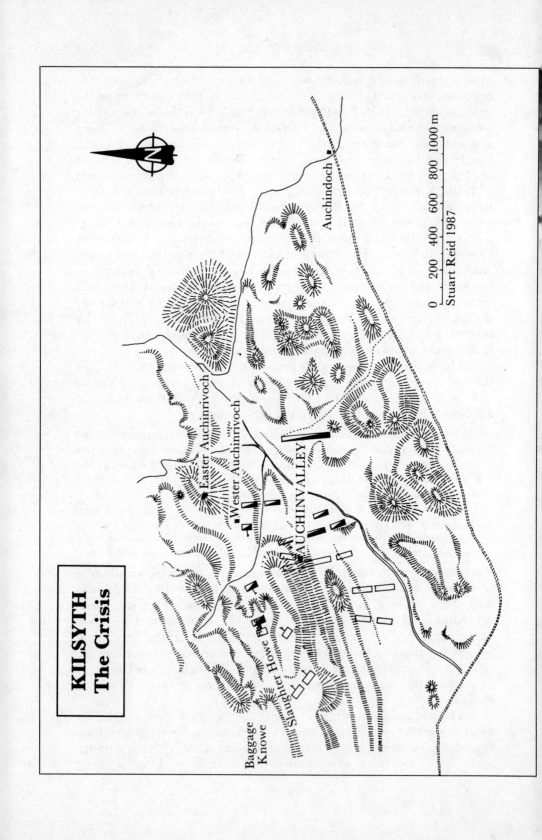

KILSYTH
The Crisis

Baggage
Knowe

Slaughter Howe

AUCHINVALLEY

Easter Auchinrivoch

Wester Auchinrivoch

Auchindoch

N

Stuart Reid 1987

0   200   400   600   800   1000 m

what the Irish and the Gordon infantry did during the battle, and it seems likely that Inverey led them against the Fife regiments. How much of a fight the levies put up will probably never be known—had it been considerable the rebels would surely have noted their prowess in overcoming it—but Baillie provides a hint in replying to the charge that his men were so unprepared that they had not even lit their slow match:

> The fire given by the first five regiments will sufficiently answer what concerns them: and for the other three, I humbly intreat your Honours to inform yourselves of Generall-Major Leslie, the adjutant, and the chief officers of these severall regiments: if they doe not satisfie yow therein, then I shall answer for myself.[19]

Whatever their resistance, it proved unavailing, and having once broken they could not be rallied again despite all the efforts of Baillie and his officers. He and Holburn overtook Major Inglis and some of the Fife officers and tried to halt their men at the 'brook', which must be the stream which crosses the A803 at Auchincloch, 'bot all in vaine'. The mounted officers then retired to the Bridge of Denny and from there went their separate ways. Baillie and Holburn rode for their part to Stirling, where a fresh attempt was made to rally the fugitives. Naturally the cavalry, who had been chased as far as Falkirk, were the first to arrive; but although relatively unscathed they were badly shaken, and refused to follow Baillie into Clydesdale, so he instead settled for securing Stirling.

Being mounted it was relatively easy for the government cavalry to escape from the battlefield, but in order to complete this re-assessment of the battle of Kilsyth it is necessary to examine the fate of Baillie's infantry, and in particular to challenge the assumption that nearly all of them were slain.

As with the fate of Campbell of Lawers' Regiment at Auldearn, the popular tale that all or most of them perished does not stand up under close examination. A considerable number of officers at least are known to have survived, and not all of them can have been mounted. Argyle's Regiment, allocated reinforcements from Dunbartonshire in October and November 1645, was in sufficiently good shape to be sent into England after Montrose's defeat at Philiphaugh. Baillie himself mentions a Captain Ludovick Maitland of Lauderdale's Regiment, who with Major Inglis of the same accompanied him to Stirling, and the regiment had certainly recovered by the following year. Oddly enough its Lieutenant Colonel at Kilsyth, Colin Pitscottie, was to command a brigade of highlanders at Worcester in 1651 which included MacDonalds and MacLeans. The Earl of Cassillis' Regiment is unlikely to have mustered more than 100 men at Kilsyth, yet enough of them remained afterwards to provide a sufficient nucleus for new recruits, and it was preparing to return to England in November. The survivors of Alford were obviously a hardy lot. Glencairn's Regiment too survived the battle, although equally weak. A petition by the survivors stated that most of the officers had been slain at Alford and Kilsyth, but enough of them still remained to have Robert Cunningham appointed Colonel over them. Loudon's, the third of the under-strength units, also survived, and was not disbanded until the formation of the Scots new model army in 1647. Haldane was appointed Lieutenant Colonel then to Colonel Walter Scott.[20]

Baillie's army was destroyed, but not massacred, and Stirling was not to be taken.

10

The Government Counter-Attack: Philiphaugh 13 September 1645

The battle of Kilsyth was followed by something not unlike a stunned silence. The rebels remained there for two days, which rather argues for their not having emerged unscathed from what was by most accounts some very heavy fighting, but their subsequent advance on Glasgow was unopposed save by political considerations. The remains of Baillie's army had taken refuge in Stirling, and although the rebels at no time appear to have contemplated going after it, it would clearly be out of action for the forseeable future. Baillie had hoped to take the cavalry into Clydesdale with a view to joining with Lanark's forces, but they refused to go, and Lanark, left unsupported, fled to Berwick. His regiments however must have retired into upper Clydesdale, for they were certainly still in existence the following month (and indeed subsequently served in England), and Sir John Browne was awarded £100 sterling on 30 October 'In thankful remembrance of [his] good service with his dragoons against the rebels since 15th August last'.[1] Other than Lanark's regiments however, the government, itself scattered to the four winds, had no forces remaining in the field in Scotland, and no resistance could be made either to a rebel cavalry raid on Edinburgh (the Castle, however, stoutly held out) led by Nathaniel Gordon and Lord Napier, or to a rather larger scale raid on Kilmarnock and the Ayrshire coast led by MacColla.

Paradoxically though, both raids contributed to the break-up of the rebel army. Montrose had withdrawn almost at once from Glasgow and established a camp at Bothwell, and in MacColla's absence the clans, already unhappy at being denied the sack of Glasgow and the non-appearance of the 'storm-money' promised in lieu, had been growing increasingly restless and had been steadily deserting. Indeed it would appear that most of them had gone by the time MacColla returned, and on 2 or 3 September the last of them departed for the west coast led by MacColla himself and Sir James Lamont, who had been commissioned by Montrose to raise Cowal for the King. MacColla (knighted by Montrose on either 18 August or 2 September) also took off with him 120 of the best of the Irish to serve as his lifeguard. Although the Irish were of course his to command, in as much as he was their brigade commander, this marked the beginning of a new status for the Irish, serving not in their original, now much reduced regiments, but in small mercenary bands. No sooner had the high-landers gone but the Gordons departed also, although the reasons for their going were rather more complex. In the first place, Aboyne had received word from his father, now returned to Strathbogie, ordering him to return to the north-east, and his men were only too eager to go with him since their homes had been left unprotected against the indefatigable northern Covenanters; secondly, Aboyne was himself very unhappy about the publication of an account of the campaign written by Sir William Rollo, which made scant mention of the important contribution made by the Gordon contingent to the rebel victory; but the final straw was the appointment of the Earl of Crawford to command the rebel cavalry.

Crawford had been languishing in the Edinburgh Tolbooth since his capture at the fall of Newcastle Upon Tyne at the end of October 1644, but along with a considerable number of others, including the elder Gight, Sir Alexander Gordon of Cluny and Airlie's eldest son, Lord Ogilvy, he had been released during the rebel raid on the capital in late August. His appointment as commander of the rebel cavalry should not, with a little tact, have proved overly objectionable, and had much to recommend it. Although his career had to date been undistinguished if not a little unfortunate, he was an experienced cavalry officer; and with Lord Gordon dead at Alford, Montrose, with hundreds of cavalry recruits expected from the borders, needed a competent brigade commander for his cavalry. The appointment however was very badly timed, being made when the rebel cavalry still only comprised Aboyne's Regiment and Airlie's Troop, and Aboyne in consequence, perhaps not unnaturally, took it as a personal affront. The result was that at the end of the first day's march after abandoning the camp at Bothwell, Aboyne took his leave of Montrose at Calder Castle, and retired homewards accompanied by all his men, horse and foot, save for Colonel Nathaniel Gordon's Troop.

This left Montrose with only 500 Irish infantry, and not much more than 100 or so cavalry led by Airlie and Nathaniel Gordon. He had of course been reduced to less men than this in the past, but then had never marched far from the hills; now he was in the far from friendly lowlands, and having summoned a parliament to meet at Glasgow on 20 October was politically committed to remaining there. It was therefore all the more imperative to gather in the men promised by the Marquis of Douglas and other of the border Earls; and still avoiding plague-stricken Edinburgh, the rebels turned south from Dalkeith on 6 September, bent upon a rendezvous at Galashiels. Douglas met them there on the 7th with around 1,000 troopers, but there was, ominously, no response from the Earls of Home and Roxburgh at Kelso the next day. With the exception of Douglas, all the noblemen who had turned up were only the sons of lords, their sires having prudently remained at home. Montrose nonetheless cannot have been too disappointed by the accession of more cavalry than he had ever commanded before, but at the same time must have been only too well aware that it was still far too small a force with which to take on David Leslie's army, which, he must by this time have been aware, had returned to Scotland.

Leslie in fact crossed the border at Berwick on 6 September with at least four regiments of infantry and six regiments of cavalry. His first objective appears to have been the relief of Edinburgh, for he stuck by the coast all the way to Gladsmuir in East Lothian, halfway between Tranent and Haddington, which he reached late on 11 September. There he received word, traditionally from the Earl of Traquair, that the rebels were still lurking to the south of him, and immediately set off after them, leaving most of his infantry behind in order to march the faster.

The rebels were at Jedburgh on the 10th or 11th,[2] but afterwards began marching westwards, probably with the intention of swinging clear of Leslie's men, still thought to be in the Edinburgh area, and eventually returning to the north. The following afternoon, 12 September, the rebels marched into Selkirk, and while some of the cavalry quartered in the burgh itself, most of them bivouacked on the levels of Philiphaugh, and the foot were quartered in a wood.[3] There then followed a characteristic failure of intelligence by the rebels which on this occasion proved catastrophic. Ogilvy of Powrie, whom Spalding had described in 1639 as a 'strong Covenanter',[4] was sent out with a small party of horse on a clearance patrol, but returned before nightfall with the happy news that there was not an enemy within ten miles. In so reporting, Powrie clearly failed in his duty, and Ruthven admits that he simply asked the country people if they had seen anything of Leslie's men.[5] Not surprisingly they told him nothing of the government forces, who were by this time actually only a short distance away, and later that night an even more serious failure took place which was inexcusable. A rebel officer, Charteris of Amisfield, and his troop, were actually surprised in their quarters by some of Leslie's men at the small village of Sunderland about five kilometres north of Selkirk. Presumably they had been posted there as a standing patrol, but since the survivors— only Amisfield himself and two or three of his men escaped—were

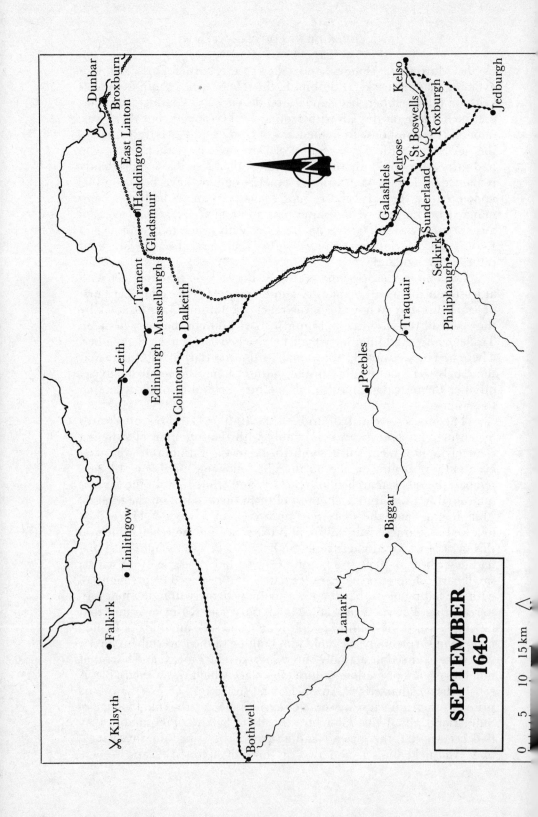

SEPTEMBER
1645

0   5   10   15km

Dunbar
Broxburn
East Linton
Haddington
Tranent
Gladsmuir
Musselburgh
Edinburgh
Leith
Dalkeith
Colinton
Linlithgow
Falkirk
Kilsyth
Bothwell
Lanark
Biggar
Peebles
Traquair
Galashiels
Melrose
Sunderland
Selkirk
Philiphaugh
St Boswells
Kelso
Roxburgh
Jedburgh

assumed to have been involved in some sort of drunken brawl, it may fairly be assumed that far from keeping a good watch they had given themselves over to carousing. Their report that Leslie's men were at hand was therefore dismissed as an alcoholic fantasy, and no action was taken, although Leslie's men stood to arms all night and presumed the rebels to have done likewise.[6] It is possible that Montrose wilfully refused to believe that Leslie could be so close, but one would have thought a drunk and incapable picquet to be a serious enough matter in itself: the lack of action taken suggests that such a state of affairs was far from uncommon amongst the rebels.

Having thus dealt with Amisfield's men, it is then suggested in some reconstructions that Leslie spent the rest of the night at Sunderland before advancing again next morning, but it seems rather unlikely that they should have remained there after having, as they not unreasonably supposed, alerted the rebels. No location is in fact given in any of the government accounts of the action, save that they were a few miles off from the rebels (and certainly not sleeping in Melrose as at one time used to be believed). In any case government sources make it clear that it was only a detachment which did for Amisfield's picquet. Wishart again merely says that Leslie spent the night 'four miles from Selkirk', but Ruthven, while agreeing, also gives the crucial information that Leslie's men lay hidden 'invironed with woodes in a deep wallay',[7] which rather suggests the valley of the Tweed between Linglie Hill and Meigle Hill, just a little upstream from its confluence with the Ettrick.

The course of events the following morning is by no means straightforward, and before considering them the composition of the government forces might usefully be described.

Leslie's army can be reconstructed with a fair degree of accuracy, through the government's generosity in awarding a bounty of a month's pay to the regiments which fought there, so great was their relief at the victory. (This generosity did not extend to a prompt payment of the bounty, and the veterans had to wait until their regiments were disbanded at the beginning of 1647 before receiving it, and even then were only paid at the prevailing rate, which was some 25% less than in 1645.) From the sums disbursed to each individual regiment, it is possible to establish not only which units were present, but also to arrive at a pretty close estimate of their strength on the morning of 13 September 1645.[8]

The Earl of Leven's, David Leslie's and John Middleton's regiments between them mustered something in the region of 1,500 troopers. To judge from muster reports of the following January, the first two had something like 550 apiece, while Middleton's had only about 400. Lord Kirkcudbright's Regiment had about 600 men, while Lord Montgomery's contributed a further 470 or so. All five of these regiments had previously been serving in England, Leven's, Leslie's and Kirkcudbright's being veterans of Marston Moor, and were brought north by Leslie: but at Gladsmuir he was evidently joined by two others who had been serving in Scotland. These were 40 troopers of Colonel Harie Barclay's still incomplete regiment, and around 330 of the Earl of Dalhousie's. This should have given Leslie a total of 3,000 or so cavalry, but his effective strength may have been slightly lower. In February 1645 Spalding commented that Dalhousie's and Hamilton's Regiments had gone to pieces while quartered in Aberdeenshire that winter,[9] and this is confirmed not only by their low turnout at Philiphaugh but by a muster report of 11 December 1645, which noted that the regiment then comprised 324 troopers but had only 84 horses fit for service.[10] Dalhousie's Regiment was almost certainly therefore left in reserve at Philiphaugh.

Besides these Leslie had two other regiments which had accompanied him from England: Colonel Hugh Fraser's Dragoons and Lord Coupar's Regiment of Foot, amounting, according to the monies disbursed, to some 400 dragooners and perhaps 700 infantry. Whether all of Lord Coupar's Regiment actually fought at Philiphaugh is open to a little doubt. It is the only infantry unit known to have been present, yet had Leslie been willing to slow his march to infantry pace there is no real reason why he should not have brought other regiments with him also. It is possible that this unit's participation in the battle may have been limited to a party of dragooners—musketeers temporarily mounted on horseback to speed their march—and there are in fact references to such a unit, led by a Captain Grierson, in the Ordnance Papers.[11]

PHILIPHAUGH, 13 SEPTEMBER 1645

A misinterpretation of the well known ballad concerning the battle has suggested that Leslie divided his army in two, and sent half of them around Linglie Hill to fall upon the rebels' rear, while he himself pushed straight down Ettrick Water. If he was indeed lying in the Tweed valley at the back of Linglie Hill, this would certainly be possible, and giving this detachment time to get into position over the hill might in part account for his delay in beginning the battle until 10 o'clock. Had this indeed been the case, however, it is inconceivable that Leslie, or indeed any of the contemporary chroniclers, should not have mentioned such a bold movement, and it is indeed explicitly contradicted by most accounts, including Wishart, who as an eyewitness is rather more reliable than usual.

Rebel accounts, particularly Ruthven's with its graphic description of Captain Blackadder's bursting in on Montrose at breakfast 'in a great fright' with the news that Leslie was almost upon them, suggest that the battle began shortly after first light; but while Leslie would have set his army in motion then, it is evident that he held off from attacking the rebels until the early morning mists lifted from the valleys, for one of the government accounts of the battle states quite cat-egorically that they came in sight of the rebels at 10 o'clock.[12] This delay at least gave the rebels a chance to pull themselves together. Alerted by Captain Blackadder, Montrose mounted the first horse he could find and galloped across to Philiphaugh, where, far from finding his forces drawn up in good order, 'he found all in uproar and confusion'. The bulk of the cavalry, having no experienced officers (some may have been trapped in Selkirk, for Wishart says that many were absent and never reached the field), were scattered about the haugh in parties of 50, 60, 100 or even 200, but all prudently remaining well out of the way and showing no inclination to come forward. The majority of the cavalry were of course the untrained border levies, but even the Irish veterans were in some disorder, many of them according to Wishart intent only on saving their personal baggage, and in consequence Laghtman and O'Cahan could only assemble about half of them, or even less, to face Leslie's men. At the outset of the fight therefore Montrose had only 200 infantry, and no more than 100 cavalry, with which to fight off over 4,000 government troops;[13] but the rebels were at least well posted.

> According to their usual manner they had made choice of a most advan-tageous ground wherein they had entrenched themselves, having upon one hand an impassable ditch and on the other dikes and hedges, and where these were not strong enough they further fortified them by casting up ditches and lined their hedges with musketeers.[14]

The 'impassable ditch' may, as Colonel Fitzwilliam Elliot suggests, have been the Linglie Burn, joining the Ettrick about a kilometre north of Selkirk; but this is almost certainly too far north, and the prominent re-entrant of the Philhope Burn, opposite Selkirk itself, seems a rather likelier site. Anchoring their left flank on this re-entrant or 'ditch', the rebel foot, or at least those who could be persuaded to stand, took post in or behind what were obviously some agricultural enclosures facing northwards, while between them and the Ettrick were the rebel cavalry under Lord Ogilvy and Colonel Nathaniel Gordon.

Leslie for his part had divided his army in two—at the Linglie Burn if ballad evidence is to be believed—and while a part of it led by Lieutenant Colonel James Agnew of Lord Kirkcudbright's crossed the Ettrick and cleared Selkirk, Leslie led the remainder round the base of Linglie Hill ('Let ae half keep the waterside, The rest gae round the hill') and straight at the rebels.

In an attempt to delay Leslie's approach, three parties of rebel horse came forward to skirmish, but within quarter of an hour were driven in by Leslie's skirmishers. At this point, according to the Haddington dispatch, 200 rebel musketeers pushed forward for some reason, but were 'forced by ours to retreat in great disorder', 'ours' presumably being Lord Coupar's men; although this is the only reference which might be applied to Leslie's infantry, and 'ours' may well in fact have been cavalry. With the rebels thus smartly rapped over the knuckles, the battle then began in earnest.

First a regiment, 400 strong according to Ruthven, which must mean John Middleton's or perhaps Lord Montgomery's, fell on but was repulsed, as was another regiment which seconded them. In this second charge, however, the rebels crossed the ditch (which in this context must be the lower reaches of the Philhope Burn), and finding themselves unable to retire back across it safely, pressed on instead, and some of them, Lord Ogilvy and Colonel Gordon amongst them, managed to fight their way through Leslie's men and then attempted to escape northwards. This was at about noon, and within a few minutes it was all over. Montrose now had only forty or fifty horse left with which to hold the gap between the foot and the Ettrick, but Leslie, instead of charging him, instead wheeled to his right and: 'charging very desperately upon the head of his own regiment, broke the body of the enemy's Foot, after which they all went in confusion and disorder'.[15]

At the same time, Lieutenant Colonel Agnew, having cleared Selkirk, recrossed the Ettrick with his men and fell upon the right flank and rear of the rebel horse, whereupon, not surprisingly, they broke and ran, though many, perhaps even a majority, were taken or slain. The border levies too, still standing irresolutely in the rear, turned and fled at this point. Stewart, the Adjutant General, rallied some of the Irish, no more than a hundred of them, at Philiphaugh farm; but charged again by Leslie's men, surrendered on promise of quarter. With their surrender the battle was over, but urged on by the ministers accompanying the army, the government troops, instead of pursuing the rebels, busied themselves in shooting the Irish prisoners and murdering the camp-followers, men, women and children, arguing that quarter had only been granted to the three senior officers: Stewart, Laghtman and O'Cahan.[16]

Rebel casualties in the battle (and afterwards) were not considerable, and Wishart's contention was that 'Almost none of the horse, and very few of the foot, excepting those who had surrendered on terms, fell in fight. As they [the foot] were not more than 500 in all, and of those 250 rejoined Montrose before the next day, all armed with their swords, we may conjecture that those who were missing did not exceed that number'.[17] The Haddington dispatch, although absurdly optimistic in claiming between two and three thousand rebel casualties, gives 100 as the number of Irish 'shot at a post', which allowing for other stragglers captured is not incompatible with the 50 said by Ruthven to have surrendered with Stewart.[18] Despite Ruthven's surprisingly unsympathetic condemnation of the Irish for their cruelty and barbarity, Leslie's execution of the Irish prisoners has generally been condemned.

Government casualties were rather lighter, as might be expected. The Haddington dispatch gives a Captain Barclay and a Captain Dundas (neither of whom can be identified) and a few soldiers slain, but avers that the total number of killed and wounded did not exceed 100 in all.[19]

The fortunes of the fleeing rebels were mixed. Those who had broken out to the north, including Nathaniel Gordon and Lord Ogilvy, were eventually, lost and on foundered horses, captured by country people; but those who fled westward for the most part escaped. Montrose's own party even went so far as to capture a Captain Bruce and a couple of cornets who had pursued too eagerly.[20] Having overtaken a number of fugitives a short distance from the battlefield, Montrose then proceeded at a more leisurely pace to Peebles, where a halt was made outside the burgh; more stragglers, including presumably the surviving infantry, were gathered in, and they afterwards spent the night there. Peebles, it has been suggested, was too close to Philiphaugh, and with the fighting over by noon Montrose must surely have been able to have made his way as far as Biggar; but in reality there is little reason to disbelieve Wishart's explicit statement about the night's halt being made at Peebles.[21] Leslie's men were far too busy plundering the rebel baggage train and slaughtering their prisoners to mount a determined pursuit (and in any case afterwards returned up Gala Water to Haddington), and there was therefore no urgency for Montrose to press on to Biggar. Moreover it is clear from Wishart's eyewitness account that some time was spent in gathering in fugitives and awaiting the infantry, and in any case 25 kilometres was a good afternoon's march for the infantry after fighting a battle. Pressing on the next morning, the rebels crossed the Clyde, picking up Airlie and Crawford with 200 horse at the ford, and then swung north across the Forth and the Earn and by the 19th were safe in Atholl.

Having effected his escape back to the highlands, Montrose immediately set about trying to raise another army, but with mixed success. The noble lords recalled their sons, and there was no response to Montrose's letters summoning MacColla back from the west. The rebel losses at Philiphaugh, while representing a substantial proportion of those engaged, were far from considerable—there were probably more killed and wounded at Auldearn—but the defeat obviously undermined confidence in Montrose, and it may not be going too far to suggest that it destroyed his credibility. Without MacColla the western clans would not come in, but enough Athollmen were raised to bring Montrose's infantry up to 800 men, and with these and 200 horse he moved northwards in an attempt to enlist the aid of the Gordons once again.

The Gordons however were somewhat preoccupied. Returning home from Kilsyth in mid-September, Aboyne had quite fortuitously seized the Earl Marischal at Rickarton near Fettereso, the rebels getting within the gates before he and the other committee members with him realised they were about. The Earl Marischal was released on parole (afterwards a matter of some dissension between Aboyne and Montrose since he failed to honour it), but the others, John Forbes of Leslie, Alexander and Thomas Jaffrey, and Andrew Cant, were taken off by Gordon of Newton and Leith of Harthill and imprisoned in Pitcaple Castle.[22] Next day, 15 September, Aboyne moved on to Aberdeen and demanded that the burgh militia should be mobilised and captains appointed to command it, failing which he threatened to inflict a garrison of his own upon the burgh. Captain William Gordon of Arradoul was left behind to ensure compliance in this, and the council, 'finding no possibilitie for the present to resist the same, resolved and concludit to give way thairto for the tyme'.[23] Captains were appointed the next day, but the only real result of all this activity was to cause Leslie to send Major General Middleton north with 800 cavalry— presumably his own and Lord Montgomery's regiments. He was in the north-east before the end of the month, and although too weak to attack the Gordons, at least kept them out of Aberdeen and provided a focus for a revival in the government's fortunes in the area. Indeed sometime around the beginning of October, Pitcaple Castle had been recaptured by the Master of Forbes, or more accurately by the prisoners who managed to shut the garrison out (while they were preoccupied with skinning an ox), and then held on for 24 hours until Forbes arrived 'in the verie nick of tyme' with 30 horse and 50 to 60 foot.[24] It was against the background of this revival that Montrose arrived, demanding that the Gordons should march south again.

Aboyne, despite his father's disapproval, was at first inclined to co-operate, and joined Montrose at Drumminor Castle with 1,500 foot and 3 to 500 horse led by his wild younger brother, Lord Lewis Gordon. No sooner were they joined, but a dispute broke out as to whether they should march south directly, with the aim of recapturing Glasgow in time for the Parliament which Montrose had called to meet there on 20 October, or whether they should first deal with Middleton, then lying at Turriff. The latter course of action was, according to Ruthven, agreed upon at a council of war, but Montrose still insisted on moving south, 'fyndeing himselfe now stronge eneugh to giue his enemies a day'. Aboyne consented reluctantly, but Montrose, at a moment when tact was essential, put Lord Lewis Gordon under the command of the Earl of Crawford; and at Kintore Lord Lewis, intent on asserting his independence, went off and attacked one of Middleton's patrols. Middleton's men, considerably outnumbered, promptly took to their heels, and returned to Turriff in such a fright that Middleton withdrew northwards in some disorder to Banff. Lord Lewis then returned to Strathbogie, taking the cavalry with him. This untimely withdrawal of the Gordon horse deprived Montrose of sufficient cavalry with which to continue his advance down the east coast, and instead he doubled back to Alford where Aboyne too broke away with his infantry.[25] Reduced once more to between 5 and 600 highlanders, 200 Irish and a similar number of cavalry, Montrose reached Braemar on 23 October, and from there despatched a letter to Robertson of Inver at Blair Castle, instructing him to assemble an army at Dunkeld and asking for news of MacColla.

Somehow a few hundred more men were raised, and with their aid Montrose hung around Buchanan for nearly a week threatening Glasgow; but Leslie's forces were strong enough to keep him in the hills, and when Middleton's two regiments were recalled from Aberdeenshire (thus vindicating Montrose's argument) he withdrew northwards in increasingly bitter weather, through Atholl and up to Keith. Here the army was quartered while Montrose rode to meet Huntly at the Bog of Gight, and discuss how best to conduct the war.

11

The End of the Rebellion

On 31 October 1645, with the immediate threat to Glasgow having receded, Leslie was ordered back to England with his own, Leven's and most of Middleton's regiments of horse. Before embarking upon an account of subsequent events, it may be useful to review briefly the dispositions of the government forces then remaining in Scotland.

Having suffered a bit of a scare when the rebels unexpectedly reappeared before Glasgow, within such a short time of having apparently been given their quietus by David Leslie at Philiphaugh, the Estates ordered the fortification of the burgh on 6 November. All fencible men in the presbytery of Glasgow were to begin work on the following Monday and labour until noon on Saturday. The sabbath was of course to be left free for matters spiritual, and then the fencibles of Paisley and Hamilton were to take their turn from 17 and 24 November respectively, being followed in succeeding weeks by those of Irvine, Ayr and Lanark. The Glaswegians themselves were to labour alongside the countrymen on Mondays and Saturdays, and the works were scheduled to be completed by 20 December. Given the degree of organisation and the confidence with which the project was ordered, one would be surprised to learn of anything being allowed to delay this completion date. In the meantime the burgh depended for its defence upon a militia regiment led by Colonel George Porterfield and Lieutenant Colonel William Dick. The unit had earlier been conspicuous by its absence in the weeks after Kilsyth, and as Porterfield and some of his officers were evidently seconded from the General of the Artillery's Regiment (now commanded by Lindsay of Bellstanes), it is evident that some stiffening had been necessary. Further stiffening was provided by the remains of Cassillis' Regiment of foot, together with Lord Coupar's Dragoons and Sir John Browne's Horse and Dragoons.

Lanark's Horse and Dragoons meanwhile were still in Clydesdale, and Colonel Robert Montgomery's (formerly the Earl of Eglinton's)

Regiment of horse was quartered in Ayr and Renfrew. The greatest concentrations of troops were, however, around the Forth crossings; Dalhousie's Regiment together with Argyle's and Callendar's Troops was in the Stirling area, while Lord Montgomery's and Colonel Hugh Fraser's Regiments lay in Clackmannan. Lord Kirkcudbright's Regiment was pushed forward to Baillie's old camp at Bridge of Earn, where it could maintain contact with the Earl of Moray's Regiment watching the highland passes out of Atholl, with Sir James Lindsay of Bellstane's Regiment of foot at Falkland in Fife and with the Dundee garrison under a Colonel Lyell. This latter comprised a militia regiment under Lyell and Colonel George Milne's Dragoons. Stirling itself was of course well garrisoned with the remains of Baillie's army, but to the north only Perth, Dundee, Inverness (and shortly St. Andrews where the Estates were to move to escape the plague) were garrisoned, and generally lightly at that. Clearly this state of affairs was most unsatisfactory, and Middleton was appointed to command the army in Scotland—in place of Robert Monro, left to the Irish bogs—and the necessary preparations made for yet another expedition into Aberdeenshire.[1]

The forces made available for this expedition were far from numerous, and the fact that they eventually proved sufficient for the task illustrates well just how far rebel fortunes had sunk. Sensibly enough it was felt that those units which had already been mauled by the rebels had done enough, and as soon as they were strong enough to go they were sent back to join Leven's army in England. In their place, two regular infantry regiments lately returned from England with David Leslie, Colonel William Stewart's and Viscount Kenmure's, were lying in Forfarshire by mid-December; the first at Arbroath and the second at Montrose.[2] (Lord Coupar's men were ordered to Perth at the same time, but do not appear to have taken much part in the subsequent operations.) Both were intended not to sit in garrisons but to take the field against the rebels, and with a view to establishing a forward base at Aberdeen, Colonel Harie Barclay was ordered to raise a regiment of foot in addition to his horse, and given his marching orders on 27 December. He arrived in Aberdeen on 2 January 1646,[3] having, it seems, mounted his foot on ponies to speed his march, for when they arrived they were noted by the town council as being dragooners. This indicates that by now the government was acting with a very proper sense of urgency—wholly lacking amongst the rebels. Barclay's men were followed into Aberdeen the next day by Colonel Stewart's and Lord Kenmure's Regiments of foot and Colonel Robert Montgomery's Horse,[4] but a further advance was delayed until the spring while some overdue taxes were gathered, and, of some more immediate importance, at least two local units raised. The Master of Forbes became Colonel

163

William Forbes, leading all the old Aberdeenshire Horse including Craigievar's Troop, while Colonel George Forbes of Mill Buie raised a foot regiment.

By this time most of the rebels were over the Spey. Montrose, in a distinctly uneasy partnership with Huntly, was intent on taking Inverness. The Gordons, on the other hand, contended that the burgh should be bypassed and Seaforth compelled to rise together with the other northern clans, arguing that in such a case Inverness would then of necessity have to surrender without a long and costly siege. The bad wintry weather precluded much action, however, and while Huntly began reducing various small castles in Moray, Montrose busied himself in some ultimately fruitless recruiting, writing to clan chiefs demanding their support and, as ever, enquiring for news of MacColla. Aberdeenshire in the meantime was left to the Earl of Crawford, who at first proved surprisingly energetic. Ruthven unfortunately gives no indication as to the dates upon which the skirmishes he records took place, although they must have been sometime in February or March of 1646.[5]

Fyvie Castle had been re-fortified by Aboyne on his return from Kilsyth, and a strong garrison left there under one of the Strathbogie officers, Captain John Gordon of Knockespock. Hearing of a government foraging party at Old Meldrum, he sent out a mixed party of horse and commanded musketeers who routed them, and captured both baggage and forage. Next, Sir Alexander Irvine of Drum with a troop of horse, and Farquharson of Inverey with his 200 highland foot from Braemar, swept down Deeside and beat up some government quarters at Murtle, not far from Aberdeen, causing Barclay to draw in his outposts; but the final straw was a raid by Captain Blackadder with men from the Fyvie garrison on a detachment at Esslemont near Ellon, which left 36 dead. Barclay then decided that enough was enough and sallied forth with 600 cavalry—probably all that he could muster—not to Fyvie but to Crawford's headquarters at Banff. There were some 240 rebels there under both the elder and younger lairds of Gight, Captain William Gordon of Arradoul, and two Irish officers who had escaped from Philiphaugh, Captain John Mortimer and a Captain McDonnell. Barclay evidently marched around the coast, for the first intimation the rebels had of his approach was when he stumbled across a standing patrol in Doune (now Macduff). One reads with no surprise that the patrol, far from keeping a good watch, 'ware carruseing'. Had Barclay's men merely slit their throats all might have been well; but as it was, the sound of pistol shots carried across the bay, and the rebels had time to get their baggage away and organise a rearguard led by Crawford himself. There was a brief skirmish and then the rebels fled away up Speyside to join Montrose's army. Barclay for his part then left a small garrison in Banff and returned to Aberdeen to await the arrival of Middleton.

Ruthven ascribes Middleton's arrival in the north to a lack of confidence by the government in Barclay, but he had always intended to come north to deal with Montrose, and had only been delayed by the need to deal with a couple of rebel incursions on the fringes of the highlands. Nevertheless there may be some truth in the story, for when Aberdeen was stormed by the rebels in May 1646, Barclay was actually serving under Lieutenant Colonel Hew Montgomery of Robert Montgomery's Horse.

In the first of these incursions 1,200 Campbells under the Laird of Ardkinglas—armed refugees rather than soldiers—who were plundering in Mentieth, were set upon and routed near Callendar on 13 February by 700 Athollmen, led by Graham of Inchbrackie and Drummond of Balloch. The refugees fled to Stirling, where Argyle found them starving, and the rebels prudently retired into the hills again only to re-emerge at the beginning of March. This time Balloch and Lord Napier threw a garrison into Kincardine Castle outside Auchterarder, and cannot have been too surprised when Middleton laid siege to it on 2 March. They held out for two weeks, but at length on the night of 15 March, with supplies of both food and water running short, Balloch, Napier and the Laird of McNab galloped out and through Middleton's lines, leaving the fifty strong garrison to surrender the next day. The whole affair looks at first to have been rather pointless, but it did at least prevent Middleton from moving north for two weeks, and the hope of achieving this or a longer delay may have been behind it. Whether the rebel soldiers abandoned by their officers, and in particular the twelve Irish mercenaries summarily executed by Middleton, appreciated this, is altogether another matter.

In the meantime things in the north for a time got out of hand and anarchy prevailed. At their December meeting Huntly and Montrose had agreed on the need to secure the north before moving south, but Huntly had resisted Montrose's blandishments to accept his orders, and in the end stood on his dignity and evidenced his commission to command as Lieutenant General in the north. Montrose, having lost his Viceregal commission in the baggage train at Philiphaugh, was unable to pull rank on him, and retired in some pique up Speyside to Ballachastell with 800 foot and 200 horse. Ruthven believed that it had been agreed that he would support Huntly, but it was not in Montrose's nature to support anyone and it seems rather unlikely. Indeed it is quite evident that neither party was capable of co-operating with the other, far less acknowledging one or other as being the commander in chief. Montrose spent some time in trying to persuade the western clans to rally to his banner, but by March was intent on besieging Inverness, and to that end appealed to Huntly for support, intending that his forces should block up the burgh on the west while the Gordons blocked up the east. Huntly, however, not surprisingly, refused to co-operate.[6]

Until now his campaign in Moray had been pretty successful, and a number of small garrisons had been cleaned out. Spynie Castle, though, still held out for the government under the command of young Grant of Ballendalloch, and Lord Lewis Gordon was left behind at Rothes Castle to keep the garrison in check. Because of the bitter wintry weather, no attempt was made by either party to besiege the other, and instead the two played the part of robber barons, issuing forth from their strongholds to plunder, burn and bicker with each other. Lord Lewis, by the general consent of contemporaries, was undoubtedly the worse scourge of the two, and according to Fraser even employed in his train a Master Burner, 'who uppon the sign given him would instantly set fire to the cornstacks, and put all in a flame'.[7] Huntly for his part busied himself in besieging Lethen, near Auldearn, defended by the Laird of Brodie. Although Ruthven defends the decision to lay siege to it without battering pieces, there is little doubt that the three months which Huntly spent before Lethen could have been used more profitably. At length, despairing of assistance from Huntly, Montrose attempted to force the issue by laying siege to Inverness on his own. Doing so without first having defeated Middleton was a dangerous move, and Ruthven is probably correct in ascribing the decision to a wilful perversity and a desire to assert his authority. When he began the siege on 29 April though it was already too late.

The rebels planted two brass cannon on the old castle hill under a hawthorn tree, and proceeded to batter the town, while raiding parties crossed the River Ness and plundered the Aird bare, forcing the local people to take refuge in a number of outlying earthen forts. In this the rebels were soon joined by some McKenzies and MacDonalds, but otherwise little progress was made, for the garrison had time to burn the suburbs before retiring behind their earthworks. Huntly has been criticised for not aiding Montrose at this time, but the wonder is that the siege was undertaken at all, for Middleton had by now returned to the north and was marching hard for the Spey. Huntly for his part, beset by hectoring demands from Montrose, was mustering his forces at Kinermony on Speyside (near Balvenie) at the beginning of May. Middleton meanwhile was at Banff, and realising that Huntly was not yet ready to march, resolved upon a dash along the coast, leaving his foot to follow as best they could.[8]

There are two versions as to what happened next. One, Wishart's, is hostile towards the Gordons to the extent of alleging the very blackest treachery, whilst Ruthven's, although obviously motivated by a desire to refute Wishart's allegations, is altogether more convincing. According to Wishart, Montrose had three troops of horse watching the Spey, but Lord Lewis Gordon assured them that all was well and invited their commanders to a banquet at Rothes Castle, so allowing Middleton to cross the Spey undetected with 600 horse and 800 foot, very narrowly avoiding surprising Montrose. Ruthven, on the other hand, allows only two troops watching the Spey at Garmouth, and names their commanders as the two Irish officers, Captains Mortimer and McDonnell. The notion of their being detained by Lord Lewis at Rothes Castle is categorically refuted, and their failure to prevent or even detect Middleton's crossing the Spey is ascribed to their own negligence—a charge which is all too consistent with the rebels' previous record in such matters. With Middleton across the river the rebels fell back, McDonnell heading straight for Inverness to warn Montrose, while Mortimer rode to Rothes to warn Lord Lewis that Middleton was in the area. He remained there for about an hour, and it is far from impossible that this was inflated into an excuse, later seized upon by Wishart, for his negligence. Since Middleton had already marched 35 kilometres that day from Banff to reach Elgin, the rebels confidently expected that he would halt for the night there, but he confounded them by stopping only long enough to feed and water his men and their horses, and then pushed on that night a further 38 kilometres to Inverness. The result was that he arrived at the burgh only three hours behind Captain Mortimer and caught the rebels quite unawares. Alerted by Middleton's trumpets the rebels had no thought of fighting, and instead abandoned their guns and fled across the river covered by a rearguard under Crawford (who must have been getting quite used to such operations), comprising 70 or 80 horse including young Gight, Harthill and Hay of Delgatie. Once in the Aird the rebels retired westwards and took refuge in the wood of Farley above Beauly, where Middleton, having again halted only long enough to feed and water his forces, came up with them again. There they remained for two days, eyeing each other balefully, but neither side keen on forcing a battle.[9] The rebels were quite simply too weak, and to make matters worse the McKenzies and other highlanders deserted; and Middleton, initially because his men must have been exhausted, saw no reason to throw away the benefits of a hitherto successful operation on anything so chancy as a needless battle—his predecessors had done that all too frequently.

On the morning of the 10th Montrose decided that he had had enough, burnt his camp and retreated down Strathglass, winning back at length to Speyside. Middleton, for his part, made no attempt to pursue the rebels, and indeed on the contrary embarked upon a tour of Ross and Cromartie, an area which had conspicuously not supported the rebels.[10]

Had the two rebel leaders been co-operating, it is possible that Huntly might have marched at once to Montrose's aid, and between them they might have mustered sufficient forces to defeat Middleton. However, as soon as word reached him from Lord Lewis Gordon that the government forces were over the Spey, Huntly marched not west, but east for Aberdeen, sending a messenger to Aboyne to meet him at Inverurie with as many foot as he could muster. Huntly's advance was an open secret and the Aberdeenshire Covenanters also mustered their men, at Aberdeen, ready to receive him.

THE STORMING OF ABERDEEN, 14 MAY 1646

The garrison, according to Ruthven, mustered 500 horse and 1,000 foot,[11] but the town council, who ought to have known since they had to feed and house them, put it at four troops of horse numbering 240 men, with two regiments of foot adding a further 700 men.[12] The identity of the various units involved in the fighting is not entirely certain. Montgomery had four troops of his own regiment, but from other council records it would appear that they amounted to only 200 men,[13] though the other 40 may be accounted for by the timely arrival of the Master of Forbes' Troop. Colonel Barclay's Regiment of horse must therefore have been serving with Middleton, but as he himself was captured in the battle it may be concluded that one of the two foot regiments was his. The two other regular regiments then serving in the north, Lord Kenmure's and Colonel Stewart's, were also with Middleton, and so the second infantry regiment in the Aberdeen garrison must have been that of Colonel George Forbes of Mill Buie, a locally raised unit.

The rebels, for their part, are not at all adequately described by Ruthven. He states that Huntly and Lord Lewis Gordon had an unspecified number of cavalry and a smaller number of foot, while Aboyne brought in a further 2,000. Both the Council and Spalding reckoned the whole lot to amount only to 1,500 foot and 500 horse, which sounds altogether more realistic.[14] Presumably Huntly's contingent included the Strathbogie Regiment and Aboyne's, Inverey's and Minimore's men, but otherwise there is no indication as to which units were represented. Some of the Gordon cavalry were indeed still with Montrose. Although the rebel foot outnumbered the defenders by two to one, the discrepancy was not in actual fact so overwhelming, since the highlanders who formed the bulk of the rebel foot played little real part in the fighting. Moreover Montgomery's men were encouraged by a successful raid before dawn on the morning of the 14th against a rebel quarter in Kintore. It will come as no surprise to learn that the rebels were 'cairless of their watch' and twelve or fourteen of them were in consequence slain.[15]

Undismayed by this set-back Huntly ordered his forces on. In order to attack the burgh, Huntly was more or less committed by its situation to an attack from the north, since the sea lay only a short distance to the east, the harbour lay to the south, and the west was fairly well protected by the valley of the Denburn and a stagnant marsh which had once been a loch. The street plan of the burgh was in essence not unlike a hammer, the head lying parallel to the harbour, and the haft running north along a whaleback ridge. The eastern half of the head comprised the Castlegate, a large rectangular market-place help-fully described by an English traveller as being large enough to accom-modate two regiments of foot drawn up in order of battle. At the eastern extremity of the Castlegate was the Justice Port, leading out of the town on to the links (where it was customary for armies to camp and the militia to drill), and to the Heading Hill. Immediately to the west of the Castlegate was the now levelled St. Katherine's Hill, forming a vast roundabout with the Shiprow curving around it to the south leading to the harbour, and the Netherkirkgate round the north, both ultimately leading to the Green and the Bow Bridge over the Denburn which was the principal entrance to the burgh from the south. The 'haft' ran north-west out of the Castlegate, a wide street called—with a certain lack of imagination—the Broadgate (now Broad Street), and then due north up the Gallowgate. Broad Street is about 100 metres long, and the Gallowgate at that time slightly less than 200 metres.[16]

His summons to surrender rejected, Huntly began the attack by sending two parties of highlanders, one to the Justice Port and the other to the Green, to 'fyre the town'. In this they were successful, at least in setting fire to some outlying houses and barns, but notwithstanding the undoubted assistance of Lord Lewis Gordon's 'Master Burner', they were unable or unwilling to penetrate the perimeter. Nevertheless they must have distracted the defenders somewhat. A third party, probably the Strathbogie Regiment, then assaulted an entrenchment at the Gallowgate Port, the northernmost extremity of the burgh, and there effected an entrance, turning some cannon there upon the erstwhile defenders. Montgomery at once despatched a troop of horse to seal off the gap, but by the time they had arrived the rebel infantry had levelled the defences, allowing Huntly's sons, Aboyne and Lord Lewis Gordon, to get in with two troops of horse; and having the advantage of the slope (the Gallowgate Port was at the highest point of the ridge), they drove the government troops back down the street and into the Broadgate.

As soon as the rebels emerged from the Gallowgate into the wider Broadgate, they were counter-attacked by a Major Forbes at the head

169

of his Aberdeenshire cavalry, and at first driven back. Then, in a scene common to romances but rarely met with in fact, Forbes encountered Lord Lewis Gordon and engaged him in personal combat. Lord Lewis at once called upon him to surrender, but not surprisingly this summons was refused with some asperity, and thereupon losing his temper he assaulted Forbes furiously and left him dead on the ground. At this Forbes' troopers gave way, but then Montgomery himself intervened at the head of some of his own cavalry—three or four troops by Ruthven's reckoning, although it would have been difficult to cram them all into the Broadgate—and the rebels, 'with maine strength', were forced out of the town.

Aboyne would then appear to have taken no further part in the fighting, but Lord Lewis, nothing loth, twice more entered the burgh and was twice more tumbled out again by Montgomery. Huntly, meanwhile, seeing that his men were getting nowhere, began to have second thoughts and was apparently on the point of ordering a retreat; but Lord Lewis Gordon with his blood up was in no mood to do so, and determined upon another attempt. Unsupported cavalry charges down the Gallowgate were obviously getting him nowhere, and so, rather belatedly, a properly co-ordinated assault was organised.

This time when he charged down the Gallowgate at the head of a troop of volunteers, a strong party of commanded musketeers, presumably Strathbogie men, broke into the town at another point. Unfortunately neither Ruthven nor Spalding say where the infantry made their attack, but it must either have been by the Upperkirkgate Port to the west, or more likely perhaps over the garden walls to the rear of Marischal College on the east side of the Broadgate. Assailed by these musketeers Montgomery's men broke at last before Lord Lewis Gordon's charge, and fled down the Shiprow, swimming their horses across the harbour and winning away to the south. Some resistance was made thereafter by some of the infantry barricaded into the Tolbooth and two other strong houses on the Castlegate, but realising the hopelessness of their situation they soon surrendered.[17]

As to casualties Ruthven is obviously quite unreliable, claiming that between two and three hundred of the defenders were slain. Added to the 350 prisoners which the town council noted were taken, this pretty well accounts for the infantry in the garrison, but must be too high, for most of the fighting was done by the cavalry and most of the infantry in fact appear to have escaped. The council gave no estimate of the number of dead (the relevant document has a blank space here), but gives the impression that they included a high proportion of officers, including of course Major Forbes. As to rebel losses, Ruthven allows none at all, which even allowing for his tendency to count 'friendly' casualties only in terms of officers and gentlemen and to

170

ignore losses amongst the common soldiers, is ridiculous. Spalding apparently put the total number of dead on both sides at 80, the majority of them government soldiers slain after the rebels broke into the burgh.[18]

'This was thought', said a contemporary, 'to be one of the hottest pieces pieces of service that happened since this unnatural war began, both in regard to the eagerness of the pursuers and valour of the defenders'.

It proved however to have been in vain. Huntly allowed his men two hours plunder in the burgh and then withdrew, releasing Barclay and his officers on parole, and their men on promising not to take up arms again. The local leaders whom he had captured, however, amongst them Forbes of Craigievar, were sent to Auchindoun. Montrose, still smarting from his defeat at Inverness, attempted to have a meeting with Huntly at the Bog of Gight, but Huntly avoided him, and then on 31 May 1646 it was suddenly all over. The reason for Middleton's inactivity became apparent when a messenger arrived from the King, himself a prisoner of the Scots since 5 May, ordering the rebels to lay down their arms.

The King's letters to Montrose and Huntly did not end the war there and then, of course. Huntly, for the moment at least, had had enough, and disbanded his forces at once—it is possible that rumours of the King's capture had influenced his withdrawal from Aberdeen— and offered no resistance as Middleton, suddenly galvanised into action, swept past demanding the surrender of the Bog of Gight and Strathbogie Castle. Montrose, by contrast, called a council of war, and offered to keep his forces together if the King could secretly confirm that he had ordered the surrender under duress; but it was a forlorn hope, and on 15 June the King repeated his command to surrender. After a conference with Middleton to settle the terms, Montrose disbanded his forces at Rattray near Blairgowrie on 30 July 1646 and then, prudently, fled abroad.

Middleton followed up this surrender by accepting the submission of Blair Castle from John Robertson of Inver, and planting a garrison of his own there under Captain John Campbell of Crunane.[19] Problems remained, however, in the west, where MacColla had, since leaving Montrose, conquered all of Kintyre, besides gaining effective control of most of the west highland seaboard south of Lochaber. Furthermore the situation had dramatically worsened with the arrival in Kintyre of 2,000 men under the Earl of Antrim. He and MacColla proved even more unwilling to disband their forces than Montrose had been, and stronger measures were necessary.

Although these had to wait until 1647, a foretaste of them was seen when Campbell of Ardkinglas was sent in May with his ragged band of ruffians across from Ayrshire to Cowal, and besieged Sir James

Lamont and his men in Toward Castle. With the aid of some cannon Ardkinglas forced the surrender of the castle on 1 June, granting the garrison the usual terms to march out to the nearest friendly forces (which in this case meant MacColla's men); but no sooner was the castle rendered up but Sir James was forced to instruct the neighbouring garrison of Ascog Castle to likewise surrender. All the rebel prisoners were then marched to Dunoon and executed in the kirkyard, the soldiers shot and hacked to death, and the officers (with the exception of Sir James) hanged.[20] Until now only Irish prisoners had been executed out of hand, in accordance with an English parliamentarian ordinance,[21] but this was doubtless intended to be a salutary warning to MacColla's men. As is often the case, however, the reverse resulted, and seeing little prospect of good terms the rebels disobeyed the King's orders to disband. Antrim certainly returned to Ireland towards the end of the year, but MacColla with most of his men remained in Kintyre.

After the main rebel surrenders in the early summer, nearly all the non-regular forces in Scotland, such as Forbes of Mill Buie's Regiment, were likewise disbanded in August;[22] and the final phase of the counter-insurgency operation was to be entrusted to the regular army, now released from service in England by the end of the Civil War there. First, though, it had to be re-organised. By the end of 1646 the army was in a condition common to most seventeenth century armies which had been in the field for any length of time: it comprised a large number of regiments, all with their full complement of officers, or very near it, but badly under strength as to their common soldiers. Not only was this inefficient, in requiring a number of regiments to carry out an operation which should have called for only one, but from the government point of view it was very undesirable indeed. An infantry regiment at full establishment should have mustered 1,400 men, and something in the region of 50 commissioned officers, but with units reduced to two or three hundred men apiece, a force of 1,400 men in 1646 could have as many as 300 commissioned officers, and the wages bill would be correspondingly inflated. The answer to the problem was exactly the same one decided upon by the English parliament in 1645—'New Modelling'.

On 29 January 1647 the Estates laid down the establishment of the new army,[23] and ordered the disbanding of the old on 9 February (the cavalry disbanding on the following day). A hundred men were to be taken from each of the regiments and the rest of the men allowed to return home; some thirty infantry regiments were thus reduced to seven, two of them highland regiments, while fifteen cavalry regiments and a plethora of independent troops were ordered to be reduced to fifteen independent troops. Units which had originally come from Ireland were not affected, and were instead ordered back there, but in the event two, Lothian's and Sinclair's, disbanded themselves, and the third, Campbell of Lawers', was still serving in Scotland in 1651. Rather more cavalry was also retained on service, though that was only to have been expected.[24] This new army was specifically organised with counter-insurgency operations in mind, hence the employment of independent cavalry troops rather than unwieldy large regiments, and the fact that two of the seven infantry regiments were highland ones. The lowland regiments had an establishment strength of 800 men, although some appear to have failed to achieve this, but the two highland regiments, Argyle's (which had actually been commissioned in December 1645) and Ardkinglas', seem to have been regarded by Argyle as a form of charitable employment for his distressed dependants, and had in the region of 1,200 men apiece.[25] An interesting innovation in the lowland regiments was the formation of something not unlike later grenadier companies, formed of 72 men drawn from all six of the 'line' companies, and equipped not with grenades but with halberts, back, breast and headpiece.[26]

Although the Estates, in ordering the formation of this force, may have had the disposal of MacColla's rabble in mind, it was first sent north to deal with Huntly who had unexpectedly raised his forces again at the end of 1646, on receiving a message from the King indicating that he was about to try and escape; but the attempt on Christmas Eve failed, and Huntly's seizure of Banff was consequently pointless. With a few hundred horse and as many as 1,500 foot he held the burgh all winter. Sometime in March Lieutenant Colonel Thomas Craig of Riccarton arrived before it with a mixture of regulars and local levies, but hastily retired again on discovering the strength of the opposition. Nevertheless Huntly realised that the game was up, evacuated Banff, and having left garrisons in his castles, was chased into the hills by Middleton. Leslie himself soon followed with the regular army, and the by now familiar round of minor sieges followed. By the end of March most of Huntly's castles had fallen, and the Irish mercenaries found in them were executed out of hand. The Scots soldiers were generally released on the usual promise not to fight again, but the officers, amongst them Colonel William Gordon of Minimore, were imprisoned in Edinburgh. Huntly saw no point in fighting, disbanded his marching army save for a small lifeguard, and was pursued through Badenoch and into Lochaber where in November he was betrayed by the Camerons. Middleton, guided by them, took the fugitives by surprise, and although Leith of Harthill fought a gallant little rearguard action at the head of Huntly's lifeguard, only Aboyne succeeded in making his escape.[27]

Leslie meanwhile had turned his attention to the rather more important problem of MacColla, and in filthy weather marched west-wards from Dunblane on 17 May, and on the 24th forced his way into Kintyre, where his cavalry caught the rebels on open ground at Rhunahoarine Point, and routed them utterly. While waiting that night for his infantry to catch up, Leslie lost contact with the rebels and they succeeded in escaping by sea, ultimately to Ireland. An odd amphibious campaign then followed, mainly involving Leslie's highlanders, which culminated in the capture of Dunaverty Castle at the beginning of June and the massacre of its garrison. Dunyveg Castle surrendered on 5 July; oddly enough the Irish were allowed to go home, and although one or two minor garrisons still held out, its capture effectively ended three years of rebellion.[28]

MONTROSE RE-ASSESSED

Ultimately Montrose failed to win Scotland for King Charles because he was unable to secure the support of the nobility, and through them control of the Estates and the regular Scots army—something ironically which Hamilton was to achieve in 1648. Win battles though he might, he could not conquer Scotland with an undisciplined rabble of poorly armed highlanders; for that he needed cavalry and regular infantry. Although hampered by chronic indiscipline which pervaded all his forces, and time after time compromised his security, Montrose's failure at first lay in his inability to raise sufficient regular troops prepared to accept his authority and to do their job properly. The Gordons, it is true, provided at least the nucleus of such a force, but, distrusting Montrose, they invariably served as allies rather than as subordinates. In order to raise a regular army capable of taking and holding Edinburgh, he had to turn a rebellion into a civil war by holding on to enough territory over which to establish an administration capable of providing the recruits and supplies which he so desperately needed. That he was himself only too well aware of this, is evident from his not entirely unsuccessful attempt to raise the Aberdeenshire fencibles after Inverlochy in early 1645, but in the end his failure to do so must in justice be attributed not merely to his want of diplomacy, but also to the quite remarkable resilience of the government's own soldiers. Although for the space of a year continually defeated in battle, the government could always maintain sufficient forces in the field to harry the rebels, and prevent them from gaining control of an area of any size long enough to establish themselves and recruit substantial numbers of men. It is perhaps time that the Scots army was given the credit for this which it deserves. Montrose's celebrated circular tours of Scotland look impressive, and their successful execution demonstrated a certain skill, but in the end they were an admission of failure. Montrose did not go chasing around Scotland simply to give the government forces a hard time, he did it because they were giving him a hard time and would not let him rest. It would of course be going too far to say that the rising was doomed from the start, but without Montrose's tactical skill it would most likely have ended within a matter of months if not weeks. Lacking as he did any real formal training in the arts of war, Montrose was, as we have seen, fortunate enough to have some good teachers in his early campaigns, and just as importantly—Napoleon would have said more importantly—he enjoyed some very good luck.

His handling of the operations to contain Huntly and the Gordons in the north-east in 1639 was, as might be expected of a novice, rather less than inspired. There were flashes of the dash for which he later became famous, such as the rapid reinforcement of the Aberdeenshire covenanters at Turriff in February 1639, but there was also a distinct hesitancy and uncertainty. His speed in reaching Turriff in February was unfortunately matched by the speed with which he evacuated the area in May, upon receiving a much exaggerated account of Aboyne's landing with English reinforcements (not much more than sixty musketeers from Aberdeen). His first battles too were notable for his hesitancy, and the successful assault on the Bridge of Dee was actually mounted by Lieutenant Colonel John Middleton.

After his defection to the Royalists in 1643, however, a reckless, perhaps even desperate streak becomes ever more evident, and with it what was ultimately a fatal lack of patience. His abortive invasion of Scotland in April 1644 at the head of a motley band of exiles and English militiamen was ill-conceived, ill-prepared, carried out with inadequate forces and best passed over in silence. The most that can be said is that he and his men got away, but nearly surprised as they were by Callendar's forces, they had to run very fast indeed. Had he been able to persuade his little army to fight it is just possible that it might have been a different matter, for the campaign which made his reputation was begun in even less auspicious circumstances.

The military qualities, or rather more accurately the lack of military qualities, displayed by the highlanders with whom he is most readily associated, have already been discussed in as much detail as the subject warrants, and it is evident that his most notable victories were principally due not to the supposed prowess of what actually turns out to have been some very poor material indeed, but instead to Montrose's striking ability to use that unpromising material to its very best advantage. It has recently been suggested that MacColla, not Montrose, was the true architect of his victories. This was certainly the case at Tippermuir, where Montrose commanded only the Athollmen on the right wing effectively, leaving the centre and the army as a whole by implication to MacColla. It was at Tippermuir, however, that his apprenticeship ended; and in the Justice Mills fight outside Aberdeen two weeks later, we can see for the first time what became Montrose's usual tactics of first securing his own flanks and as far as possible neutralising or even driving in those of the enemy, using his best troops, before unleashing his numerous but less reliable troops in the centre upon the enemy, to finish off the job already half completed by his shock troops on the wings.

At Fyvie Castle, on the other hand, having through his own negligence got himself into a corner from which he was extremely lucky to extricate himself and his army, Montrose had no opportunity to repeat this, but at Inverlochy on Candlemas Day 1645, it was executed to perfection. The Irish regulars on either flank were committed first, in order to fight the regular companies opposite, drawn from Baillie's army, and then, only after they had been disposed of, were the rabble of highlanders in the centre sent forward. Auldearn, where the rebels came perhaps closest to defeat in battle, in what was almost certainly the hardest fight in Montrose's career, was a more complex affair which may have lasted all day; but here again we find that pains were taken to drive in Hurry's flanks, this time using Lord Gordon's superb regular cavalry regiment, before the main counter-attack was launched. Alford too was another example of this technique being employed to considerable effect, and notwithstanding Montrose's imperishable association with highlanders, it was not they but the cavalry who were the shock troops during the 1645 campaign.

Kilsyth, although acclaimed as Montrose's greatest victory, is an interesting battle in which he seems to have lost control of his army at a very early stage, after having been surprised by the direction of the government forces' advance. Baillie's appearance on the high ground to the east of his left flank, and evident preparations for turning it, necessitated a hurried change of front in order that the rebel army might face them. Had the rebel scouting been up to much, there might have been time to carry out this far from simple manoeuvre successfully; but as usual the rebel scouts proved incompetent, and the indications are that Montrose's army dissolved into a confused rabble with the result that the first counter-attack against Baillie's men was launched not by the rebel cavalry but by a pretty useless mob of peasant levies from the Western Isles. They, far from sweeping away their opponents in a 'classic highland charge', were stopped in their tracks by Baillie's veterans and reduced to hiding behind a convenient stone wall. The rest of the rebel army then appears to have been fed into the battle as soon as each individual unit could be hurried up, pointed in the right direction, and sent on its way to glory. Once again at the end of the day it was the cavalry who did most to beat Baillie's men.

Few of Montrose's battles were 'Soldiers' Battles', but if the battle of Kilsyth was not one, there is precious little evidence of Montrose managing effectively to impose his will upon the proceedings, and at best it was all down to the several regimental officers.

Impressive though Montrose's talent was for using a mixed bag of militia and regulars effectively—George Washington was later to experience similar problems—it is unfortunately quite overshadowed by his quite remarkable talent for ignoring or disregarding the importance of good and effective reconnaissance. His army was surprised at Fyvie, Dundee, Auldearn, Philiphaugh, Banff and Inverness, whilst at Alford and Kilsyth, although looking for and expecting a fight, he failed to anticipate the direction from which the government forces eventually appeared. His fighting withdrawal from Dundee has been deservedly praised (although we do not know to what extent its success was actually due to his professional officers), but it is all too easily overlooked that he should never have allowed himself to get into the position where it became necessary in the first place, and a few patrols in the direction of Perth would have prevented all manner of unpleasantness.

This was a lesson which he never seems to have learned, and instead he seems to have lurched from one near calamity to another, blaming everyone but himself for the failure to realise that the enemy was at hand, or in greater numbers than had cheerfully been supposed. Notwithstanding his brilliance as a tactician, his utter failure to grasp the importance of thorough reconnaissance must cast some doubt upon his ultimate reputation, and certainly debars him from a place amongst the great captains. The final defeat at Carbisdale on 27 April 1650 illustrates this only too clearly, since it came about solely through the failure of the rebel scouting.

Kirkwall in Orkney had been held since the previous September by a mixture of Royalist exiles (including the loquacious Welshman, Captain John Gwynne) and Danish mercenaries. Despite losing some of his ships in a storm, Montrose arrived there at the end of March with reinforcements and immediately began preparations for an invasion of the mainland. This is not the place to enter into a discussion of the prevailing political situation, but suffice it to say that Montrose was on very shaky ground, and a more prudent general might have waited in Kirkwall to see the outcome of the negotiations then being conducted between the Scottish government and the young King Charles II.

Having earlier sent Sir John Hurry, now a Royalist, across with an advance guard to secure the Ord of Caithness—a narrow defile— Montrose landed near John o' Groats on 12 April, and then moved south trying with scant success to attract recruits. Instead, on the afternoon of 27 April, he found Colonel Archibald Strachan.

Montrose was at the time under the quite erroneous impression that there was only a single troop of hostile cavalry in the area, but in fact Strachan had a fairly sizeable force, most of which had been in the area since the suppression of McKenzie of Pluscardine's rising the previous year, and which Montrose ought to have known about. Under his personal command was Colonel Gilbert Carr's small cavalry regiment comprising only two troops (Strachan was in fact at this time the Lieutenant Colonel of the regiment, although victory at Carbisdale and the later English invasion brought him promotion), and he was quickly joined by Lieutenant Colonel Robert Hackett at the head of another troop, and thirty-six musketeers of Campbell of Lawers' Regiment at Inverness, these last being led by a Captain Collace. There were also as many as 400 local levies, but they played no part in the action until Strachan's victory was assured. Montrose for his part had perhaps as many as 1,200 infantry, most of them Orcadians, but only 40 cavalry. These latter were obviously too weak to be able to accomplish much on a battlefield, but could have been used to some effect in scouting. Instead Montrose kept them close to hand, and relied as usual on picking up gossip rather than sending out patrols. He thus only had himself to blame when the rebel army was ambushed by Strachan shortly after 3 o'clock on the open strath at Carbisdale, near the present day village of Culrain. Only the Danish mercenaries put up any sort of fight, and even they quickly surrendered when assailed by the local levies.

Betrayed not by false friends or incompetent subordinates, but by his own inability to grasp the importance of thorough reconnaissance, Montrose was finished at last. Taken prisoner three days later, he was hanged in Edinburgh on Tuesday 21 May 1650.

Postscript

Even in death Montrose was to prove troublesome. Later that year, while Edinburgh Castle was under siege by Cromwell's forces, the gunner, Thomas Bynning—probably to settle a wager, although he claims nobler motives in his own account—tried to shoot the Marquis's severed head from its spike on top of the Tolbooth. Missing it narrowly, he instead dislodged a neighbouring pinnacle which crashed down upon an unfortunate English drummer shopping in the luckenbooths below.

NOTES ON THE TEXT

CHAPTER ONE: NOTES

1. James Gordon, Parson of Rothiemay, *History of Scots Affairs*, 3 vols., Spalding Club, 1842, vol. II, pp. 209–10; R. Baillie, *Letters and Journals*, 3 vols., Bannatyne Club, 1841–2, I, p. 196; Sir James Balfour, *Historical Works, Published from the Original Manuscripts in the Library of the Faculty of Advocates*, 4 vols., Edinburgh, 1842–5, II, p. 321.
2. Balfour, II, pp. 321–2.
3. *Callendar State Papers (Domestic)*, 1639, pp. 49–50, 55, 56.
4. John Spalding, *Memorials of the Trubles in Scotland 1627–1645*, 2 vols., Spalding Club, 1850–51, I, p. 136; Rothiemay, *History*, II, p. 213.
5. Patrick Gordon of Ruthven, *A Short Abridgement of Britanes Distemper*, Spalding Club, 1844, pp. 15–16.
6. Spalding, I, p. 150. Although not mentioned by Spalding, these volunteers were led by William Cuthbert, a militia Lieutenant. See *True Rehearsall: a Little Yet True Rehearsall of Severall Passages of Affairs, Collected by a Friend of Dr. Alexander's at Aberdeen*, Transactions of the Royal Historical Society, V, p. 47.
7. Spalding, I, p. 150.
8. Spalding, I, pp. 156–7; Rothiemay, *History*, II, pp. 229–32. A good modern account of the incident may be found in E.J. Cowan, *Montrose, For Covenant and King*, London, 1977, pp. 72–4.
9. Spalding, I, p. 182.
10. Spalding, I, p. 185.
11. Rothiemay, *History*, II, p. 256.
12. Ibid.
13. Ibid.
14. Spalding, I, p. 186; Ruthven, p. 19.
15. Rothiemay, *History*, II, p. 257.
16. Ibid.
17. Ruthven, p.19.
18. Rothiemay, *History*, II, p. 258.
19. Ibid, p. 260.
20. Ibid, p. 258.
21. *True Rehearsall*, p. 47.
22. Spalding, I, p. 207; *True Rehearsall*, p. 50.
23. Rothiemay, *History*, II, p. 273.
24. Ibid.
25. Rothiemay (ibid, p. 270) states that the Aberdeen men 'gott the first place of all the foote'—traditionally the right of the line.
26. Ibid, p. 273.
27. *True Rehearsall*, p. 50: he had returned with Aboyne.
28. Ibid, p. 50; Rothiemay, *History*, II, p. 276; Spalding, I, p. 209.
29. Rothiemay, *History*, II, p. 277.
30. Ibid.

31. C.S. Terry (ed.) *Papers Relating to the Army of the Solemn League and Covenant*, 2 vols., Scottish History Society, 1917–18, II, p. xxvi.
32. Rothiemay, *History*, II, pp. 277, 279.
33. Spalding, II, p. 210.
34. Ibid.
35. Rothiemay, *History*, I, pp. 277–8.
36. Ibid; Spalding, I, pp. 210–11.
37. Rothiemay, *History*, II, p. 280.
38. Spalding, I, p. 211.
39. Rothiemay, *History*, II, p. 279, nota.
40. Ibid.
41. Ibid.
42. Baillie, I, pp. 186–7.
43. *True Rehearsall*, p. 51.
44. Baillie, I, p. 219.
45. *True Rehearsall*, p. 46.
46. D. Stevenson, *The Scottish Revolution 1637–44*, London, 1973, pp. 151–82.
47. *Historical Manuscripts Commission 3*, 4th Report, 'Argyll', pp. 491–2.
48. *True Rehearsall*, p. 53.
49. Rothiemay, *History*, II, p. 211.
50. Spalding, II, pp. 65, 86–7.
51. Stevenson, *The Scottish Revolution*, pp. 208–13.

CHAPTER TWO: NOTES

1. Home's had originally been commanded by Colonel John Cochrane, but he was dismissed after being implicated in the abortive Royalist coup known as 'The Incident'. See D. Stevenson, *Scottish Covenanters and Irish Confederates*, Belfast, 1981.
2. Edward Peacock, *Army Lists of the Roundheads and Cavaliers*, London, 1874 and 1983, p. 57.
3. *A List of Officers Claiming to the Sixty Thousand Pounds etc. Granted by His Sacred Majesty for the Relief of His Truly-Loyal and Indigent Party*, London, 1663.
4. Royal Commission on Historic Monuments, *Newark on Trent, the Civil War Siegeworks*, 1974, pp. 54–5.
5. See Stevenson, *Scottish Covenanters*.
6. *Acts of the Parliament of Scotland* VI, part I, pp. 20, 43–7; various Acts reprinted in Sir James Balfour, *Historical Works, Published from the Original Manuscripts in the Library of the Faculty of Advocates*, 4 vols., Edinburgh, 1825, see III, pp. 194, 258 and 296.
7. Terry, *Army of the Covenant*, I, Introduction.
8. Terry, ibid, pp. xxiv-xxv, provides a useful list of the field officers of Leven's army in 1644, identifying the professional soldiers amongst them.
9. Stevenson, *Scottish Covenanters*, p. 76.
10. Spalding, II, p. 320.
11. Terry, *Army of the Covenant*, I, various warrants.
12. Spalding, II, p. 352.
13. D. Stevenson and D.H. Caldwell, *Leather Guns and Other Light Artillery in*

Seventeenth Century Scotland, Proceedings of the Societies of Antiquaries of Scotland, 1976–7, pp. 300–17.

14. Spalding, II, pp. 320–1.
15. George Wishart, *Memoirs of James, Marquis of Montrose, 1639–1650*, trans. Rev. G. Murdoch, with Morland and Simpson, London, 1893, p. 42.
16. Ibid.
17. *List of Officers.*
18. Wishart, p. 43.
19. Ibid.
20. Sir James Turner, *Memoirs of His Own Life and Times*, Bannatyne Club, 1829, pp. 35–8; Stevenson, *Scottish Covenanters*, pp. 153–6.
21. Spalding, II, pp. 319–20.
22. Ibid, pp. 324–5.
23. Ibid, p. 342—Gight kept the money.
24. Ibid, p. 346.
25. Ibid, p. 335.
26. Ibid, p. 343.
27. Ibid, pp. 346–7.
28. Ibid, p. 347; Ruthven, p. 51.
29. Spalding, II, p. 347.
30. Ibid, pp. 347–9.
31. Ibid, pp. 351–2.
32. Ruthven, pp. 52–3.
33. Ibid, p. 53.

CHAPTER THREE: NOTES

1. Lord Somerville, *Memorie of the Somervilles*, 2 vols., Edinburgh, 1815, II, pp. 288–331; M. Napier, *Memorials of Montrose*, 2 vols., Maitland Club, 1848, II, pp. 135–7.
2. Balfour, III, p. 186.
3. Terry, *Army of the Covenant*, I, pp. 108–9, 115, 116, 140.
4. T. Carte (ed.), *A Collection of Original Letters and Papers*, 2 vols., London, 1739. A more accessible list of company commanders appears in I. Ryder, *An English Army for Ireland*, Partisan Press, 1987.
5. Ruthven, pp. 68–9.
6. James Fraser, *Chronicles of the Frasers: the Wardlaw Manuscript*, Scottish History Society, 1905, p. 286 (6,000 foot, 700 horse); Ruthven, p. 73 (6,000 foot, 1,000 horse); Spalding, II, p. 403 (6,000 foot, 800 horse); Wishart, pp. 58–9 (6,000 foot, 700 horse). The degree of correlation between these figures is remarkable, particularly since none of the chroniclers were present. A strong suspicion must exist that the three former took their cue from Wishart.
7. See Chapter Two.
8. Ruthven, p. 74, assigns the Badenoch men to the rebels' right wing under Montrose, leaving the centre entirely to the Irish. This would have made the right at least twice as strong as the left and almost as strong as the

181

centre, though if this was the case it may have been done to offset the fact that the highlanders were poorly armed.

9. D. Stevenson, *Alasdair MacColla and the Highland Problem in the Seventeenth Century*, Edinburgh, 1980, pp. 106–7.
10. Wishart, pp. 58, 61.
11. Ruthven, pp. 72–4; Wishart, p. 61.
12. Ruthven, p. 74.
13. *Extracts from the Council Register of the Burgh of Aberdeen, 1625–1747*, 2 vols., Scottish Burgh Records Society, 1871–2, II, p. 28.
14. Fraser, p. 287; *True Rehearsall*, p. 60; Ruthven, p. 75; Wishart, pp. 61–2; Spalding, II, p. 403.
15. Stevenson, *MacColla*, pp. 83–4.
16. John, Duke of Atholl, *Chronicles of the Atholl and Tullibardine Families*, Edinburgh, 1908, Appendix.

CHAPTER FOUR: NOTES

1. Spalding, II, pp. 401–2.
2. Ibid, p. 402; Ruthven, p. 81.
3. Spalding, II, pp. 401, 405; *Extracts from the Council Register*, II, p. 29.
4. Spalding, II, pp. 404–5.
5. Ruthven, p. 81.
6. Spalding, II, p. 405. Both Ruthven and Wishart give higher figures, but Spalding was better placed to know and is normally most reliable.
7. Spalding, II, p. 406; *Extracts from the Council Register*, II, p. 29; Ruthven, pp. 80–1. Most modern writers have added colour to this incident by assuming that the drummer was a child, but in fact seventeenth century drummers were normally quite mature men employed for their skill and diplomacy, and paid accordingly.
8. S. R. Gardiner, *History of the Great Civil War*, Windrush, 1987, vol. II, p. 144. The error may easily be seen by the fact that the distance from where the Hardgate crosses the How Burn to the north of the 'Y' junction by the Crabstane is exactly 200 metres.
9. Ruthven, p. 81; Wishart, pp. 66–7.
10. Details of the dispositions of both armies have been established both from clues contained in accounts of the fighting and by applying knowledge of the likely frontages of the units concerned.

    Briefly, in theory infantry should have been drawn up six ranks deep; but few units ever attained their theoretical establishment of over 1,000 men, and so a depth of only five men has been assumed for the larger units and four or even three for the smaller ones, since it was generally preferred to maintain a unit's frontage at the expense of depth where possible. I have assumed for the purposes of this exercise a frontage of 1·5 metres per soldier on foot, and two metres for each cavalryman.
11. Ruthven, pp. 81–2. Forbes' Regiment is presumed to have been the one in reserve used for the flanking attack, since it was a regular formation and so rather more reliable than the other northern levies.
12. Wishart, pp. 67–8.

13. Ruthven, p. 82.
14. Wishart, p. 68.
15. Ruthven, p. 82; Wishart, pp. 67–8.
16. Ruthven, p. 82; Spalding, II, p. 406; *Extracts from the Council Register*, II, p. 29. Although not giving much of an account of the battle, the last says that the government forces 'wer forced to tak the retrait', which again is not quite consistent with the notion of their having been swept away by a wild charge.
17. Ruthven, p. 83.
18. *True Rehearsall*, p. 60; Spalding, II, pp. 410–12; *Extracts from the Council Register*, II, p. 29, gives eight score (160).
19. Wishart, pp. 68–9; Ruthven, p. 84; *Extracts from the Council Register*, pp. 56–7.
20. Wishart, p. 69; Fraser, p. 287. The latter, although describing the fugitives being slaughtered in the streets, makes no mention of other atrocities; the sack, although all too horrific for those caught up in it, evidently made little impression elsewhere.
21. Letter to Ormonde in Carte, I, pp. 73–4.
22. Spalding, II, pp. 414–17.
23. Fraser, p. 387. The garrison is given by Fraser as comprising Lawers' and Lothian's regiments, but as will be seen the latter remained in the field. Spalding confirms Buchanan's as being the second regiment.
24. Spalding, II, pp. 421–2.
25. Ibid, pp. 422–4.
26. Wishart, pp. 72–3.
27. Ruthven, p. 89.
28. J. M. Bulloch, *The House of Gordon*, 3 vols., Spalding Club, 1903–12, II, p. 517.
29. Spalding,II, p. 426.
30. Ruthven, pp. 90–1; Wishart, p. 73; *True Rehearsall*, p. 60; Fraser, p. 291; Spalding, II, p. 426.
31. Wishart, pp. 74–5; Ruthven, pp. 90–1; Sir Robert Ker, *Correspondence of Sir Robert Ker, First Earl of Ancrum, and his Son William, Third Earl of Lothian*, ed. D. Laing, 2 vols., Edinburgh, 1875, I, p. 178.
32. Spalding, II, p. 426.
33. Ibid.

CHAPTER FIVE: NOTES

1. *Acts*, 6, p. 176. Forbes himself had gone to Germany.
2. Spalding, II, p. 432.
3. Baillie, II, pp. 417, 417 footnote.
4. *Acts*, 6, p. 182.
5. Baillie, II, p. 417.
6. Carte, I, pp. 73–4.
7. Thirty members of the English Civil War Society quite fortuitously spent a night in the barn whilst retracing the march in 1980.
8. Spalding, II, p. 445.

9. Candlemas Day was a Scottish Quarter Day.
10. Spalding, II, p. 444; Ruthven, p. 101; Bulloch, 'Gordons under Arms', no. 835 (a).
11. Ruthven, p. 101.
12. Terry, *Army of the Covenant*, I, p. xlii; *Acts*, VI, p. 684.
13. Fraser, p. 292.
14. Ruthven, p. 101.
15. Ruthven, p. 102; Spalding, II, p. 444.
16. C. Tomasson and F. Buist, *Battles of the '45*, London, Batsford, 1962, pp. 93–4.
17. Atholl, I, Appendix.
18. Balfour, II, p. 296.
19. Spalding, II, p. 448; Ruthven (pp. 105–9) discourses upon this defection at some length, but does not add substantially to Spalding's account, and it is hard to escape the conclusion that Ruthven was as baffled by it as everyone else.

CHAPTER SIX: NOTES

1. Spalding, II, p. 449.
2. Ibid, p. 453.
3. Ibid, pp. 454–5; Ruthven, pp. 110–13.
4. Ruthven, p. 112. This is an interesting reference showing that some of the Irish were equipped with pikes and were not all musketeers as many allege.
5. Ruthven, p. 114. The presence of Monaltrie's battalion is uncertain.
6. Baillie's order of battle can be reconstructed from the first of his two papers explaining the debacle at Kilsyth, and other official documents. In addition to these units he was shortly to be joined by 1,500 men from Ireland under Colonel Home.
7. Wishart alleges that the Gordons had deserted earlier, but there is ample testimony to their presence. Wishart as ever is quite unreliable in his discussion of the part played by the Gordons in these campaigns.
8. Ruthven, pp.116–7; Wishart, p. 93; *An Extract of Severall Letters from Scotland concerning the Defeat given to the Rebel Forces under the Command of James Graham at Dundee*, London, 1645. This last is also summarised in *Mercurius Aulicus*, 4 vols., London, Cornmarket Press, 1971 (24 April 1645), with the customary sarcastic commentary.
9. The location of this clash is unknown, but it may well have been at the junction of either the present B978 or the B961 with the A92, thus preventing the rebels from taking the direct route to Brechin.
10. Baillie, II, p. 418.
11. The error is pointed out in Cowan, pp. 197–8.
12. H. C. B. Rogers, *Battles and Generals of the Civil War 1642–51*, London, 1968, p. 220.
13. Baillie, II, p. 418. His estimate of 1,200 infantry is perhaps a little generous. Lothian's had mustered only 500 men before the onset of winter, and Loudon's is unlikely to have been much stronger.
14. The letter was published in *Mercurius Aulicus*, 10 May 1645.

15. Spalding, II, pp. 463–6.
16. Ruthven, p. 121.
17. Stevenson, *MacColla*, pp. 176–7. Montrose's own account was published in *Mercurius Aulicus*, 2 June 1645.
18. Fraser, p. 294.
19. Spalding, II, p. 473.
20. Oddly enough Rogers (p. 222) places Hurry not at Inverness but only four miles west of Nairn. No source is given for this statement but it does fit with the facts as outlined, and certainly makes more sense than a 30 kilometre night march from Inverness to Auldearn in bad weather.

CHAPTER SEVEN: NOTES

1. Stevenson, *MacColla*, pp. 166–94.
2. Ruthven, p. 122.
3. *Acts*, VI, p. 176.
4. Fraser, p. 294 (see also p. 287); *Mercurius Aulicus*, p. 1611, 2 June 1645.
5. Balfour, III, p. 296.
6. Spalding, II, p. 473.
7. Ibid, p. 463.
8. Ruthven, p. 122; *Mercurius Aulicus*, p. 1612, 2 June 1645; Spalding, II, p. 473.
9. Fraser, p. 294.
10. Ruthven, p. 130, states that Minimore was in 'all the expeditiones'.
11. Stevenson, *MacColla*, pp. 166–94.
12. Fraser, p. 295. Hurry may have been approaching Auldearn over open country, avoiding the road in case it should be watched. Fraser later says that he retreated over Howford a little to the north of the road, and it would have been natural for him to have gone back by the way he came.
13. Ruthven, p. 123.
14. Ibid; Fraser, p. 295.
15. Ruthven, p. 124.
16. *Mercurius Aulicus*, p. 1612, 2 June 1645.
17. Fraser, p. 295.
18. Ruthven, pp. 124–5.
19. Ibid, pp. 125–6.
20. Fraser, p. 296.
21. Ruthven, pp. 123–4.
22. *Mercurius Aulicus*, p. 1612, 2 June 1645.
23. Spalding, II, p. 473; Fraser, p. 295; Ruthven, p. 126.
24. Fraser, p. 296; Sir Thomas Hope, *A Diary of the Public Correspondence etc., 1633–1645*, Bannatyne Club, 1843, p. 220.
25. Fraser, p. 296; *Acts*, VI, pp. 194–5; Terry, *Army of the Covenant*, I, p. lix.
26. Spalding, II, p. 474; John Buchan, *Montrose*, London, 1948, p. 249; Terry, *Army of the Covenant*, I and II. Drummond and the Murrays are buried at Auldearn.
27. Baillie, II, p. 419, implies that they were new recruits at Kilsyth, but as

THE CAMPAIGNS OF MONTROSE

the officers belonged to the original regiment it may be concluded that they represented the survivors of Auldearn.

28. Fraser, p. 296; *Acts*, VI, pp. 194–5.
29. Ruthven, pp. 126–7; Spalding, II, p. 473; Gilbert Gordon of Sallagh, *Continuation of a History of the Earldom of Sutherland by Sir Robert Gordon of Gordonstoun*, Edinburgh, 1813, p. 525.

CHAPTER EIGHT: NOTES

1. Baillie, II, p. 418.
2. Rhynie had been wounded during the crossing of the Spey before Auldearn and carried to Strudders. A raiding party out of Spynie Castle led by a Major Sutherland murdered him there in cold blood.
3. Spalding, II, p. 465. The castle had been seized by John Gordon of Buckie about 8 April.
4. Spalding, II, p. 476; Baillie, II, p. 418.
5. Wishart as ever ascribes this to jealousy or treachery on the part of Huntly and Lord Lewis Gordon, making no allowance for the Gordons' vulnerability.
6. Spalding, II, p. 479.
7. Ruthven, p. 128. Baillie, understandably, makes no mention of this little contretemps.
8. Baillie, II, pp. 418–19.
9. Wishart, p.108.
10. Ibid.
11. The ballad was first published in Alexander Laing, *The Thistle of Scotland: a Selection of Ancient Ballads*, Aberdeen, 1823, although it has been reprinted more recently in Michael Brander, *Scottish and Border Ballads*, London, Seely Service, 1975, p. 148. Two stanzas are particularly important, and although the ballad goes on to confuse the names of the rebel commanders, these stanzas have a very authentic ring:

    'We lay at Lesly a' that nicht,
    They camped at Asloun,
    And up we rose afore daylicht,
    Tae ding the beggars doun.

    Afore we was in battle rank,
    We were anent Mill Hill,
    I wat fu' weel they garr'd us rue,
    We gat fechtin' oor fill.'

12. Buchan, p. 255. Gardiner however examined the battlefield in the early 1880's, conducted over it by a local man named Farquharson who provided him with a great deal of topographical information. It is inconceivable that had the village indeed been only twenty years old Gardiner would not have been told of it. See S. Wood, *The Shaping of Nineteenth Century Aberdeenshire*, Stevenage, Spa Books, 1985, p. 34, for a description of Alford before the coming of the railway.

13. Cassillis' Regiment is specifically mentioned by Baillie, and the presence of the others may be inferred from their being allocated substantial reinforcements in August (*Acts*, VI, pp. 194–5), and a pretty unequivocal petition from the surviving officers of Glencairn's Regiment stating that most of their comrades had been killed at Alford and Kilsyth.
14. Baillie, II, p. 419.
15. Ibid. The presence of some Aberdeenshire cavalry is implicitly confirmed by the wording, and perhaps even by the very existence, of the ballad already referred to.
16. Ruthven, pp. 129–30; Wishart, p. 109.
17. Baillie, II, p. 419.
18. Fraser, p. 299; Wishart, p. 109.
19. Ruthven, pp. 129–30; Wishart, p. 110; Baillie, II, p. 419; Balfour, III, p. 293. William Gordon (p. 468) quotes Spalding to the effect that Aboyne charged Hackett's men with 'equal vigour' to his brother, which would at first sight agree with Ruthven, but all three accounts are not irreconcilable.
20. *True Rehearsall*, p. 61. He is mistakenly identified as Cassilis' brother, but the unknown author also picturesquely notes that he was 'ane man of huge stature'.
21. Baillie, II, p. 419.
22. *Acts*, VI, pp. 194–5.
23. Fraser, op. cit.
24. Ruthven, p. 135; Wishart, p. 111; *True Rehearsall*, p. 61. William Gordon, *The History of the Ancient, Noble and Illustrious Family of Gordon*, Edinburgh, 1727, p. 469, quotes Spalding as giving seven dead including Lord Gordon, Mowat of Balwholly and Ogilvy of Milton. It is likely however that he was indulging in the deplorable seventeenth century habit of counting only those of any consequence slain and ignoring the common soldiers.
25. Ruthven, p. 136.
26. Baillie, II, pp. 419 footnote, and 424 footnote. It is possible that the luckless camp-followers failed to get away because the rebel dragooners were mounted on the pack and riding ponies belonging to the baggage train.
27. Ruthven, p. 137.
28. Baillie, II, pp. 420–420 (pagination of this volume is somewhat eccentric).

CHAPTER NINE: NOTES

1. Baillie, II, pp. 424–5.
2. Ibid, p. 419 footnote.
3. Ibid, p. 420 footnote.
4. Ibid, p. 421.
5. Ibid.
6. Ibid, p. 421 footnote.
7. The widow of Captain Lieutenant Suyne of Cambo's Regiment said that he had been serving him for six months before being killed at Kilsyth (*Acts*, VI, p. 468).
8. Ruthven, p. 145.
9. Wishart, pp. 138–43.

10. Ruthven is less than clear on this point, although he implies their presence, and it is otherwise hard to account for the total rebel numbers.
11. Ruthven, p. 136. Wishart gives only 200 cavalry and 120 dragooners, and makes no mention of the foot, although they of course will have joined the army some time after the cavalry. Sir Thomas Hope, the Lord Advocate, estimated the rebels at 600 cavalry (Scottish History Society, *Miscellany*, 1892, I, p. 128).
12. Baillie, II, p. 422.
13. Ibid.
14. Ibid.
15. Ibid.
16. Ruthven, p. 140. The identity of Captain Adjutant Gordon is not given, but his career would appear to fit that of Colonel John Gordon of Littlemill.
17. Ibid.
18. Baillie, II, p. 422.
19. Ibid, p. 422 footnote.
20. See Terry, *Army of the Covenant*, I, and various *Acts* etc.

CHAPTER TEN: NOTES

1. D. Stevenson (ed.), *Government of Scotland under the Covenanters*, Scottish History Society, 1982, p. 21.
2. The precise movements of the rebel army are a little uncertain, but Wishart (p. 143) says that they marched from Jedburgh on the same day Leslie was at Gladsmuir.
3. Wishart, p. 142. The wood is identified in a footnote as Harehead Wood, but Colonel Fitzwilliam Elliot (*The Trustworthiness of Border Ballads*, 1906) points out that it had not been planted in 1645.
4. Spalding, I, pp. 208–9.
5. Ruthven, p. 158. Wishart (pp. 142–3) says that the patrol was carried out at daybreak on the 13th, which given that Leslie did not attack until 10 o'clock is possible.
6. Ruthven, p. 158; 'Haddington dispatch' in Elliot, pp. 109–10.
7. Ruthven, op. cit.
8. *Acts*, VI, pp. 246–7. It is possible that Balcarres' Regiment may also have been present, but this is unclear in the *Acts*.
9. Spalding, II, p. 449.
10. Terry, *Army of the Covenant*, I, p. 1.
11. Ibid, p. lxix. See also p. 181: money was paid to soldiers of Coupar's Regiment digging trenches at the siege of Hereford on 11 September.
12. 'Haddington dispatch', Elliot, pp. 109–10.
13. Wishart, p. 144; Ruthven, pp. 158–9.
14. Elliot, p. 109.
15. Ibid. Government and rebel accounts of the battle are entirely compatible. The fact that such a 'simple' engagement lasted two hours before the rebel foot were broken is interesting, and supports the case that other battles lasted rather longer than might be suggested in rebel accounts—particularly Auldearn.

16. Laghtman and O'Cahan were subsequently hanged at Edinburgh, but Stewart escaped. Lord Ogilvy also escaped, but Nathaniel Gordon was executed at St. Andrew's in January 1646.
17. Wishart, p. 145.
18. Elliot, p. 109; Ruthven, p. 160.
19. Elliot, pp. 109–10.
20. Wishart, pp. 146–7. Captain Bruce may have been Michael Bruce of Fraser's Dragoons, or more likely Hendrie Bruce of Middleton's Regiment. He is unlikely to have been Harie Bruce of Barclay's Regiment, since it would appear from the *Acts* that the 40 troopers at Philiphaugh were led by a Lieutenant and a Cornet only.
21. Wishart, p. 147. A halt at Biggar may have been none too safe if Lanark's and Browne's regiments were still lurking in upper Clydesdale.
22. Ruthven (p. 155) places the incident at 'Haccartoune', which might be Halderton near Laurencekirk, but Alexander Jaffrey said that he was captured at Fetteresso (Rickarton is nearby). It is possible that there were two separate incidents, but it seems unlikely.
23. *Extracts from the Council Register*, I, p. 578.
24. Two accounts of this affair by Alexander Jaffrey are extant, one in *Acts*, VI, p. 394, and a rather more embroidered one in his 'diary' (reprinted in Spalding, II, pp. 505–6). The seizure of the castle was probably in fact organised by one of Middleton's troopers also held there.
25. Wishart, p. 153; Ruthven, pp. 164–6. The two accounts are in some measure incompatible concerning the rebel movements. Wishart places the rendezvous at Drumminor, while Ruthven places it at Kintore, but since on Wishart's chronology the rebels took three days to march from Drumminor to Alford, the course suggested in the text would reconcile the two accounts.

CHAPTER ELEVEN: NOTES

1. Stevenson, *Government Under the Covenanters*, pp. 9–55, passim.
2. Balfour, III, p. 333.
3. *Extracts from the Council Register*, II, p. 60.
4. Ibid.
5. Ruthven, pp. 175–7.
6. Ibid, pp. 168–73.
7. Fraser, pp. 313–14.
8. Ibid, pp. 314–15; Ruthven, pp. 183–4.
9. Fraser, pp. 315–16; Ruthven, pp. 184–7. Fraser repeats Wishart's allegations almost verbatim, and was clearly influenced by his version of events.
10. Fraser, pp. 316–17, 318.
11. Ruthven, p. 187.
12. Spalding, II, p. 499, Appendix 16.
13. *Extracts from the Council Register*, II, p. 63.
14. Ruthven, p. 187; Spalding, II, p. 499.
15. Ruthven, pp. 187–8.

16. James Gordon, Parson of Rothiemay's 1661 map of the burgh (available from Aberdeen Art Galleries and Museums) gives a pretty good idea of its appearance during the civil war, and may usefully be examined in reading this part of the chapter.
17. This account is based primarily upon that in Ruthven, pp. 188–9, with additional material from the various sources already mentioned and the account given by William Gordon (pp. 511–3), which is, we are assured, closely based on Spalding's narrative, Gordon having had access to a now missing portion of the manuscript.
18. Ruthven, pp. 189–90; Spalding, II, p. 499; William Gordon, p. 513. A number of skeletons were discovered in the Gallowgate in the nineteenth century and assumed to have been Huntly's dead. All were young men with their hair tied back.
19. *Acts*, VI, p. 245.
20. Sir Norman Lamont, *An Inventory of Lamont Papers*, Scottish Records Society, 1914, pp. 419–34.
21. Balfour, III, p. 341.
22. *Acts*, VI, p. 284. Forbes had just equipped some soldiers recruited in Banff with a loan from the burgh, and the government had to bail him out.
23. Ibid, pp. 242–44.
24. Ibid. Leslie's old regiment of horse had included a troop of dragooners, and this was at his request retained in service. Local levies were also raised somewhat haphazardly for specific operations.
25. Ibid; Baillie, III, p. 6; Turner, p. 45. Ardkinglas' Regiment was to have been raised from highlanders serving in Tullibardine's and Campbell of Lawers' Regiments and from independent companies led by the Lairds of Glenorchy and Wemyss. It must therefore have been a predominantly Perthshire formation.
26. *Acts*, VI, p. 254. The soldiers volunteering to wear armour were to be paid an extra two shillings (Scots) per day. It was clearly felt to be something of an imposition.
27. Ruthven, pp. 196, 197–200, 204–5. Huntly was subsequently executed, and Aboyne died in exile, leaving Lord Lewis Gordon to succeed in time as 3rd Marquis of Huntly.
28. A full account of these operations is to be found in Stevenson, *MacColla*, pp. 232–41. MacColla himself was killed at Knocknanus near Mallow on 12 November 1647, probably murdered after being granted quarter.

Bibliography

PRIMARY SOURCES

Acts of the Parliament of Scotland, vol. VI, Record Commission, 1835.

Baillie, R. *Letters and Journals*, 3 vols., Bannatyne Club, 1841–2.

Balfour, Sir James. *Historical Works, Published from the Original Manuscripts in the Library of the Faculty of Advocates*, 4 vols., Edinburgh, 1825.

Barriffe, William. *Militarie Discipline, or the Young Artillery-man*, 6th edition, Leigh on Sea, Partisan Press, 1989.

Callendar State Papers (Domestic), various vols.

Carte, T. (ed.) *A Collection of Original Letters and Papers*, 2 vols., London, 1739.

Cruso, John. *Militarie Instructions for the Cavallrie* (original edn. 1632), Kineton, 1972.

De Gheyn, Jacob. *Exercise of Armes* (1607), McGraw-Hill, 1971.

Directions for Musters, Cambridge, 1638.

Extracts from the Council Register of the Burgh of Aberdeen 1625–1747, 2 vols., Scottish Burgh Records Society, 1871–2.

Firth, C. H. (ed.) *The Life of William Cavendish, Duke of Newcastle*, London, 1886.

Fraser, James. *Chronicles of the Frasers: the Wardlaw Manuscript*, Scottish History Society, 1906.

Gordon, James, Parson of Rothiemay. *History of Scots Affairs*, 3 vols., Spalding Club, 1841.

    A Description of Both Towns of Aberdeen, Spalding Club, 1842.

Gordon, Gilbert of Sallagh. *Continuation of a History of the Earldom of Sutherland by Sir Robert Gordon of Gordonstoun*, Edinburgh, 1813.

Gordon, Patrick of Ruthven. *A Short Abridgement of Britanes Distemper*, Spalding Club, 1844.

Gordon, Robert of Straloch. 'The Straloch Papers' in *Spalding Club Miscellany*, vol. I, Spalding Club, 1841.

Gordon, William. *The History of the Ancient, Noble and Illustrious Family of Gordon*, Edinburgh, 1727. (Begun about 1700, this is technically a secondary source, but is included here since it makes some considerable use of the now missing continuation of Spalding's *Trubles*.)

Historical Manuscripts Commission, various Reports.

Hope, Sir Thomas. *A Diary of the Public Correspondence, etc. 1633 to 1645*, Bannatyne Club, 1843.

Jaffrey, Alexander. *Diary*, Aberdeen, 1855. (Substantial portions also in Spalding's *Trubles*, vol. II, Appendix.)

Ker, Sir Robert. *Correspondence of Sir Robert Ker, First Earl of Ancrum, and his Son William, Third Earl of Lothian*, ed. D. Laing, 2 vols., Edinburgh, 1875.

Lamont, Sir Norman. *An Inventory of Lamont Papers*, Scottish Records Society, 1914.

A List of Officers Claiming to the Sixty Thousand Pounds etc. Granted by His Sacred Majesty for the Relief of His Truly-Loyal and Indigent Party, London, 1663.

Mercurius Aulicus (Royalist newsbook), 4 vols., London, Cornmarket Press, 1971.

Military Discipline, London, T. Jenner, 1642.

Records of Old Aberdeen 1157–1905, 2 vols., Spalding Club, 1899 and 1909.

Spalding, John. *Memorialls of the Trubles in Scotland 1627–1645*, 2 vols., Spalding Club, 1850–51.

Stevenson, D. (ed.) *Government of Scotland Under the Covenanters*, Scottish History Society, 1982. (Mainly military papers.)

Terry, C.S. (ed.) *Papers Relating to the Army of the Solemn League and Covenant*, 2 vols., Scottish History Society, 1917–18.

True Description of the Discipline of War, York (?), 1644.

True Rehearsall: a Little Yet True Rehearsall of Severall Passages of Affairs, Collected by a Friend of Doctor Alexander's at Aberdeen, Transactions of the Royal Historical Society, vol. V.

Turner, Sir James. *Memoirs of His Own Life and Times*, Bannatyne Club, 1829.

Ward, Robert. *Animadversions of Warre*, 1639.

Wishart, George. *Memoirs of James, Marquis of Montrose, 1639–1650*, trans. Rev. G. Murdoch with Morland and Simpson, London, 1893.

SECONDARY SOURCES

Atholl, John Duke of. *Chronicles of the Atholl and Tullibardine Families*, Edinburgh, 1908.

Baynes, J. C. M. *The Jacobite Rising of 1715*, London, 1970.

Boynton, Lindsay. *The Elizabethan Militia 1558–1638*, London, 1971.

Buchan, John. *Montrose*, London, 1928.

Bulloch, J. M. *The House of Gordon*, 3 vols., Spalding Club, 1903–12.

Caldwell, D. H. (ed.) *Scottish Weapons and Fortifications 1100–1800*, Edinburgh, 1981.

Cowan, E. J. *Montrose, For Covenant and King*, London, 1977.

Dow, F. D. *Cromwellian Scotland 1651–1660*, Edinburgh, 1979.

Dunbar, J. T. *History of Highland Dress*, Edinburgh, 1962.

Elliot, Col. Fitzwilliam. *The Trustworthiness of Border Ballads*, 1906.

Firth, C. H. *Cromwell's Army*, London, 1967.

Gardiner, S. R. *History of the Great Civil War*, Windrush, 1987 (Vols. I and II only).

Hastings, M. *Montrose, The King's Champion*, London, 1977.

Haythornthwaite, P. *The English Civil War 1642–1651*, Poole, 1983.

Hill, J. M. *Celtic Warfare 1595–1763*, Edinburgh, 1986.

Hughes, Major General B. P. *Firepower, Weapon Effectiveness on the Battlefield*, London, 1974.

Livingston, A., Aikman and Hart. *Muster Roll of Prince Edward Stuart's Army*, Aberdeen, 1984.

McClintock, D. F. *Old Irish and Highland Dress*, Dundalk, 1944.

Napier, M. *Memorials of Montrose*, 2 vols., Maitland Club, 1848.

Newman, P. R. *The Battle of Marston Moor*, Chichester, 1981.

Peachy, S. and Turton, A. *Old Robin's Foot*, Leigh on Sea, Partisan Press, 1987.

Peacock, E. *Army Lists of the Roundheads and Cavaliers*, London, 1874 and 1983.

Potter, R. and Embleton, G. *The English Civil War 1642–51*, London, 1973.

Reid, S. *Gunpowder Triumphant*, Leigh on Sea, Partisan Press, 1987. *The Scots Army in the Seventeenth Century*, 4 vols, Leigh on Sea, Partisan Press, 1989.

Rogers, H. C. B. *Battles and Generals of the Civil War 1642–1651*, London, 1968.

Ryder, I. *An English Army for Ireland*, Leigh on Sea, Partisan Press, 1987.

Seton, B. G. and Arnot, J. G. *Prisoners of the '45*, 3 vols., Scottish History Society, 1928.

Smout, T. C. *A History of the Scottish People 1560–1830*, London, 1969.

Sotheby's. *The Contents of Littlecote House*, London, 1985 (Vol. II only).

Stevenson, D. *Alasdair MacColla and the Highland Problem in the 17th Century*, Edinburgh, 1980.
   Revolution and Counter-Revolution in Scotland 1644–51, London, 1977.
   Scottish Covenanters and Irish Confederates, Belfast, 1981.
   The Scottish Revolution 1637–44, London, 1973.

Stevenson, D. and Caldwell, D. H. *Leather Guns and Other Light Artillery* in *Seventeenth Century Scotland*, Proceedings of the Societies of Anti-quaries of Scotland, 1976–7.

Stewart, Col. D. *Sketches of the Highlanders of Scotland*, 2 vols., Edinburgh, 1977.

Terry, C. S. *The Scottish Campaign in Northumberland and Durham*, Archae-ologia Aeliana, 1899.

Tomasson, C. and Buist, F. *Battles of the '45*, London, Batsford, 1962.

Tucker, J. and Winstock, L. S. (eds.) *The English Civil War, a Military Handbook*, London, 1972.

Williams, R. *Montrose, Cavalier in Mourning*, London, 1975.

Young, Brigadier P. *Edgehill 1642*, Kineton, 1967.

English Civil War Armies, London, 1973.

Marston Moor 1644, Kineton, 1970.

Young, Brigadier P. and Adair, J. *From Hastings to Culloden*, Kineton, 1979.

Young, Brigadier P. and Emberton, W. *The Cavalier Army*, London, 1974.

INDEX

Abercrombie, Alexander of Birkenbog, 41, 65, 187

Aberdeen, 13, 14, 20, 21, 23, 24, 28, 31, 37, 38, 41–3, 45, 46, 60–3, 65, 67–71, 73, 77–9, 92–5, 102, 123, 132, 160, 163–5, 168–71, 175

Aberdeen Militia, 23–8, 41, 42, 61, 65, 69, 93, 94, 160, 179

Aberfeldy, 49

Aboyne, Viscount see Gordon, James

Agnew, Lt. Col. James, 157, 158

Airlie [Forfarshire], 30, 96

Airlie, Earl of see Ogilvy, James

Aleiss, Captain, 73

Alford, 124–6, 128–31, 134, 141, 142, 152, 161, 176, 177

Antrim, Earl of see McDonnell, Randal

Arbroath, 98, 99, 101, 163

Arbuthnott, Viscount, 45

Argyle, Marquis of see Campbell, Archibald

Argyllshire, 70, 80, 81

Arnott, Lt. Col. Sir Charles, 61, 144

Arnott, Colonel James, of Ferny, 141

Ascog Castle, 172

Asloun Castle, 121

Athole, Earl of see Murray, John

Atholl [northern Perthshire], 49, 57, 71, 89, 101, 120, 122, 124, 159, 161, 163

Athollmen, 49, 51, 52, 55, 58, 74, 77, 84, 89, 95, 97, 108, 120, 132, 142, 160, 165, 175

Auchindoun Castle, 31, 45, 78, 102, 171

Auchterless [Aberdeenshire], 74, 75

Auldearn, 8, 103–8, 110–14, 116, 118–23, 131, 141, 166, 176, 177

Ayr, 162, 163

Badenoch, 49, 71, 122, 173, 181

Baillie, General William, 69, 80, 81, 84, 85, 92, 93, 96–9, 101, 108, 119–26, 128–38, 140–7, 149, 151, 163, 176

Balcarres, Earl of see Lindsay, Alexander

Balfour, Robert, Lord, of Burleigh, 50, 56, 61, 65, 135, 138, 140

Ballachestell [Grantown on Spey], 90, 165

Ballachroan, 49

Balvenie Castle, 78, 90, 122, 166

Banchory Devenick [Deeside], 24, 27

Banff, 31, 45, 161, 164–6, 173, 177

Barclay, Colonel Harie, 142, 156, 163–5, 168, 171

Berwick upon Tweed, 29, 36, 151, 153

Biggar [Lanarkshire], 159

Birkenbog [Banffshire], 121, 122

Blackadder, Captain, 156, 164

Blair, Captain, 144

Blair Atholl, 49, 50, 75, 78, 80, 81, 97, 120, 161, 171

Blairgowrie, 97, 171

Bog of Gight Castle, 121, 161, 171

Boldon Hill [Co. Durham], 39, 128

Boner, Captain, 26

Bothwell [Lanarkshire], 151, 152

Braemar, 73, 75, 101, 161, 164

Brechin [Forfarshire], 96, 97, 99, 101

Bridge of Dee, 24–7, 62, 71, 73, 93, 175

Bridge of Earn, 132, 133, 138, 163

Browne, Col. Sir John, 151, 162

Bruce, Captain, 159, 188

Bruce, Captain William, 118

Buchanan, Col. Sir Gorge, 71, 79, 107, 183

Buchanty [Perthshire], 49, 50, 51

Burleigh, Lord see Balfour, Robert

Burnett, Alexander, 44

Caerlaverock Castle, 31

Calder Castle, 152

Callendar [Perthshire], 165

Callendar, Earl of see James Livingston

Campbell, Archibald, Marquis of Argyle, 30, 32, 33, 42–6, 59, 60, 70, 71, 73–5, 77–9, 80, 82, 84, 89, 124, 135–8, 165

Regiment, 46, 84, 87, 90, 141, 143, 145, 147, 149, 163, 173

Campbell, John, Earl of Loudon, 96, 101, 102, 107, 116, 119, 123, 141, 150, 184

Campbell Lairds:

Ardkinglas, Colonel James of, 165, 171–3

Auchinbreck, Colonel Sir Duncan of, 84, 88, 90

Crunane, Captain John, of, 171

Lawers, Colonel Sir James of, 173, 178

Lawers, Colonel Sir Mungo of, 8, 42, 46, 70, 71, 79, 107, 110, 111, 113, 114, 116, 118, 119, 149, 183

Campbell, Lt. Col. William, 118

Campbell, Captain, 118

Carbisdale, 177, 178

Careston Castle, 99

Carlisle, 31, 40, 48, 101

Carr, Colonel Gilbert, 178

Cashore, Captain, 118

Cassillis, Earl of see Kennedy, John

Cavendish, William, Marquis of Newcastle, 35, 39, 40

Cawdor Castle, 103, 104, 106, 108, 118

Charles I, 3, 4, 28, 29, 31–3, 35, 132, 171, 174

Charles II, 177

Charteris of Amisfield, 153, 155

195

Rattray [Perthshire], 171
Reay, Lord *see* Mackay, Donald
Rhunahoarine Point [Kintyre], 174
Rickarton [Mearns], 160
Ripon, Treaty of, 32
Robertson, John, of Inver, 161, 171
Robertson, Donald, Tutor of Struan, 44, 49
Rollo, Sir William, 63, 66, 152
Rosneath, 81
Rossie [Fife], 133
Rothes Castle, 166, 167
Roughe, Lt. Col. Lachlan, 84, 87
Rupert, Prince, 47
Rutherford, Captain Thomas, of Ranfertlie, 47
Ruthven, Patrick, Earl of Forth, 29, 30, 34

St. Andrews, 163, 188
Scott, James, 44
Scott, Colonel Sir James, of Rossie, 50, 52, 54, 55, 58
Scott, Colonel Walter, 150
Seaforth, Earl of, *see* McKenzie, George
Selkirk, 153, 157, 158
Seton, John of Pitmeddan, 27
Seton, William, of Schethin, 22, 41
Shaw, Captain, 118
Sinclair, Francis, 46
Sinclair, Lord [Regiment], 31, 36, 40, 173
Skene, James, of Skene, 16, 19
Solemn League and Covenant, 35, 36
South Shields Fort [Co. Durham], 47
Spynie Castle, 31, 91, 103, 166
Spynie, Lord, 71
Stewart [rebel Adjutant General], 158, 159, 188
Stewart, Colonel Francis, 35
Stewart, Colonel James, Earl of Moray [Regiment], 128, 131, 163
Stewart, Major James, of Ardvorlich, 56
Stewart, John, Earl of Traquair, 153
Stewart, Captain Thomas, 85
Stewart, Colonel William, 163, 168

Stonehaven [Mearns], 21, 22, 45
Stirling, 40, 59, 60, 133, 135, 136, 149, 151, 163, 165
Strachan, Colonel Archibald, 177, 178
Strachan, Captain John, 38
Strathardle, 123
Strathaven, 49, 73, 75
Strathbogie, 15, 17, 31, 41, 49, 73, 74, 78, 81, 101, 121–3, 152, 161, 171
Strathbogie Regiment, 16–19, 23–7, 75, 93, 95, 108, 113, 116, 128, 129, 142, 164, 168, 169, 170
Strathearn, 101
Strathnavar, 46, 107
Suie Road, 125, 126
Sunderland [Selkirk], 153, 155
Sunderland [Co. Durham], 39, 47
Sutherland, Earl of [Regiment], 102, 107
Suyne, Captain-Lieutenant John, 188

Tarland [Aberdeenshire], 120
Threave Castle, 31
Tippermuir, 50–6, 58, 59, 60, 62, 63, 66, 175
Toward Castle, 72
Towie Barclay Castle, 15
Traquair, Earl of *see* Stewart, John
Tullibody, 133
Turing, Sir James, of Foveran, 14, 16
Turriff [Aberdeenshire], 13, 16–19, 20, 77, 93, 160, 175

Udny, Colonel John, of Udny, 60, 61, 69, 70
Ulster, 34, 36, 38, 39, 40, 84, 121
Urquhart of Craghouse, 43
Urquhart, Sir Thomas, of Cromartie, 16

Wauchope, Sir John of Niddrie, 85
Wemyss, Colonel David, Lord Elcho, 42, 50, 52, 55, 56, 61, 69, 128, 131, 138, 141
Wemyss, Colonel James, 38
Wentworth, Thomas, Earl of Strafford [English], 10, 11, 31